JA74.5 .H58 2

M000169048

WHEN THE ROMANCE
ENDED

rvine Sullivan Ingram Library
DISCARD

IRVINE SULLIVAN INGRAM LIBRARY
STATE UNIVERSITY OF WEST GEORGIA
CARROLLTON GEORGIA

WHEN THE ROMANCE

ENDED:
LEADERS OF THE
CHILEAN LEFT, 1968–1998

**KATHERINE
HITE**

Columbia University Press / New York

IRVINE SULLIVAN INGRAM LIBRARY
STATE UNIVERSITY OF WEST GEORGIA
CARROLLTON GEORGIA

Columbia University Press
Publishers Since 1893
New York   Chichester, West Sussex

Copyright © 2000 Columbia University Press
All rights reserved

An earlier version of chapter 1 appeared as "The Formation and Transformation of Political Identity: Leaders of the Chilean Left, 1968–1990," in *Journal
of Latin American Studies* 28, pt. 2 (May 1996): 299–328. Reprinted by permission of Cambridge University Press.

Photo of Patricio Rivas courtesy of Rivas.
All other photos courtesy of COPESA.

Library of Congress Cataloging-in-Publication Data
Hite, Katherine.
    When the romance ended : leaders of the Chilean left, 1968–1998 /
Katherine Hite.
        p.   cm.
    Includes bibliographical references and index.
    ISBN 0–231–11016–2 (alk. paper). — ISBN 0–231–11017–0 (pbk. :
alk. paper)
        1. Political psychology—Chile. 2. Politicians—Chile—
Psychology. 3. Right and left (Political science)—Psychological
aspects. 4. Political culture—Chile. I. Title.
JA74.5.H58 2000
324.2'2'092283—dc21   99-38567

Casebound editions of Columbia University Press books are printed on
permanent and durable acid-free paper.
Printed in the United States of America
c 10 9 8 7 6 5 4 3 2 1
p 10 9 8 7 6 5 4 3 2 1

CONTENTS

For Rob

ACKNOWLEDGMENTS

■ Over the many years that I have been engaged in this book, I have benefited from an enormously rich and diverse range of intellectual, personal, and institutional support.

In 1983, Arturo Valenzuela, my professor when I was an undergraduate at Duke University, convinced me that I should join his three-month academic exchange program in Santiago. He offered me a Duke fellowship to participate, and I reluctantly agreed. That period deeply influenced my subsequent professional interests and direction. The program gathered a group of undergraduate and graduate students from around the United States to study with professors who were prohibited from teaching in Chilean universities, including Manuel Antonio Garretón, Norbert Lechner, and Tomás Moulián of the Facultad Latinoamericana de Ciencias Sociales–Chile (FLAC-SO–Chile), all of whom would later assist my graduate research.

When the program ended, I returned to Washington, D.C., where I worked with the U.S.-based human rights community for the next several years. Human rights and feminist activist Isabel Morel Letelier became a central teacher of my life. I also enjoyed the professional guidance and friendship of Eliana Loveluck, and I learned a good deal from working with such people as Joe Eldridge, Virginia Bouvier, and Cynthia Brown, and from my colleagues at the Institute for Policy Studies, including Robert Borosage, John Cavanagh, Peter Kornbluh, Saul Landau, and Nancy Lewis.

I was able to return to Chile several times, and in 1991, I began extensive dissertation research with support from the Fulbright Foundation. SUR Profesionales and its director, Carlos Vergara, gave me an institutional home in Santiago, where I benefited from the colleagueship of Carmen Barrera, Alvaro Boehme, Alvaro Díaz, Javier Martínez, and Darío Vergara.

In addition to those listed above and the central members presented in detail in this study, I am particularly indebted to the Chilean academics, activists, and officials who over the years discussed crucial aspects of my work with me: Felipe Aguero, John Biehl, Josefina Bilbao, Sergio Bitar, José Joaquín Brunner, María Isabel Castillo, Ernesto Galáz, Josefina Guzmán, Carlos Huneeus, Iván Jaksic, Marta Lagos, Juan Pablo Letelier, Elizabeth Lira, Cecilia Medina, Juan Enrique Miquel, Roberto Moreno, Gabriel Palma, Osvaldo Puccio, Martín Rodríguez, Juan Somavía, Cecilia Valdés and Teresa Valdés.

During my growing family's stay in Chile, two individuals were a constant source of intellectual and personal companionship: Sergio Baeza, a steadfast friend who has continued to joust with me over Chilean politics, and Cynthia Sanborn, who arrived in Chile and underwent the "immersion-into-Chile" process with me. I am also deeply appreciative to the Letelier family for taking our family under their wing during its expansion, and to the Guzmán-Bilbao family for adopting us as well.

For my writing I found a welcome home at the Institute of Latin American and Iberian Studies (ILAIS) of Columbia University, and to ILAIS I am especially thankful for all of the personal as well as professional support. Douglas Chalmers was enormously supportive in his roles as my academic adviser and my boss. Andrea Hetling and Judy Rein were also supportive colleagues. I took full advantage of the ILAIS community of visiting faculty and associates, including Robert Kaufman, Peter Winn, Susan Eckstein, Nora Hamilton, and Eric Hershberg. Above all else, I thank ILAIS visiting faculty member Margaret Crahan for her mentoring, patience and friendship. I also received invaluable suggestions from the institute's visiting Tinker professors, including Atilio Borón, Maria do Carmen Campello de Souza, Carlos Iván Degregori, María del Carmen Feijoo, José María Maravall, Gonzalo Portocarrero, and Carlos Vilas. And last, but certainly not least, I gained a great deal from ILAIS's Ph.D. group, in particular from past members Jo-Marie Burt, Brian Ford, Martín Gargiulo, José María Ghio, Ed Gibson, Blanca Heredia, Scott Martin, Kerianne Piester, Hector Schamis, Rob Smith, and especially Monique Segarra. I also wish to thank Claire Ullman for her colleagueship and her friendship through our graduate school careers.

Regarding the larger Columbia community, I especially thank Alfred Stepan for his intellectual challenge, support, and mentoring, and Lisa Anderson, Michael Delli Carpini, Mark Kesselman, Anthony Marx, and Kelly Moore. Others who have given their time to help me think pieces of this project through include Nancy Bermeo, Terry Lynn Karl, Ron Kassimir, Kenneth Roberts, Philippe Schmitter, Eric Selbin, Yossi Shain, Michael Shifter, and Alexander Wilde. I also thank the staff of Columbia University Press, including editor John Michel for his early support, and Alexander Thorp and Jan McInroy for helping to see this through.

Vassar College has proved to be a supportive environment for finishing this work, and I am grateful to my colleagues in the political science department, to the Vassar Faculty Research Committee for funding my 1998 return to Chile, and to Caleb Elfenbeim for taking on the index.

Finally, I thank my family. Richard Roberts came through for me as a brilliant intellectual and a loving father, and I cannot thank him enough. My grandfather Clifford Carpenter challenged me and continued to remind me of the humanity and bravery of my subjects. My mother, Deborah Fields, is a powerful presence in this work and in my life. I realized, particularly after her death, how much my parents' and grandparents' examples were the inspiration for this study.

I do not know how to begin to thank Robert Hite. His friendship, humor, and love as my husband and the father of our amazing children, Aidan Carpenter Hite and Adeline Roberts Hite, are a constant marvel. To Rob I dedicate this book.

■ In 1973 Chile experienced the most cataclysmic event in her history, a violent military coup d'état that abruptly ended decades of democratic rule. The military strafed and bombed the presidential palace, and amid the shelling and flames Chilean president Salvador Allende ended his life. Over the next several years the military junta led by General Augusto Pinochet imprisoned, tortured, exiled, and disappeared thousands of Chilean citizens. The dictatorship lasted for seventeen years. During the final years, cracks began to appear in the regime, and the military oversaw a gradual, controlled transition to democracy. In the 1989 national elections, leaders of the opposition movement, many of whom had been in the Allende government that the military had overthrown, emerged euphoric in their victory yet haunted by a painful past. Out of the disaster of dictatorship came a democratic rebirth not unlike many of the democratization movements that have taken place or are taking place internationally.

It has now been ten years since the passing of the presidential sash from Pinochet to a democratically elected civilian, Patricio Aylwin, and a good twenty-five years since the coup. Yet arguably only today have Chileans truly begun to engage in a public, collective—albeit divided—remembrance of the tragedy and brutality of the overthrow of Allende and the Popular Unity government. The unanticipated October 16, 1998, arrest of Pinochet in London most forcefully contributed to what began with the twenty-fifth anniversary of the September 11 coup: a steadily increasing series of explorations, interviews, and images in the popular press and media unearthing the horrors of the dictatorship and those who defended it. With Pinochet's arrest, debates about the past have moved quite perceptibly beyond the private spaces of homes and gatherings of close friends to the public sphere and the streets.

As the Chilean political class engages in the 1999–2000 presidential campaign and pending change of administration, such revelations and debates have made for a tense political scenario. The arrest of Pinochet has placed many members of the political left who are government officials in a strange position: several of today's left leaders are now defending the right to sovereign immunity from prosecution of the man who led their overthrow and persecution twenty-five years ago. Moreover, the Pinochet arrest came at a time when a popular Socialist Party leader, Ricardo Lagos, was attempting to run for the presidency with a focus on the future rather than the past. Lagos was trying to avoid the bitter and well-worn debates over the responsibilities and errors of his party's leadership in the early 1970s, including the governing Socialist Party's role in the tremendous economic and political turmoil that preceded the coup.

This book is about a unique group of young sixties-generation national leaders of the left who came to power with Allende's 1970 election, who were proponents of a program for revolutionary social transformation, and who were part of the short-lived experiment that failed. Within this group, many experienced imprisonment and torture, and all of those on whom this book focuses spent years in exile. During their exile, they played a crucial role in defining opposition politics at home. In addition to raising funds and fomenting international opposition to the regime, the exiled leadership developed both doctrine and strategy to fight the dictatorship and effect the return to democracy in Chile. They are currently involved in the rebuilding and consolidation of Chile's democratic institutions. The purpose of this book is to examine what happens to the political identities of leaders such as these in a context of traumatic political upheaval and change.

During the political transition of the mid- to late 1980s and the first year of return to democratic rule, the Chilean press often referred to some formerly exiled politicians as "the Europeans," because they had spent much of their exile in Rome, Paris, London, and Madrid; others were categorized as the "Bolches," or "Bolsheviks," an allusion not only to their Stalinist politics but also to their place of exile—Moscow. Such labeling connoted, first, that these political actors had lived in and experienced distinct political as well as geographic arenas of the world and, second, that they brought back the influences of these arenas to their postexile politics. I was intrigued by the notion of tracing and differentiating these influences, examining how exile in Rome carried a different set of political influences and experiences than did exile in East Berlin or Mexico City, for example. Thus my empirical sample, those men and women who became the basis of my study, are all former exiles who returned from different regions of the world to Chile to play important roles in politics.

When I began interviewing, however, it quickly became apparent that while exile was often an important influence on the political thinking and behavior of my subjects, to focus on exile was far too limiting if my objective was to understand how this group's politics had evolved and been transformed. The point of departure became not exile but home and family, childhood, and peers. It involved early exposure to politics at the kitchen table, in the neighborhood, in the workplace, in school, and, particularly for the 1960s generation, in the streets. For the men and women whose lives are the focus of this book, I found, the most salient indicators of political identity were their early experiences in national politics, experiences that seared their memories and defined their political priorities and relationships to politics in unique ways. Such defining experiences also reflected individual community, class, and educational backgrounds.

Through the 1990s I conducted many interviews with Chilean leaders, including a significant portion of the exiled political leadership who had returned to Chile, and I conducted intensive life history interviews with twenty-five political leaders in that group. The texts of the intensive interviews form the basis of my conceptualization of individual political identity and its relationship to political process, and the experiences of fifteen of the twenty-five interviewees are used extensively in this book.

The most striking thing to emerge from my interviews, observations, and analysis was how little political leaders' cognitive understandings and approaches to politics change, even in the face of traumatic political experiences. I expected to see fundamental change not only in their ideologies from the 1960s to the 1990s but also in the ways they approached political practice. I did not. Instead, distinct patterns for processing politics, what I call "cognitive frameworks," seemed to remain constant through the course of these individuals' political lives. Cognitive frameworks are understood as basic approaches to ideas, organization, and relationships to fellow political leaders and activists.[1] I propose four cognitive orientations: political party loyalist, personal loyalist, political thinker, and political entrepreneur. The four cognitive types form a basis for predicting the patterns and dynamics of changes and continuities in individual political thinking and action. In addition, I have found that over the decades, from the 1960s through the 1990s, each of the four cognitive types proposed here has flourished at particular historical and political moments.

I examine herein how the four types are embedded in particular social and political structures and institutions. As network theorists argue and as this study suggests, individuals' identities are very much shaped by their early and intense relationships to the predominant groups and structures of their lives.[2] Following Karl Mannheim's claim that ideological identity "is always bound up with the existing life situation of the thinker," this book examines the individual political identities of leaders as framed by their family, class, generation, and political party, by their major political experiences of victory and defeat, and by their own understandings of their contributions to a political project.[3] For this study, family, class, generational, and political party identification emerged as the most important forms of embeddedness. Family and class embeddedness shapes individuals' cognitive frameworks. Generational status situates the individuals of this study as young people in an ideologically charged moment that had lasting repercussions throughout their political lives. And individual political leaders both shape and are shaped by their affiliations with political parties, the central political institution for those in this study.

Finally, this book examines the relationships between cognitive frameworks and traumatic political experiences. Traumatic life experiences, such as political victory and defeat, imprisonment and exile, and the collapse of the international left, are catalysts for ideological and role transformation. Such experiences also serve to affirm ideological and role convictions, depending on the types of cognitive frameworks individuals possess. I conclude with the argument that despite heart-wrenching experiences, the political identities of these highly political, sixties-generation individuals—including their fundamental approaches to politics, to their immediate political communities, and to their understandings of their own images and roles in politics—have changed very little.

The categories of cognitive orientation that I have developed come from intense engagement with each of the individuals in this book and represent interpretation of the patterns that emerged from this engagement. Given that many of the Chileans in this book are well-known political figures, I have no doubt that there will be vehement disagreement with my categorizations, even from the interviewees themselves. No theoretical modeling can explain all political behavior. Indeed, this book challenges rational-choice attempts to do just that. Nevertheless, the categorizations developed here serve as a powerful heuristic device for understanding political leader identity and political process amid political trauma and change.

Political identity studies are booming in academia, as vastly distinct groups across the globe struggle to redefine themselves. The issues of gender, ethnic, racial, religious, national, and even transnational identity have emerged with explosive force. Clearly, many of the conflicts over identity have endured for centuries. Yet the combination of the recent collapses of regimes and a technology that has contributed to heightened global awareness and involvement in conflicts has created a series of new challenges, for scholars, policy makers, and the world citizenry.

Within the scholarly community, formulations of the question of identity span the disciplines, from more established traditions in psychology, comparative literature, and anthropology to a fairly recent range of explorations in political science. Psychologist Erik Erikson's works on individual identity, for example, are major references for students in several fields.[4] In comparative literature, a significant body of theoretical work has emerged on individual, ethnic, and racial identity in the United States and elsewhere. Within the field of anthropology, such thinkers as Clifford Geertz, Virginia Domínguez, Kay Warren, and others have played decisive roles in inspiring a literature on ethnic identity in regions around the world, from Southeast Asia, the Middle East, and northern Africa to the Central American and Andean countries of Latin America.[5] The literature explores such interrelated questions as the relationships among ethnic, religious, and national identity, the subordination of ethnic groups to dominant societies that are not ethnically defined, and the gradual yet steady transformation of ethnic identities.

Political scientists such as David Laitin, Juan Linz, and Alfred Stepan have pioneered new terrain in the field regarding the conceptualization of political identity as it is associated with national identity struggles in Africa, Southern Europe, and the former Soviet Union.[6] Apparent in much of this literature is a clear normative concern, as well as a deliberate search for workable political solutions in these regions. The questions that orient the literature include the following: Are identities fixed and primordial, or do members of the citizenry possess and internalize multiple identities that can accommodate greater flexibility regarding territorial boundaries? What kind of statecrafting is required to incorporate competing national identities? In yet another vein, scholars across the disciplines are exploring the question of transnational identity.[7] Such literature examines how communities are defined and constructed when the concept of sovereignty is of little meaning to the definition, as when tight networks of families and governing bodies extend across national boundaries.

This book is about the formation and transformation of individual political identity, with a focus on ideology and political roles. Such a focus raises questions that are distinct from those of literatures on national, ethnic, and transnational identity. Based on intensive interviews and the study of a generation of leaders of the Chilean left, it closely examines how individual political leaders conceptualize their politics and the meanings they derive from their political practices. It explores the process of identity formation and the transformation and reformulation of political identity. Competing national visions of polity and society play a central role in this process, including individual leaders' understandings of democracy and participation, social justice, the roles of parties and party leaders, and what is possible in their given societies.

This book is meant to deepen our understanding of political identity, leadership, and change in three ways. First, by focusing on the identity formation and transformation of Chilean political leaders, it will offer a lens through which the transformation of Chilean political culture itself can be more carefully examined and analyzed. As many classic studies of leading thinkers and politicians have demonstrated, there is a powerful dynamic between elite thought and action and the political culture of which elites are a part.[8]

Second, the study will contribute to our understanding of the transformations on the left universally. Debates within the international left heavily influenced leaders of the Chilean left in a variety of ways, and the Chilean socialist experience (1970–1973) had an important impact on the thinking and strategy of the international left. Insight into the sixties generation of Chilean left leaders will contribute in comparative terms to analysis of a series of broader, global transformations on the left, from European left intellectual currents to contemporary debates on modernization and the left in Latin America. Just as the Chilean left acts within a political culture wounded by authoritarianism, the left internationally has yet to emerge in any clear way from deep-rooted crises and from tremendous challenges to left models. Yet this study will challenge "end of ideology" claims and will assert that while the left continues to be engaged in soul-searching processes, left thinkers and politicians have not abandoned democratic socialist visions.

Third, the book will argue that the conceptualization of individual political identity is a powerful explanatory framework for understanding the formulation and reformulation of political thinking and action, particularly during periods when political institutions are in a state of flux or crisis. Political leaders are the protagonists of both the breakdowns and the recompositions of the major political institutions of their countries, and it is therefore important that we understand how such leaders define their visions and roles. Yet one cannot understand contemporary Chilean political history without understanding the influence of distinct ideologies on its political leaders, and I argue that this is also true for understanding political dynamics across the globe. This study has found that for those whose identities have been strongly defined by ideological beliefs and political activism, cognitive frameworks do not disappear in the process of dramatic political transformations. Yet traumatic experience does bring about identity change. New contexts bring about new adaptations, as rational-choice theorists assert. There is a dialectical tension between one's political identity and changing social and political demands. The individuals studied here fall along a continuum between the pole of strong attachment to initial ideologies and roles and the abandonment of ideologies once held to be universal, particularly Leninism. The model of individual political identity forwarded in this study offers a lens through which to examine larger political processes, where identities are aggregated and distributed in positions of formal political power, shaping the institutions and the very political cultures in which they are embedded.

POLITICAL AUTOBIOGRAPHY AS METHOD

From 1990 to 1998 I conducted approximately one hundred interviews of Chilean leaders and activists. While they do not represent a random sample, they include approximately one-quarter of the top Chilean left political leadership forced into exile during the Pinochet dictatorship. Between 1991 and 1993, I conducted intensive interviews with the fifteen individuals on whom I focus, and I have continued to follow their political trajectories through correspondence, brief personal contacts, and research since that time. In addition, I formally reinterviewed eight of the fifteen in Chile in 1998.

During the interviews, I asked individuals to recount their life histories and then to discuss their views of democracy, socialism, the role of the party and party leaders in the polity and society, and their visions and concerns for Chile's future. While I used a questionnaire to ensure that basic themes and issues were addressed in the sessions, my questions were primarily open-ended and the sessions were free-flowing.

The objectives of this method were twofold: First, I sought to explore and analyze the individuals' own understandings of their political life trajectories, including why they had come to think about politics and their political roles as they did. Second, I sought to relate their narratives to the broader questions of political identity formation in their historical and political contexts.

This method is quite similar to that used by political scientists Robert Lane and Jennifer Hochschild in their respective works, *Political Ideology* and *What's Fair?* In an attempt to reveal the processes by which the so-called common man comes to formulate ways of thinking about the world in political terms, Lane created fifteen "political autobiographies" based on a series of intensive interviews with fifteen American men.[9] To examine U.S. notions of distributive justice, Hochschild conducted a similar study with a group of twenty-eight men and women.[10]

As Lane and Hochschild argue, this kind of qualitative approach allows for a depth that is difficult, if not impossible, to achieve in vast survey studies. What the method perhaps sacrifices in parsimony, it gains in richness, texture, nuance, and comparative content. It uncovers the silences and surprises, as well as the expected. As Italian social historian Luisa Passerini argues, intensive interviewing for individuals' life histories captures the unique as well as the conventional:

> The request for personal histories, while designed to inquire into everyday life, stimulates references to the exceptional—the things that make one individual different from another. A questionnaire, however, implicitly suggests that it is uniformity that counts, along with numbers and classifications over and above the individual. By encouraging subjects to present themselves as unique and irreplaceable through an autobiographical account, therefore, it induces them to reveal their cultural values, and hence, paradoxically, throws light on stereotypes and shared ideas.[11]

My "autobiographies" of the Chilean political class reveal a great deal of deliberation, ambivalence, and inner conflict over individuals' political choices, trajectories, and ideologies. The research design allowed members of the study to forge their own explanations of their political paths, a clear departure from a research design such as the survey study, which relies exclusively on inferring those links.[12]

For my methodological design, I have also drawn from select works on the question of memory, particularly the works of oral historians Alessandro Portelli and Luisa Passerini. As is the case with all oral historians, Portelli and Passerini rely almost exclusively on individual memories of the past to uncover previously unexplored aspects of history, politics, and culture. They reveal that memory can represent the imaginary as well as the actual, reflecting how an individual wished an event had taken place rather than how it did take place.[13] In the course of recounting such memories, interpreters such as Passerini uncover memory reconstructions as individuals' attempts to preserve or meld their past and present identities.

As will be evident throughout the book, my approach also relies extensively on memory. I, too, have found an intimate relationship between memory and individual political identity, shown in accounts of participation in student and worker movements, political roles during the Allende years, imprisonment and/or exile, and return. In the texts, I have found both conscious and unconscious efforts by individuals to claim a kind of continuity for their lives, even if their political lives have, in fact, been transformed. Later, I explore the relationships between individual and collective memories and political identity.

ORGANIZATION OF THE BOOK

Chapter 1 elaborates on the notion of individual political identity. It briefly examines rational-choice and identitarian debates concerning political thinking and behavior and asserts that while rational-choice approaches are useful for studies of particular kinds of political behavior, they fail to capture critical aspects of political thinking and behavior, namely, action on behalf of the collective, action that appears contradictory and irrational, as well as action in the face of powerlessness. The chapter argues that the keys to understanding the formation of the individual political identities of the Chilean leaders on whom I focus lie in the stories shared by the individuals themselves, in the meanings that they assign to particular ideas, experiences, and relationships. The chapter also introduces the four cognitive orientations that will be explored through the course of the study.

Chapter 2 provides a context for the individuals covered in this study by examining Chilean political culture and the left's role within it from the 1960s to the postauthoritarian period of the early 1990s, thereby setting the stage for an analysis of the formation and transformation of the political identities of Chilean left leaders over the past thirty years. The chapter also suggests that while valuable contributions have been made to understanding left thought and the trends among left political organizations in Chile, a crucial element of the equation is missing, namely, study of the individuals themselves as central units of analysis.

Chapters 3–6 present the cognitive orientations themselves, highlighting each cognitive type in the context of political moments in which each of the types was of particular political prominence. Chapter 3 focuses on political party loyalists and their centrality in the pre-1973 period and the early years of the coup. Chapter 4 examines personal loyalists—that is, those loyal to the leader Salvador Allende—and explores the shaping of their political identities during the Popular Unity (1970–1973) period. Chapter 5 is a look at the thinkers discussed in this study, using the lens of their exiles from the mid-1970s to the mid-1980s to examine transformations in political identity and highlight their political roles during that period. Chapter 6 focuses on the study's political entrepreneurs and on the critical roles they have played in Chile's redemocratization process.

The concluding chapter reexamines the four cognitive types and the struggles of people within each type to redefine their individual political identities in Chile today. Focusing on what emerged as the central preoccupation of all those included in this study—the nature and meaning of democracy, as well as democracy's relationship to the processes of modernization—it explores what the model of individual political identity reveals about prospects for the Chilean left and for contemporary Chilean politics in ways that invite comparative case reflections.

One final note: In this book, I quite consciously include extensive excerpts of the interviews I conducted. While I am aware that I am selecting and shaping the narratives that constitute the book, I give the leaders ample space because they have powerful, eloquent voices and this study is at its core theirs. I sense that readers of this book may appreciate the leaders' expressions of their political experiences and beliefs, their sentiments of joy, pain, disappointment, and love for politics, as much as I have.

WHEN THE ROMANCE ENDED

CHAPTER 1

INTERPRETING POLITICAL IDENTITY

■ The generation of activists who entered politics in the 1960s inspired by a revolutionary socialist project have seen their aspirations challenged at the very core by the events and transformations of the past thirty years. The once massive movements demanding radical social change have all but disappeared or have given way to far less visible, ideologically ill-defined, and isolated struggles. National regimes that claimed socialism to be their governing principle have, for the most part, collapsed. For the past several years, neoliberal conservative projects have universally dominated economic policy making and discourse. For those who for three decades have defined themselves as part of a collective ideological left, the meaning of that identity has become unclear. This absence of viable collective left projects, accompanied by what might be termed a shrinking of the political imagination, comes at a time, paradoxically, when members of the sixties revolutionary generation have assumed the reins of political society in countries across the globe.

In this context of uncertainty over what it means to be part of a collective left, this study analyzes the individual search for political ideology and meaning among former revolutionaries of the sixties generation. To do so, it focuses on the concept of individual political identity, treated here as the result of specific processes that individuals undergo to define their political ideas and roles. These processes involve a dynamic interplay among individuals' embeddedness in particular political and social structures and institutions, their cognitive beliefs and approaches to politics, and the major political experiences of their lives, which together influence their political ideologies and roles. Ideology, as it is used here, is understood as an individual's articulated set of visions for society, a kind of program that encompasses individual understandings of democracy, leadership, participation, social justice, and the roles of parties and party leaders and of what is possible in their societies. Roles are understood as the broad and varied ways in which individuals participate in politics.

The primary contribution of this study is to sharpen the concept of political identity by proposing a set of cognitive orientations that, I argue, can be used to describe the core political identities of individual political leaders. The orientation typology focuses on the values that individuals assign to ideas, political organization, and their relationships to fellow political leaders and activists. This book centers on the formation of four types of core orientation: political party loyalist, personal loyalist, political thinker, and political entrepreneur. I argue that these cognitive orientations remain constant over the lifetimes of individuals and condition the ways individuals think and act politically at given political moments. In current debates regarding the nature of political identity, the typology of this study clarifies what remains fixed about individual political identity and what transforms according to the political moment. Through an intense examination of the lives of several Chilean left leaders, I will explore, first, how cognitive orientations are formed, and, second, why individuals act politically in the ways that they do.

A well-established literature on political leadership also advances sets of ideal-types or categories of leadership.[1] The ideal-types of political leaders developed in this literature are used to hypothesize about leadership performance and survival. Yet the literature does not address the question of the relationship between leadership types and identity formation, including transformations in ideologies as well as roles.[2] This book will systematically address such relationships.

The conceptualization of individual political identity and the four cognitive orientation types proposed here grew from my intensive interviews and study of a generation of leaders of the Chilean left political class, a generation that played a central role in the rise and fall of the 1970–1973 leftist Popular Unity government of Salvador Allende, as well as the end of the dictatorship of General Augusto Pinochet (1973–1990). The people on whom this study focuses were in the national left leadership at the time of the brutal 1973 military coup d'état, some as leaders and organizers of party youth branches, but most as national political party and government figures. Many were imprisoned and tortured. All spent from five to fifteen years in exile. All returned to Chile to assume active political roles in the struggle against the dictatorship, which in 1990 ceded power to the democratically elected Concertación coalition. Now at the close of its second term, the Concertación government represents an unprecedented alliance forged between centrists and many of the left leaders covered in this study, including several who, two decades ago, were bitter political and ideological enemies.

Today, the majority of the men and women discussed here hold central positions in the executive or legislative branches of the Chilean government, as well as in their political parties. All claim to be heirs of a left tradition, yet the contemporary expressions of that tradition vary enormously. While almost all are members of recognized left political parties, the meanings they attach to that membership vary in dramatic ways. Beneath the surface-level political trajectories of these people are also quite divergent class and cultural contexts, memories and life experiences, and senses of self and the self's relation to others.

As a result of wrenching historical and political change, these former revolutionaries have undergone profound ideological and role transformations. Nevertheless, their fundamental approaches to ideology and political organization during their early political lives continue to serve as essential referents that define their political identities today. For example, those who were inspired by the notion of a vanguard party and devoted all their energies in the 1960s to organizing and recruiting for their parties continue to play those roles, albeit in a dramatically changed political moment. In contrast, others who were the idea men for the new society in the 1960s continue to focus on new political visions and are less concerned with party organization and mobilization. The 1960s' ideas of radical social change continue both to inspire and to haunt that generation's proponents, mediated through the lenses of their core political identities. I suggest here that early and intense political socialization in an ideologically charged moment is extraordinarily important for ongoing political identity.

One cannot understand the last three decades of Chilean political history without understanding the influence of ideas and movements for revolutionary change on its leading political actors. While my typology focuses on individuals, it also underscores the importance of the political organizations and projects that infuse meaning into individual political actions across the political spectrum. This suggests that the typology could be used to examine the ideological and role transformations of leaders and activists in a range of cases, from the changes and continuities within the leadership of South Africa's antiapartheid movement to the influence and logic of the political right in the United States. Erik Erikson has argued that "youth is one stage of life naturally (and sometimes even morbidly) open to insight, because insight emerges from passionate experience as much as from the structure of things."[3] My study of the sixties generation of Chilean left leaders leads me to contend that the profound immersion in and commitment to a revolutionary program of this group as young people, however ill-defined at the time, serves as a fundamental referent even in today's climate, in which the notion of totalizing projects meets with skepticism and disregard.

In order to describe better the process by which political identity is formed, this chapter examines specific rational-choice and identitarian approaches to political thinking and action currently used by political philosophers and social movements theorists who examine individual political behavior on behalf of the so-called common good. The term *the common good* is understood here to mean the good of others or the welfare of society as a whole. In choosing to examine such debates, I am assuming that individuals who are members of the left have framed their thinking and behavior largely in terms of action on behalf of the common good. Such altruistic thinking and behavior can hypothetically occur either out of pure self-interest or not.[4]

Drawing from but moving beyond rational-choice and identitarian literature, I propose an alternative model that focuses on individual political identity formation and advances a typology of core cognitive orientations. I argue that class, education, and political party are the crucial variables of early political identity formation, though the dramatic and traumatic experiences of the revolutionary 1960s generation did have a lasting effect on the identities of its activist members. To illustrate the political identity formation process and the typology, I use observations and narratives from interviews with Chilean political leaders from research and interviews that I conducted between 1990 and 1998. I conclude that individual cognitive political orientations form early in life and condition the kinds of political activities and directions that individuals pursue. The typology is a heuristic tool for understanding why people behave politically in the ways that they do.

RATIONAL-CHOICE APPROACHES TO INDIVIDUAL POLITICAL BEHAVIOR AND THE COMMON GOOD

As Kristen Renwick Monroe has succinctly stated, the theory of rational action "can best be understood by assuming individuals pursue their self-interest, subject to information and opportunity costs."[5] The theory assumes that individuals have fairly clear and ordered sets of values, priorities, and preferences and that they will act to maximize those preferences.

While the concepts of "rationality" and "self-interest" are distinct from one another, there is a certain tendency for both rational-actor theorists and their critics to conflate the two. As Norman Frohlich has stated, "economic models using the assumptions of rationality and self-interest have been so successful that economists have become accustomed to using the two assumptions as if they were a single assumption."[6] Economists in this vein include Anthony Downs and Mancur Olson, who have turned to studies of politics and have served as founding fathers for subsequent rational-choice theorists across the political science field.[7]

The notions of rationality and self-interest have struck a deep chord with those working in the area of social movements. Olson's *The Logic of Collective Action* inspired impressive new work in the theoretical literature on the relationship between the individual and collective action. His removal of value concerns from a model of individual behavior did a great deal to jettison theories based on "mob" behavior—behavior based on "feelings of alienation."[8] Collective action theorists such as Anthony Oberschall, Charles Tilly, and John McCarthy and Mayer Zald now focus on resource mobilization and individual calculations of perceived benefits from choices to participate in collective action. Social movements and social movement organizations themselves have come to be treated as rational actors.

In the area of political philosophy, rational-actor theorists have attempted to address behavior on behalf of the common good that seems far from self-interested. They argue that while such individual political behavior often appears to be selfless, it is, in fact, self-interested. Rational-actor conceptualizations of altruistic behavior include: (1) goods altruism, that is, the expectation of some kind of reward for having chosen to act on behalf of others; (2) participation altruism, the notion that individuals help others in order to feel good about themselves; (3) psychic goods altruism, a kind of taste for being altruistic; and (4) altruist clusters, the idea that altruists in close proximity motivate one another.[9]

THE IDENTITARIAN CRITIQUE

Powerful critiques have emerged to challenge rational-choice approaches to political behavior, both in the field of collective action scholarship and in political philosophy. Underlying the critiques in the collective action literature is the basic concern that in the dramatic shift from emotive, value-based arguments about collective action to economistic, self-interest arguments, social movement theorists "threw the baby out with the bath water by excluding the analysis of values, norms, ideologies, projects, culture, and identity in other than instrumental terms."[10]

Identity-oriented theorists of collective action, such as Jean Cohen (who coined the term *identity-oriented*), Alain Touraine, Aldon Morris, and others fault rational-actor approaches for their failure to explain the very basis or logic for group formation and group solidarity.[11] They charge that models of collective action grounded in rational choice skirt the so-called free rider paradox—that is, they avoid coming to terms with why an individual would join a group when there are no obvious incentives to do so. Those known as social constructionists, such as Bert Klandermans, assert that because social crises "do not *inevitably* generate a social movement," the way that individuals perceive reality—the "mediating process through which people attribute meaning to events and interpret situations"—is a crucial dimension of collective action missed by resource mobilization theory.[12] Some collective action theorists, such as Michael Schwartz and Shuva Paul, argue that individual identity can be "supplanted by group logic in a context of personal relationships in which individual ties among members activate obligations of each to the group."[13]

Paralleling such a focus on the dynamic process of individual identification with a collective is philosopher Jürgen Habermas's concern for that "generalized identification which is made between an individual and the most diffuse culture of which s/he is a member."[14] Habermas termed this generalized identification an "identity-securing interpretive system."[15] He contends that "humans and society seek actively to 'find'—both in terms of locating and creating—their 'proper' and 'true' identity."[16] When the identity-securing system (including institutional and normative structures) between humans and their social structures proves incompatible, a "legitimation crisis" occurs, forcing either change or a demand for change in the social structure.[17]

In efforts to unmask those "identity-securing interpretive systems" as they exist in the political sphere, a number of political scientists have advanced political identity frameworks. These frameworks go considerably beyond U.S. political science's traditional understanding of political identity primarily as individual voter or party identity. The theoretical and methodological approaches employed draw from rational-actor, game theory approaches to institutionalist studies and survey research as well as culturally oriented ethnographic research.

In *Hegemony and Culture: Politics and Religious Change Among the Yoruba*, David Laitin delves heavily into debates between social systems–oriented and rational choice-oriented studies to advance what he terms a "Janus-faced" explanation of Yoruban political identity.[18] Borrowing from Antonio Gramsci, Laitin develops a hegemonic explanatory framework, arguing that the British imposed a stratification system on the basis of identification with particular ancestral cities. The British privileging of ethnicity over religion, Laitin argues, provides the key to the nonpoliticization of religion for the Yoruba.[19]

Laitin uses the comparative method to make his case, and he gathers his evidence through historical and ethnographic research together with small formal surveys among the Christian and Muslim communities of Ile-Ife, located in rural southwestern Nigeria.[20] Theoretically, Laitin's work is quite engaging, as he encourages a rather hybrid approach to understanding the complex relationships among ethnic, religious, and political identities. Yet he offers no real hypothesis. Like many studies of identity, Laitin's is a study of process, an ambitious attempt to understand the formation of contemporary political culture, borrowing from both rational-choice and identitarian explanations of individual and group behavior. This hybrid approach has influenced my conceptual design, which also borrows from both rational-choice and identitarian frameworks to explain a range of individual and collective political behaviors.

In a distinctly institutionalist vein, political scientists Juan Linz and Alfred Stepan approach political identity by examining the potential for recrafting citizens' self-defined national identities through electoral institutions.[21] They argue that "the sequence of elections, per se, can help construct or dissolve identities."[22] In their comparison, the authors suggest that there is a strong correlation between the holding of unionwide elections at the outset of regime transition and the surfacing of "complementary multiple identities" conducive to democratization. Using the outcomes from successive unionwide and regional elections and survey data on national identity, Linz and Stepan contrast the successful Spanish case with the bitter fragmentation of what were Yugoslavia and the USSR.

The utility of Linz and Stepan's approach is their demonstration of the power of macro institutions in forming collective political identity. While they do not deny that feelings about territorial identity are important, they stress that such feelings are largely social and political constructions and that there is more flexibility in national identity than conventional wisdom has recognized.[23]

In my study of the individual political identities of Chilean leaders I, too, place great weight on the power of institutions, particularly educational institutions and political parties. In contrast to Linz and Stepan's argument that territorially or ethnically based national identity is not so fixed or primordial as has often been assumed, I have found that individuals' approaches to politics are often not so fluid or flexible as is conventionally asserted.

This conclusion is, in part, influenced by William Bloom's *Personal Identity, National Identity, and International Relations,* an explicitly psychological conceptualization of political identity. Bloom's work is an effort to provide international relations theory with a framework that "explains how to argue coherently from the individual to aggregate group or mass behaviour, which explains political integration and mobilisation."[24] Drawing extensively from psychologists Sigmund Freud, George Mead, and Erik Erikson, as well as from social systems theorists Talcott Parsons and Jürgen Habermas, Bloom develops a model based on individuals' needs to identify with and internalize the actions and attitudes of prominent figures in their environments.[25] On this basis Bloom attempts to explain what he terms a "national identity dynamic," in which citizens of nations "act together to protect and to enhance their shared identity."[26] As evidence of this process, he analyzes how political elites evoked national identity sentiment in medieval England and France.

Bloom's is an ambitious effort to address the perennial failure within international relations theory to account for intrastate identity formation. Yet in attempting to shrink the unit of analysis to the individual in order then to return to the state aggregate level, Bloom succumbs to a similar shortcoming. He recognizes no intrastate identity conflict, only identity with the nation. In providing a framework for individual political identity, Bloom loses the richness of difference, of a dialectical interplay between individuals and their identifications with others. My approach to individual identity is based on a more complex range of political positions, sentiments, and behavior revealed in identities that may lend themselves to distinct understandings of the meaning of loyalty to the nation-state.

Underlying the past decade's scholarly turn to identity is a fundamental disenchantment with purely materialist explanations for individual and collective action. In a sense, identity studies "bring culture back in" as a crucial dimension of the interpretive framework, a dimension virtually discarded in the backlash to modernization theories of the 1950s and 1960s.

This does not mean, however, that materialist interests are no longer an important part of explanatory frameworks based on identity. My own work signals class background, for example, as a crucial variable of political identity formation. Moreover, many theorists have advanced arguments regarding individual political behavior that implicitly or explicitly draw from both rational-action and identitarian approaches. In their critique of rational-choice theory, therefore, identitarians by no means discard the notion that individuals think and behave in commonsensical, rational ways. Rather, questions such as values, ideology, and culture are explicitly incorporated in identitarian approaches.

Critics of the attempts of rational-choice theory to explain altruistic behavior do challenge such efforts explicitly on normative grounds. Such critics charge first, that rational-choice attempts to explain all forms of individual political behavior lead to no more than tautologies; second, that the notion of "choice" itself is problematic in many cases of individual behavior; and third—and most fundamentally—that models that exclude individual sentiments of love, duty, and concern for those other than self not only are inaccurate reflections of society and community but also lead to highly problematic prescriptions for the polity and society.

In their study of the usefulness of rational-choice explanations of altruistic behavior for explaining the cases of rescuers of Jews under Nazism, for example, political theorists Kristen Renwick Monroe, Michael Barton, and Ute Klingemann have found the notions of "participation altruism" or "psychic goods" to be "frustratingly tautological," largely because of their difficulty to operationalize. They write that "the idea of psychic goods is so all-encompassing that it can mean anything and thus cannot be tested reliably."[27] In order to understand political action in the face of traumatic events, they advance the notion of cognitive frameworks, understood as "that particular part of an individual's beliefs about how the world works that is used to organize and make sense of reality."[28] They argue that one's sense of self and one's self in relation to others "acts to delineate and define the boundaries of possible behavior." Through interpretation and discourse analysis of the narratives of intensive interviews conducted with both rescuers and nonrescuers of Jews in Nazi Germany, Monroe et al. determined that the rescuers demonstrated a "perception of self as part of a common humanity" so pronounced that it consistently produced behavior on behalf of others and limited the range of perceived options for action when, objectively, the range for action was far greater. For example, rescuers did not see *not* aiding Jews in determined situations as an option, despite the fact that it was an option and that to participate in such rescues could (and often did) result in extremely negative consequences for the rescuers and their families.

In my own study of Chilean left leaders, I, too, have found a clear distinction between those whose sense of self appears virtually inseparable from particular collectivities and those who are individualist in their cognitive ori-

entation. Those who are individualist emphasize in their discourse and behavior their own stature and that of other individuals in society. In contrast,
others clearly identify themselves with particular collectivities, such as the
working class, and that identification is evident in the way they express themselves. Eduardo Reyes, for example, whose father was an illiterate farm-
worker in the province of Bio Bio, favored first person plural throughout the
entire interview. It was "we working people," or "we students," or "we socialists," rather than "I." As described in chapter 4, Reyes, today a member of
the Socialist Party Central Committee, risked his life during the early years
of the dictatorship in clandestine efforts to organize the party; he was captured, imprisoned, tortured, and exiled. Reyes's identification with the actions and beliefs of former president Salvador Allende on behalf of the
Chilean working class continues to define his own political ideas and roles.

Jane Mansbridge deems theory based solely on self-interest to be of little use: "The claim that self-interest alone motivates political behavior must
either be vacuous, if self-interest can encompass any motive, or false, if
self-interest means behavior that consciously intends only self as the ben-
eficiary."[29] My own study of the Chilean left leadership clearly questions
the rational-choice premise, which claims self-interest as the sole explanation for political action. As I describe in subsequent chapters, there is a
good deal of evidence to demonstrate that individuals like Reyes act on behalf of a collective or an ideal even when those actions are pursued at personal cost—taking an "unpopular but principled" stance as a candidate in
an election campaign and organizing politically under tremendously repressive conditions are two common examples.

On the question of the *empirical* accuracy of individual action's being
guided by "choice," critics such as David Johnston argue that a great deal
of individual behavior is not a product of choice, and that where choice is,
in fact, involved, the process of choice is far less ordered and clear than rational-choice models allow.[30] Johnston suggests, in part, that individuals
live multiple roles, roles that often possess distinct, and conflicting, "value
structures" and that therefore require constant internal deliberation and
result in constant ambivalence regarding choice of action. Individual political behavior, then, is the result of an unending and extremely dynamic
process of defining individual identity. Johnston and others cite the classic
case of a person who is both a parent and a professional. The demands of
a career are often diametrically opposed to the needs of children.

My study supports the concepts of competing roles, distinct value structures, and the constant need for deliberation within individuals' political

identities. A common "two personae" dilemma occurs for the individual who is both an intellectual and a professional politician. Throughout his political career, for example, Chile's ambassador to Mexico Luis Maira has consistently deliberated between his hierarchy of values as a visionary thinker and the needs and priorities of political party leadership. This deliberation often surfaces publicly, and Maira's proposals and decisions are perceived as either "intellectually appealing" but "bad political judgment" or "a sell-out to political interests over political principles."

A second such dilemma occurs for an individual who is both a professional politician and a feminist. As described in chapter 6, former Socialist Party Central Committee member Clarisa Hardy expresses enormous frustration with her party and her society's "backwardness" regarding women's rights. She admits to questioning herself daily regarding her continued presence and activism within her party because of these issues, and since 1990 she has announced her exit from the party several times. In short, there is no neat hierarchy of values that individuals internalize and express; rather, individuals constantly wrestle with multiple value hierarchies, ideas, and roles. Nevertheless, it is possible to detect individual patterns of political approach and behavior that reflect core cognitive orientations over considerable spans of time, from early involvement in national politics to political behavior in far later years. Despite her frustrations with the Socialist Party's failure to respond adequately to women's issues, for example, Hardy remains in the party because it is to her mind the best organizational vehicle for her professional and intellectual priorities and values.

A normative set of questions underlies all these debates among rational-choice theorists, identitarians, social constructionists, and other students of political thinking and behavior. The questions center, fundamentally, on what we hold to be the essence of human nature and, therefore, to be "the possible" for an ideal politics and society. Are individuals so motivated by self-interest concerns that political theorists can reduce political behavior models to this premise? Or is individual political action so inspired by concern for the collective that models of political behavior must incorporate such dimensions at the risk of losing clarity and explanatory power? Or is neither option sufficiently descriptive of reality?

My study suggests that analyses of political thinking and action require a multilevel approach that incorporates cognitive, structural, institutional, and experiential dimensions. Such an approach reveals motivations that are self-interested and collectively oriented, that are always *cognizant* both of fellow leaders and activists and of a larger community, and that are ideologically as well as organizationally driven. I argue that structures and institutions influence the early development of individuals' cognitive beliefs and actions, while individuals' memories of their first public political experiences sear their consciences and are lasting influences on their political identities.

For leaders of the 1960s Chilean revolutionary generation, moreover, I argue that the core political identities formed in the late 1960s have specific consequences for Chile's political climate today. I will show how the traumatic events of the late 1960s and the rise and fall of the Allende administration forever marked the political identities of those examined in this study, freezing the ideologies and roles of some, transforming the ideologies and roles of others, all mediated by cognitive orientations formed early in their political lives. Cognitive orientations, understood as the values that individuals assign to ideas, organizations, and their relationships to fellow leaders and activists, remain complicated yet unchanged. In today's Chile, for example, collective identities based on the working class, such as trade unions and working-class political parties, are no longer powerful features of Chilean political culture. Those whose cognitive orientations are intimately associated with such collective identities are on the margins of politics and policy making. In contrast, those whose cognitive frameworks have lent themselves to greater organizational and ideational adaptability, whose networks are based on ties with the universities, who have shed past political loyalties (and animosities) in the interests of producing winning political coalitions, have emerged as the leaders of today's Chile.

THE FORMATION OF INDIVIDUAL POLITICAL IDENTITY

It was psychologist Erik Erikson who held that the key to individuals' psychological development or breakdown rests in their continuing efforts through their lives to define themselves in relation to the collective.[31] For Erikson, who popularized the term *identity crisis*, the formation of an "ego identity" is a dynamic, ever-evolving process relating the self's inner drives to the external world, the other. "Indeed," Erikson wrote, "in the social jungle of human existence, there is no feeling of being alive without a sense of ego identity."[32] How that identity is formed depends on what Erikson sees as three interwoven aspects of the self: "the personal coherence of the individual and role integration in his group; his guiding images and the ideologies of his time; his life history—and the historical moment."[33] Individuals find self-fulfillment and meaning in their ability to identify with others, and individuals will hold fast to those identifications when their well-being is threatened.

The key to revealing the process of identity formation is uncovering those "external worlds," worlds that represent individuals' fundamental referents in the formation of their political identities. Such worlds shape both individuals' opportunity structures and their cognitive beliefs about politics and their political relationships. For the Chilean leaders of this study, the crucial worlds are class, education, and political party. In addition, the Chileans here are members of the sixties generation: their first experiences in the public arena took place in a period of powerful revolutionary ideologies, parties, and movements, infused with totalizing visions of a collective struggle for social transformation. Membership in the sixties generation forever distinguishes these leaders from those of other generations that preceded and follow them. They are passionate about politics, and they have been major players in politics of the most varied sort, from revolutionary political movements under democratic regimes, to their brutal defeat under dictatorship, to a far more guarded, cautious activism in the return to democratic rule.

Social network theorists have signaled the importance of framing individual action within varied types of social "embeddedness."[34] According to network theorists, this embeddedness in social networks, such as class, educational, and career networks, largely determines collective identities, which, in turn, mediate individual identity and action. Embeddedness within class, education, party, and generation is the striking definitional characteristic of the Chilean politicians interviewed for this study.

THE INFLUENCE OF CLASS ON POLITICAL IDENTITY

In what is now a classic critique of a classic examination of political culture and political socialization, theorist Carole Pateman challenges Gabriel Almond and Sidney Verba to analyze a fundamental finding that they merely report—namely, that there is a link between class and political views.[35] Pateman reminds us that the relationships among socioeconomic status, political thinking, and political behavior are "one of the best-attested findings in political science."[36]

Class stratification has been a marked feature of Chilean society. According to Markos J. Mamalakis's seminal study of the Chilean economy, the Chilean income distribution pattern by the 1960s was best illustrated by the fact that "nine percent of the population controlled forty-three percent of the national income."[37] Moreover, within the Chilean working class, there were marked differences in income and opportunity between blue-collar and white-collar workers. White-collar workers, who composed roughly 10 percent of the Chilean labor force, earned 17.8 percent of the national income, while manual workers, who composed 56.9 percent of the labor force, earned only 23.8 percent of the national income.[38] As will be illustrated in subsequent chapters, inter- and intraclass disparities undergirded distinct social and political cultures, collective identities, and opportunity structures for their individual members.

Until the mid- to late 1960s, for example, political leaders from the Chilean working classes were concentrated in the Chilean Communist Party and to a lesser, but important, degree in the Chilean Socialist Party, as well as in their unions. Class embeddedness fundamentally shapes cognitive frameworks, structurally granting and limiting individual access to a range of networks and opportunities.

Related to, though distinct from, the influence of class identification is identification within "political families." This study reveals that the family has had a central significance for many. Indeed, for one of the interviewees family is the defining feature of her role in Chilean politics today—Congresswoman Isabel Allende, the daughter of Salvador Allende.[39] Chilean ambassador to Austria Osvaldo Puccio, whose father was Salvador Allende's chief aide, does not remember a family discussion that was not political:

> In terms of my family there was a great deal of stability with a good deal of economic instability. I would say that our family biography went from Allende campaign to Allende campaign and that in the campaign year my father dedicated himself exclusively to politics based on whatever resources he had, which inevitably ran out. . . . We were a family quite open to social life, all kinds of people passed through our home. I remember well, we are three brothers and sisters, when we celebrated a night when only the five of us ate together and we realized it was the first time in more than a year that the five of us ate at home alone. . . . This was basically my family life, with a *high* level of politicization, a family that *lived* for politics.

Political families do carry important weight in terms of identity formation and structures of opportunities afforded members of those families.

EDUCATION AS AN INDICATOR OF IDENTITY

Also related to, but distinct from, class embeddedness is the importance of educational opportunities and networks. Until the 1973 coup, which marked an end to many traditional forms of entry into national politics, high schools and universities represented crucial loci of political as well as educational training.[40] The most well-known centers included the National Institute (the leading public high school of the 1960s), the Catholic University, and the University of Chile (particularly their law schools). High school and university leadership in the nation's top public and private educational institutions launched several prominent national political careers.

It was primarily in school where the individuals of this study were first exposed to serious ideological debate, and it was the network of school companions that most influenced their decisions to join a particular political party. Individual—and, at times, collective—decisions to enter the Radical, Christian Democratic, Communist, or Socialist Party, or later the Revolutionary Left Movement (MIR), the United Popular Action Movement (MAPU), or the Christian Left (IC) were made on the basis of the parties' direct influence and strength among high school and university friendship circles. The latter New Left parties were, in large part, products of a 1960s radicalized elite university climate.

Moreover, the interparty alliances and battles of the Federation of Students of the University of Chile (FECH) mirrored those at the national party level. As former Communist Raúl Oliva describes, elections to determine the FECH leadership also served as bellwethers for upcoming national elections:

> In 1969 we won the FECH elections. We achieved the unity of the
> PSCH with the MAPU as well. I was the First Political Commissioner
> of the Federation. . . . The victory of the FECH in '69 was seen as
> the antecedent of what was going to happen in '70. It was such that
> when Allende won, they called us at the UP student headquarters
> announcing that Allende wanted to give his first speech from the
> FECH balcony. It was a symbol. He had lived his young political life
> in the FECH.

University training through degree completion in the 1960s and early 1970s separates the distinct cognitive types of this study. Along with the elitism that upper-class status allows, the university afforded its students access to a range of professional, political, and intellectual networks that were unavailable to the less privileged and less educated.

THE POWER OF THE PARTY IN POLITICAL IDENTITY FORMATION

There is no greater organizational referent for Chilean political activists than their political parties. The party constitutes the central institutional network in which individual political actors are embedded. In the words of several participants in this study, the party is like "a second family," "a stepfamily," "*the* family." The texts of interviews for this study recount distinct political party cultures, as well as dynamic individual-party relationships.

According to Ernesto Galaz, the son of a military commander, joining the New Left (MAPU) at sixteen was one of the most important decisions of his life:

> [MAPU] was tremendously religious, mystical, with a heavy dose of messianism. Politics were understood as the sublimation of man, of soul and society, it was everything. As a militant, politics weren't merely a segment of your life, no, it affected your entire life, your family relations and everything else. . . .
>
> [Together with being from a military family,] entering the MAPU was the most important formative influence on my life.

While Chilean political parties are still highly institutionalized, intra-party dynamics have changed in important ways. From the years of repression, when entire directorates were physically eliminated, to the contemporary period, Chilean New Left party networks have created much more fluid and somewhat uncertain forms of individual embeddedness. This is best symbolized by the close and often uneasy relationship between the historic Chilean Socialist Party (PSCH) and the instrumentalist party it created during the final year of the dictatorship, the Party for Democracy (PPD). For Vice President of the House of Representatives Adriana Muñoz, for example, the PPD served as a successful alternative for leadership in a 1997 run for the Congress after her defeat as an incumbent PSCH congresswoman. The intensities of the relationships between individual party members and their parties have changed considerably, as have their understandings of the role of the party in society. In addition, several participants in this study have changed parties or were in the process of deciding upon a new party. For many, political ideologies and political parties, inextricably linked in the minds of individuals in their early activism, have gradually become unlinked and reformulated. Nevertheless, the notion of political party embeddedness remains central to individual political identity because of the historic dominance of parties and the party system as the country's supreme vehicle for political expression.

THE EXPLOSIVE SIXTIES GENERATION

As many studies of the sixties generation have emphasized, and as my study has found, the influence of the ideologically charged sixties era on the identities of young people coming of political age cannot be overemphasized.[41] The "revolutionary sixties generation" represents the period of the Cuban Revolution as a catalyst for revolutionary movements throughout Latin America, of Vatican Council II and the rise of liberation theology, of international attention and protest against imperialism, triggered in large part by the Vietnam War, and of mass student protest and countercultural movements in Europe and the United States. For the subjects of this study, memories of coming of political age in this generation prove to be constant referents, gauges for measuring their perceptions of the current political moment.

Theoretical debates within generational analyses center on whether to view a generation as a biologically conceived group of individuals whose commonality is primarily age-determined, or as a sociopolitically conceived group that shares a common location in the historical process. American generationalists have tended toward the former, positivistic orientation, while the latter tendency, a view with German Romantic-historicist origins, has predominated among European and Latin American generationalists.[42] Nevertheless, contemporary generationalists such as Robert Laufer, Verna Bengston, Michael Delli Carpini, and others have attempted to couple the two approaches, examining the combination of social forces and life-cycle stages to explain the emergence of a more or less clearly defined generation.

While formulations of generational concepts continue to be murky, this study contends that the generational question is well worth pursuing in studies of identity and ideology, particularly in such cases as Chile, where major social or political events so characterize a given period or era. This study defines a generation as starting from a dramatic political period rather than as a clearly demarcated age group. The sixties generation is thus meant to capture individuals whose early political activism takes place during the ideologically charged period of the 1960s and early 1970s, in Chile, under the political administrations of Eduardo Frei and Salvador Allende.

There is a fifteen-year span in age between the youngest and the oldest individual interviewed for this study. Nevertheless, 1960s generational referents are vivid in the texts of all those interviewed—from those who were student leaders to those who were cabinet ministers during that period. The dominant international referent is the Cuban Revolution, symbolizing both ideological and strategic inspiration and challenge. Expressing the sentiments of several of the young revolutionary activists of the time, one interviewee stated, "We all wanted to be Che Guevara." Other international referents include Vietnam and the Prague Spring. National referents are chiefly the struggles over university reform and, of course, the 1963 and 1969 campaigns and the 1970 victory of Salvador Allende.

In his reflections on political society of the preauthoritarian period, Chilean senator José Antonio Viera-Gallo places the 1960s generation, of which he was a part, within the social-historical context of the Cuban Revolution, the Vietnam War, and, in a less direct way, the Algerian independence movement. For Viera-Gallo, these political struggles inspired a "liberation ideal" with enormous and long-lasting ideological repercussions for his generation. This ideal, he claimed, consisted of three elements: "domination of natural forces by man's technology; conquest over individualism; and the struggle against social injustice."[43] Viera-Gallo writes of the student movement as the generational expression of civil society's insistence on radical social change:

> To the question, was it possible to construct a non-repressive civilization, the response was affirmative. It would be enough if the people became conscious of the possibilities of freedom that technical progress had engendered in society, and acted as a result to change profoundly the oppressive structures. Revolution was an insignia shared by all. Imagination could take us to power.[44]

In addition, it was this revolutionary sixties generation that experienced a set of particularly traumatic political events. Social psychologists, sociologists, and a handful of political scientists have studied the influences of traumatic life experiences on political socialization. These include studies of Holocaust victims, Vietnam veterans, and others who were indelibly stamped by a particular traumatic life experience and whose subsequent political beliefs and behavior reflected this.[45] Moreover, a group of Latin

American social psychologists, in a search for appropriate therapeutic methods, has explored the impact of traumatic experiences like the Salvadoran civil war and the Chilean military coup on political activists.[46]

For some members of my study, memories of the experience of political victory, namely, the 1970 victory of the Popular Unity (UP) government, represented as crucial a transformative experience as that of subsequent defeat. According to UP education minister and current ambassador to Colombia Aníbal Palma, being in power was the most profound and difficult experience in his life:

> Before the UP government, I had never held a government position. In September of 1972 Allende appointed me undersecretary of foreign affairs, and shortly thereafter minister of education in an extremely conflictive period. . . . It was extremely hard, because in addition I was a young minister, I was thirty-five years old, and I had been both a high school and a university student leader, so when I had to confront student conflicts, and I saw them marching in the streets, screaming slogans against the government exactly as I had done before, I felt as if I were living a dual personality. I remember several times receiving dispatches to go and see student demonstrations which attacked the ministry, and I had done exactly the same thing. . . . The roles had simply changed. And for the first time in Chilean history, just as there were students marching against the government, there were also students marching in support of the minister, in favor of the government. I had never imagined students breaking strikes in support of the government, we were living the world in reverse! . . . I tell you all this frankly, I believe that I have never lived more bitter moments in my entire life than in the moment that the opposition students took to the streets, and there were fights, making it necessary for the police to intervene. I always lived with the fear that at some point a student would be killed or terribly injured, and I felt responsible for whatever might happen, and each protest gave me an enormous sense of tension, and it felt so out of my hands.

I would argue that Palma's sense of role reversal in power, his sense that he had lost control of the moment, marked him in profound ways, causing him to identify all the more closely with Salvador Allende as the heroic figure of Palma's life. Palma is guarded in his hopes for change in Chile. Within his party discourse on social equality and change, Palma places strong emphasis on patience and gradualism, on compromise over confrontation. Palma is a personal loyalist who has tightly linked his identity with Allende, whom Palma holds as a defender of Chile's democratic institutions in the struggle for the peaceful road to socialism.

Thus, class, education, political party, and generational membership represent chief variables in political identity formation, reflecting both the importance of location within the social structure and the vital role of political institutions and experiences that shape identity. They relate what C. Wright Mills termed "individual milieus" to the larger "public issues" and realities, allowing us to explore the sociological imagination through the biographies and types of cognitive orientations that emerge in this interplay.

POLITICAL PARTY LOYALISTS

For those whose core political identities are rooted in their orientations as political party loyalists, activism within the political party is the all-encompassing dimension of their lives. Party loyalists believe that the key to politics and to any possibility of social transformation lies with the strength of their political parties. They possess a strong sense of organization and hierarchy, and they value internal party discipline and order. Their political discourse is collectivist in its orientation, emphasizing solidarity with what loyalists perceive as their historic bases. Party loyalists are wary of Chile's new politics of consensus, and there is a nostalgic tone in their ideological discourse. They tend to possess a subjective image of their parties that may contrast dramatically with the parties' popular image or the images held by many of the parties' most visible leaders.

In terms of roles, party loyalists tend to be keepers of the flame, those whose political behavior is inseparable from their representation of past traditions and symbols. They derive political self-worth and meaning from their identities as effective organizers and recruiters, roles that were far more valued in the 1960s, a period of mass mobilization.

PERSONAL LOYALISTS

The second primary cognitive orientation is that of personal loyalist, represented by those who define their political images by tightly aligning themselves with an individual political leader. In contrast to party loyalists, the identifications of personal loyalists with a political leader outweigh any loyalty or affinity they possess toward a political party or organization. Personal loyalists believe that social transformation must be effected by an outstanding political leader or hero. The most striking example of this in my study was the identification of personal loyalists with Salvador Allende. In recounting their associations with Allende and Allendismo, individual personal loyalists have struggled to preserve their own identities in the face of painful individual and political party setbacks and the difficult reconstruction of their political lives. Loyalists to Allende define their ideologies in terms of "Allendismo," which they interpret as progressive nationalist sentiment and a commitment to formal democratic institutions. They see themselves as preservers of Allende's vision, which they attempt to champion in their political parties. Personal loyalists to Allende rely on memories of their prominence and activism during the Popular Unity period to bolster their presence in contemporary politics. It must be noted here that while the personal loyalists among my subjects are Allende loyalists, personal loyalists as a cognitive type would not be restricted to those loyal to Allende. They can be loyal to any individual leader. In fact, as Chile engages in a new and decidedly heated contest over the next Chilean presidency, I would argue that personal loyalists play increasingly prominent political roles as spokespersons for a range of rival candidates.

POLITICAL THINKERS

The third cognitive type, the thinkers of this study, represents those who have focused on ideas and intellectual debates throughout the course of their political lives.[47] Thinkers show a tendency to privilege ideas over what might be seen as the good of the political party or their own self-interest. They believe that political vision must be the foundation for social transformation. Thinkers are capable of changing political direction as they deem historical conditions merit. Nevertheless, they consistently reveal their deliberations and struggles with the political and institutional parameters that they face in public office. The thinkers of this study have undergone varied ideological transformations and are to be found in the Chilean cabinet and legislature, and among the leaders of intellectual currents within both traditional and New Left groupings. Political thinkers now draft and defend increasingly differentiated party positions within the left, particularly with regard to such questions as political participation and citizen empowerment in the era of modernization.

POLITICAL ENTREPRENEURS

The fourth cognitive orientation, that of political entrepreneur, most closely fits rational-choice explanations of political behavior. They represent those who are "born organizers" and dealmakers, who are responsive to changing political winds, and who rise to leadership positions as a result of adept training within and use of networks outside their political parties. Political entrepreneurs believe that ideas for social transformation must be crafted within powerful organizational vehicles. The emphasis in their discourse today is on pragmatism, consensus- and coalition-building, stability, and gradualism. Compared to past ideological visions for society, their visions of "the possible" tend to be modified in tone, focused on peace and on classic liberal notions of individual freedoms and the private sphere. They tend to be wary of the very notion of "ideology." The political entrepreneurs of this study are located today in high elected and appointed public offices in the Chilean cabinet and legislature and/or are in the top groupings within the Chilean Socialist Party and the Party for Democracy.

COGNITIVE ORIENTATIONS COMPARED

Cognitive orientations are understood here as the reasoned, deliberative approaches that individuals use to process and interpret the political moment and their behavioral responses to the moment. These orientations form early in life as individuals first act in politics. The crucial variables shaping early political identity are class, education, and political party. In addition, the individuals of this study first acted politically during the turbulent 1960s; their experiences of victory and defeat during the late 1960s and 1970s represent the fourth important dimension of their political identities.

It is no small coincidence that at least half of those whom I term the personal and political party loyalists of this study are from the Chilean working class. The identification of the political party and personal loyalists of this study with the Popular Unity period links them with a period in which there is at least the perception that the Chilean working class experienced greater social and political mobility than at any time in Chilean history.

Educational and professional networks are also important sources of political identity. For example, political party and personal loyalists have relied on their parties and individual party leaders for their political education and opportunities. In contrast, those whom I term the political thinkers and entrepreneurs use their political parties as only one important source of political education, while university training and other networks often afforded by their class status weigh just as heavily in their political socialization.

The political party loyalists and personal loyalists of this study draw their strongest political roots from the left parties—the Chilean Communist (PCCH) and Socialist (PSCH) parties—historically based in the working class. The PCCH and the PSCH can be viewed as the loyalists' chief political educators, molders, and sources of their political identities. In addition, the political thinkers and entrepreneurs tended to abandon Chile's traditional political parties to found parties of the Chilean New Left, such as the MAPU, Izquierda Cristiana (IC), and MIR. While small in membership, these New Left parties proved explosive in the ideologically turbulent 1960s and 1970s, and they represented important sources for the renovated left thinking that took place in the 1980s. This study has found that while political party and ideology are inextricably linked during the process of political identity formation, over the course of time this linkage relaxes. Nevertheless, political parties remain the central political institution that shapes individuals' political roles.

Generational embeddedness has a strong impact on political identity as well. Political party loyalists, for example, tend to employ a discourse and to long for the political and cultural movements that were characteristic of the 1960s generation. Political thinkers tend to seek intellectual inspiration from the "imaginative power" a totalizing framework could provide, while they struggle to reframe their visions for new political generations and contexts. Political entrepreneurs tend to be publicly dismissive of the 1960s generation, self-consciously repackaging their discourse and action toward more "attainable" goals and away from ideological projects.

The early and particularly traumatic political experiences of individuals themselves represent an essential explanatory force in the fine-tuning of cognitive frameworks. Such experiences include major political victories as well as major political defeats. In the course of traumatic political experiences, such as the 1973 military coup d'état, entire networks, including political party, university, and even family networks, were severely restructured or eliminated. Traumatic political experiences can challenge the very core of individual political identity. They represent the transforming dimension of individual political ideology for thinkers and entrepreneurs. Nevertheless, although individual core identities, their cognitive frameworks, are threatened by traumatic political experiences, this study has found that individual cognitive frameworks remain basically intact—even affirmed—in the face of trauma. Political trauma works to transform the larger political identities for political thinkers and entrepreneurs, while it freezes those identities for political party and personal loyalists.

I argue herein that political party loyalists, when confronted with traumatic political experiences, have sought refuge in their revolutionary ideological convictions and political roles. This has manifested itself in their dedication to sustaining the preauthoritarian images of their political parties, images from a period when those parties were at the height of their visibility and prominence. In contrast, for political entrepreneurs, traumatic political experiences proved to be catalysts for dramatic ideological transformations. Entrepreneurs have consistently adapted their political discourse and programs to the tenor of the political moment.

The types represent a model that can be used to hypothesize about political leadership in larger political processes. There are two basic dimensions upon which the four ideal-types of this study vary. The first is their preoccupation with organization, and the second is their preoccupation with ideas. The party as organization is the central concern of political party loyalists, who seldom draw upon other formal networks for their political sustenance or mobility. Preoccupation with political ideas or visions tends to be much less of a daily focus for this group.

For personal loyalists, party organization is also central, but not so central as identification with an individual. Regarding ideas, personal loyalists tend to associate themselves with the ideas of the leader to whom they link themselves. For the political thinkers, of course, ideas are the central focus, while the organizational expression of those ideas is less of a concern.

Finally, it is the political entrepreneurs who are preoccupied with both organization and ideas. For political entrepreneurs, a dialectic exists between political visions as projects and the political organizations necessary to realize those projects. Political entrepreneurs are constantly anticipating the organizational networking that they perceive must encapsulate their political views.

Consequently, this study will explore several dimensions of the factors that shape individual political identity. First and foremost, it will address individual political identity formation and develop an ideal-type model of individual cognitive frameworks, that is, how individuals perceive the political world and their places in it, particularly with regard to others. Cognitive orientations, which remain relatively fixed, condition individual ideologies and roles under a variety of contexts and experiences.

Furthermore, I argue that the pre-1973 and immediate post-coup years favored the party loyalist cognitive orientation, which tends to emphasize party continuity and survival. The political thinkers of this study assumed prominence in the mid-1970s to mid-1980s, as parties reflected upon and debated new identities. Finally, the political entrepreneur orientations emerged visibly during the 1970–1973 Popular Unity years but did not come to dominate until the years of transition and postauthoritarian rule from the late 1980s through the 1990s.

Cognitive types are in and of themselves influenced by both social and political embeddedness. Family, class, and generation represent extremely important formative networks in individuals' young lives, while political parties serve as central networks as individuals define themselves politically in more specific ways.

Thus, involvement in a range of structures, institutions, and networks actively shapes distinct cognitive frameworks. Yet the relationship is a dynamic one, for many of the individuals of this study also influence the shape and character of the central networks in their lives, particularly their political parties. Political party loyalists, for example, tend to fuel their parties' militants in ways that challenge the "consensus politics" style that characterizes contemporary Chile. Political thinkers tend to push their parties to greater programmatic content and vision. In addition, these visions were mediated by individuals' cognitive identities, which altered little in the face of traumatic political experiences, including the defeat of the 1970–1973 Popular Unity project. Those who had always been adaptive strategically and ideologically simply adapted their ideologies and roles in response to new political moments. In contrast, those who placed tremendous value on particular ideologies and their political structures tended to hold fast to those loyalties, even as their own well-being was jeopardized. For many subjects of my study, traumatic political experiences affirmed their convictions.

Finally, in case after case, this study reveals that particular life experiences serve as reference points, as explanations for both freezing and transforming thinking. This study focuses particularly on the experiences of individuals in top political positions and offices during the rise and fall of the Allende government, their exile experiences, and their return to Chile to play leading roles in the transition from military rule.

While analytically distinct, these dimensions must be intertwined and, in some senses, bound together. Traumatic experiences often mean the disintegration or collapse of important networks, including family and party. Individual needs for securing identities in the face of traumatic experiences can lead either to a freezing of ideologies or to ideological transformations, depending, in large part, on their cognitive frameworks. Together, cognitive type, embeddedness, and experience allow us to conceptualize about individual political identity formation and transformation, which contributes significantly to our understanding of larger political processes.

Individual and collective memories of a turbulent, traumatic past play a crucial and undertheorized role in postauthoritarian politics. The arrest of Augusto Pinochet laid bare the ways in which authoritarian legacies can dramatically jolt as well as doggedly plague democratic regimes. In spite of the attempts of the Chilean political class to put the painful past behind, such "irruptions" as resistance to imprisonment by convicted human rights violators, protests and counterprotests on the anniversary of the military coup, and Pinochet's detention serve to unravel the efforts of the political elite to "move on."[48]

In this period of postauthoritarian transition, Latin American thinkers and political strategists are wrestling with situations in which neopopulist, authoritarian politicians have emerged in formal democratic regimes. An uneasy tension continues to shadow civil-military relations. In the wake of dramatic economic austerity programs, Latin Americans face greater social inequality than the region has ever known. The region calls out for a new period of long-term vision, tempered by past experiences yet not without a bit of utopia. In the words of Karl Mannheim:

> The disappearance of utopia brings about a static state of affairs in which man himself becomes no more than a thing. . . . Without utopia humanity would lose its will to create history, sinking into either self-pity or complacency. . . . [We] have a responsibility to defend ideals against two corrupting forces: relativism and complacency engendered by the matter-of-factness of everyday relations.[49]

In order to tease out the remnants of and the transformations in political ideology, I argue, it is necessary to unearth processes of individual political identity formation for the sixties generation of Latin America's left political elites. Such exploration has revealed a world of internal struggle and deliberation as individuals seek to mesh their past and present ideologies and roles in order to give meaning to their political practices and self-perceptions.

CHAPTER 2

CHILE'S REVOLUTIONARY GENERATION

*[On September 11, 1973, the day of the military coup,] all we had was a
pistol and a plastic bag with bullets, this was all our firepower. We left,
trying to hook up with people, there was a curfew, but we went out, something we would never do now, but we did it. The lights went out at one or
two in the morning. . . . We went to the main avenue with our little pistols
and all our little things to try to do something, and then we realized that
nothing was going on and we returned. . . .*

*That was where the romance ended, and we began to understand that
politics was something more than simply wonderful ideas, ideals, . . . and
we suffered a great deal, because if for the older [leaders] a coup wasn't
possible, for us it was completely unimaginable.*

—Eduardo Reyes, Chilean socialist

■ Among the most closely observed attempts at a socialist project in recent history was the 1970–1973 Popular Unity government in
Chile, in which Chilean Socialist Party leader Salvador Allende became the
first democratically elected Marxist president in world history. Allende's
election captured the attention, the imagination, and the hope of a universal left community of thinkers and activists, and the bloody demise of the
Popular Unity government similarly served as a catalyst for debate, analysis, and reflection.

For Eduardo Reyes, then a leader of the Chilean Young Socialists, and
for many of Reyes's generation, the military overthrow of the Popular
Unity government cut deeply into the very core of everything for which he
stood, into what had been the basis for his daily activism and existence,
into the shared beliefs, values, and motivations of Reyes and his closest
companions. For the Chilean revolutionary sixties generation, the dramatic and brutal coup d'état marked the end of the "romance," the euphoric il-

lusion that Chile was well on the road to becoming a revolutionary socialist society.

There is an abundant literature on Chilean politics of the 1960s and
1970s, and interpretations of the downfall of the Allende government vary
enormously. This chapter will provide an overview of that period and then
focus on the ideological and strategic debates, practices, and transformations within the Chilean left in the post-1973 period. In tracing the period
from the 1960s to the 1990s, I argue here that the Chilean left experienced a series of shocks that transformed its political culture from a culture based on the perception of a set of collective ideological visions that
the left believed could bring socialist transformation to Chile, to a culture
fragmented by a legacy of internal conflict, fear, and defeat. The 1960s
represented the pinnacle of Chilean left political culture, a period in which
the left perceived that, united, it had the means to lead the country toward
a revolutionary socialist society. Under the 1970–1973 Allende government, that perception was shattered and replaced by a multiparty left in
power but fraught with ideological and strategic contradictions. With
General Augusto Pinochet's 1973 overthrow of Allende, the Chilean left
physically unraveled, its leaders and militants assassinated, imprisoned,
tortured, and exiled.

Despite such repression, members of the Chilean left struggled to reconstruct their parties, analyze their own performances during the Allende
years, and rethink socialist visions for Chile.[1] In the decade following the
coup, many Chilean left thinkers and activists, influenced largely by European debates and experiences, worked to "renovate" socialism.[2] Among the
most serious theoretical reflections was a rethinking and appreciation (or
a "revaluation") of the meaning of democracy. Left leaders also engaged in
an exploration of the role of the political party and of political party alliances. At the heart of these debates was a questioning and, for many, a
gradual renunciation of Leninism. In addition, Chilean left intellectuals
produced several analytical works on the effects, both visible and latent, of
authoritarianism on Chilean culture and society. Sociologists such as Norbert Lechner and José Joaquín Brunner argued that the most enduring
legacies of the Chilean dictatorship would be the insecurities and fears
generated by the erosion of historic collective identities, which, they suggested, would produce a constant societal demand for political predictabil-
ity, political certainty, and political order.[3]

Nevertheless, beginning in 1983, the attempts of political party leaders
on the left to reconstruct an ideological, "counterhegemonic" project be-

came overshadowed by day-to-day tactical struggles.[4] The focus on tactical maneuvering and on building an alliance with the dominant Christian Democratic Party (PDC) limited much of the rethinking of a democratic socialist vision that had taken place during the dictatorship. An essential revaluation of democracy among important sectors of the left had taken place, particularly regarding the question of political compromise in order to preserve democratic institutions. Yet there was far less attention to the question of popular participation, or the "deepening" of democracy, in the postdictatorship period. Moreover, there had been little exploration of the relationship between socialism and the market or the appropriate role of the state in the economy and society. While left thinkers had produced major critiques of neoliberalism and its impact on Chile, few had seriously contemplated alternatives to neoliberalism for their country. In the Concertación campaigns to elect Patricio Aylwin in 1989 and Eduardo Frei Jr. in 1993, many left leaders embraced a discourse of modernization without an examination or critique of the relationship between modernization and democracy.[5]

In spite of impressive electoral and political gains, today's Chilean left continues to be plagued by shared memories of the chaos and drama surrounding the Allende years and the penetrating reach of the repression that followed. Through the 1990s, left leaders have been jockeying for a share of political power, with comparatively little attention to what might be considered "left visions" of Chile's future. The left also faces the challenge of framing positions within a dominant Chilean culture that emphasizes the will of the individual rather than collectivity, within a universal context in which socialist models have, for the most part, disappeared.

As subsequent chapters will illustrate, individual left leaders continue to be engaged in processes of reconstituting their political identities in a society that is painfully conscious of, yet unreconciled to, many of the realities of its past. Nevertheless, in these processes, this study has found, individual left leaders consistently draw from their ideological grounding in the 1960s for essential referents to today. Such referents may appear in individuals' discourse as signifiers of contrast between past and present identity ("I'm not the revolutionary that I once was"), as symbols of inspiration for a transformed politics ("My involvement in Catholic Action made me what I am today"), or as strong ideological attachment to a past referent ("I've always been an Allendista"). For this reason, an understanding of the historical and political contexts in which this sixties generation came of age is necessary.

THE REVOLUTIONARY GENERATION

In a certain sense, the Chile of the 1960s was a child of a world struggling to come to terms with the contradictions of modern capitalism. In the advanced industrialized countries, young people, working people, women, and minorities challenged, in disparate ways, the very premises of societies based on imperialism and material gain at the expense of class, race, gender, and community harmony. In much of the Third World, particularly in Africa and Southeast Asia, revolutionary independence movements successfully challenged colonial domination. In the Catholic world, archdioceses, local parishes, and Catholic-based political movements wrestled with the meanings of the Vatican Council II and its promotion of a preferential option for the poor.

In Latin America, the new directions in the Catholic Church had a profound influence on popular struggles for democracy and social justice. Christian-based communities proved to be a new foundation for organizing on behalf of local needs, and they provided grassroots support for many of the Catholic-based New Left parties and movements that emerged in the region in the 1960s and 1970s.

Yet it was the Cuban Revolution that influenced political discourse and political behavior in ways unparalleled in the hemisphere. In some Latin American countries, such as Argentina, Uruguay, and Guatemala, the Cuban example inspired revolutionary guerrilla movements. In Chile, the Cuban Revolution informed left discourse and debate that questioned the feasibility of a peaceful transition to socialism, as well as the need for a prolonged "bourgeois democratic" phase to oversee capitalist industrialization and modernization.

Chile in the 1960s was a country with an urbanized population and an educated and organized workforce. It was a country extremely affected by fluctuations in the global economy, particularly the world market price of copper, which accounted for approximately 80 percent of Chile's export revenues.[6] As in much of Latin America, in Chile industrialization and modernization depended upon state intervention and upon foreign capital and technology, and the country struggled incessantly with debt, inflation, and an increasingly stagnant rural economy.[7] From the 1950s through the 1970s, successive Chilean governments attempted distinct "revolutionary" economic programs to correct for such negative trends.[8]

The Chile of the 1960s possessed a solid, multiparty, democratic political system that featured a strong left.[9] Since the 1930s, the Chilean left, namely, the Chilean Socialist (PSCH) and Communist (PCCH) parties, had won representation in both the executive and the legislative branches. From 1938 to 1952, the left had formed coalitions with centrist parties that brought its representatives into the cabinet. In 1958, PSCH presidential candidate Salvador Allende came a mere 33,449 votes short of victory. In the 1961 elections for Congress, the left-dominated Popular Action Front (FRAP) coalition won 27.5 percent of the House and thirteen out of forty-five seats in the Senate.[10]

The strong showing of the left in government represented a national political culture in which the Chilean left could lay claim to a firmly established collective identity, rooted in the struggles of Chilean working people. Late-nineteenth-century capitalist expansion in the extractive sector in Chile brought proletarianization and an organized and highly class-conscious working class, a powerful Marxist labor movement unique to Latin America.[11] In Chile's northern mines, the combination of difficult working conditions, collective geographic isolation, and employment in foreign-owned companies generated early radicalization. At the turn of the century, the Chilean nitrate workers formed the political base for the founding of the Socialist Workers Party (POS), later to become the Chilean Communist Party.

The miners proved extremely effective in organizing both workers in the transport sector that serviced exports and rural workers in close proximity to the mines. Charles Bergquist, in an analysis of the early Chilean labor movement, argues that from 1880 to 1930 the ability of the nitrate workers to organize, to ally themselves with and mobilize other working-class sectors, and to build a radical labor movement caused a major crisis for the state in the 1920s. This crisis forced a restructuring of the state that moved the entire political debate to the left over the coming decades.[12]

Powerful links developed between unions and political parties. Unions depended upon parties as sources of financial support during strikes and as sympathetic interpreters during the arduous negotiation periods. Parties mobilized unions for support in the electoral process and for backing both inside and outside the state. Although the 1925 Chilean labor code attempted to restrict mass organizing through laws that barred organizing in plants with fewer than twenty-five workers, union-official salaries, collective bargaining, and the formation of labor federations, the net effect was to politicize the labor movement. Writing in 1972, Regis Debray affirmed the ties of the workers' movement to political parties: "Chile is the only country in the continent . . . in which those parties which are referred to as 'workers' parties because of their ideology, are actually organically workers organizations by extraction and social base."[13]

As noted above, the Chilean Communist Party was born in the nitrate mines as the Socialist Workers Party (POS), led by printer and journalist Luis Emilio Recabarren.[14] The POS successfully established branches in working-class sectors of Santiago and other cities throughout the country, and in 1906 Recabarren was elected to Congress (though he was not allowed to serve). After an initial period in which the PCCH adopted a maximalist, Comintern position calling for an immediate struggle for socialism, the party moved in the early 1930s to the antifascist, Popular Front strategy of the post-1935 Comintern, a position that characterized the PCCH for many decades to come.[15] In fact, between 1933 and 1973, the Chilean Communists altered their positions on class and party alliances very little, advocating a broad-based alliance among the middle and popular classes and center-left political party coalitions that would seek representation within a bourgeois democratic framework. This stance endured in spite of the ten-year Permanent Law in Defense of Democracy, which outlawed the PCCH from 1948 to 1958.

The PCCH was never recognized as a party of theoretical richness. The Chilean Communist Party, however, represented both an extremely disciplined left political organization and a bedrock of Chilean working-class and popular culture. Among the Chilean Communist Party's ranks of the 1960s were some of the most popular performers in the country, including singers Violeta Parra, Victor Jara, and the group Quilapayún. The Nobel laureate, poet Pablo Neruda, was also a Communist and a foreign diplomat. Through their songs and ballads, such artists gave popular expression to worker and peasant struggles for social justice. An estimated seventy thousand young people joined the PCCH over the course of the 1960s.[16] Artists, actors, writers, musicians, and others of enormous talent contributed to a rich Chilean left culture, which, in turn, became a highly visible part of the Chilean national cultural fabric.

Unlike the homogeneous, highly unified, and disciplined organizational and ideological PCCH, the Chilean Socialist Party has been characterized historically as heterogeneous and factionalized. The PSCH was founded in the aftermath of the short-lived Socialist Republic of 1932, a twelve-day progressive nationalist experiment led by the idealistic military leader and subsequent PSCH cofounder Marmaduke Grove.[17] In 1933 the newly founded PSCH joined several smaller revolutionary parties, aggregating, as Kenneth Roberts describes, "left-wing masons, populists, and democratic socialists under the same flag as revolutionary Marxists, Trotskyists and anarcho-syndicalists."[18] In contrast to the Chilean Communist

Party, the PSCH opposed alliances with the Third International or any of the socialist internationals. The Chilean Socialist Party embraced a strong nationalist and Latin American identity, often advocating Marxism-Leninism as a general interpretive framework while emphasizing the particularity of Chilean class dynamics. The PSCH leadership represented a peculiar brand of national populist figures who found strong resonance within the Chilean polity and society in both the middle and the working classes.[19] Again in contrast to the Chilean Communist Party, throughout much of the pre-1973 period the PSCH adopted a revolutionary doctrinal program that dismissed the possibility of socialism through bourgeois democratic means. Between 1934 and 1957, internal party struggles over class and party alliances and the means toward socialist transformation formally split the PSCH several times.

In 1957 Socialist Party leader Eugenio González, together with others of his generation, reunited the PSCH under a Workers' Front program, eschewing alliances with the petite bourgeoisie and other middle sectors and their political party representatives, while moving toward an uneasy alliance with the "proletarian party," the PCCH.[20] While the PSCH continued to house several competing factions, the radicalized Workers' Front position was strengthened by the narrow loss of the left FRAP coalition in the 1958 presidential elections, as well as by the victory of the Cuban Revolution in 1959.

Allende's loss to Christian Democratic leader Eduardo Frei in the 1964 presidential elections further fueled those within the PSCH who believed revolutionary transformation through existing political institutions was impossible. The Socialists proclaimed the victorious Christian Democratic Party no more than "a new political vehicle" for imperialists and the national bourgeoisie.[21] In 1967, at its XXII National Congress in Chillán, the PSCH passed resolutions claiming that "revolutionary violence is inevitable and legitimate" and that "peaceful or legal forms of struggle (reivindicative, ideological, electoral, etc.) will not lead by themselves to power."[22] Moreover, sectors within the PSCH successfully passed resolutions establishing it as the vanguard of the working class, democratic centralism, careful selection of cadres, increased internal discipline—in short, the Leninization of the party.[23] Thus, while the Socialist Party continued to be an active participant in Chile's electoral process, internal party positions questioned the legitimacy of such a strategy.[24] From the mid-1960s to the early 1970s, several Chilean New Left movements and parties emerged, primarily as splits from the Socialist, Communist, and Christian Democratic parties. In

1964, twenty-three young Socialist militants left the psch and, together with a handful of young Communists, founded the Revolutionary Left Movement (mir).[25] The mir denounced the "revisionism and reformism" of the leading left parties, advocating armed struggle as an appropriate path toward revolution in Chile. When asked for this study his opinion of the Frei government in that period, former Mirista Osvaldo Puccio remembered his utter disdain:

> It was the worst. It was a government without results and in my very ideologized opinion, it was part of the Alliance for Progress that the Americans had invented to stop the Cuban Revolution. It was a very antipopular government, with a, well, now that I am older, I see that it did have a progressive content, even a popular content. Now, what I was saying when I was seventeen, eighteen years old is not so disastrous in comparison to what some senators of the Republic were saying.

While quite small in number, the mir had a clear appeal for young left militants, and Mirista positions echoed an important faction within the psch. In fact, several psch members practiced a *doble militancia*, appearing as militants in both the mir and the psch.

The Chilean Catholic Left became another crucial source of the country's New Left. The two most important Catholic Left groups of the period were the Unitary Popular Action Movement (mapu, founded in 1969 and split in 1972 into the mapu and the mapu-oc, or mapu–Worker Peasant Party) and the Christian Left (ic, founded in 1971), both of them products of splits, primarily from the Chilean Christian Democratic Party. mapu and ic leaders were among the most influential left political thinkers and politicians in the country, quick to rise to the vanguard of the pre-1973 revolutionary left (and, many years later, to the leadership of the left during the 1980s transition from authoritarian rule).

Youthful energy and revolutionary zeal characterized these Catholic and secular New Left parties. As subsequent chapters will reveal in greater detail, among the young leaders of these parties, best exemplified by the mapu, were what this study characterizes as thinkers and political entrepreneurs. The thinkers were those who focused on advancing revolutionary ideas but lacked the political know-how, machinery, and support to bring them to fruition. The political entrepreneurs were adept at building revolutionary coalitions as representative organizations to house their ideas, yet they had little or no experience in governance. Together the two groups symbolized a new breed of political actors and organizations that combined intellectual brilliance with a heady drive and little political experience.

The 1960s were years in which democratic rights were vastly expanded in Chile, particularly in the countryside. In 1958 the government passed laws making the vote compulsory and guaranteeing the right to a secret ballot, electoral reforms that would dramatically weaken landowners' control over much of the rural vote. A 1962 electoral reform law further weakened the rural oligarchy. In 1970 Chile granted illiterates the right to vote.

In addition to expanding voters' rights, in 1962 Chile passed historic legislation to legalize unionization in the countryside and to transfer land to the rural poor. The Christian Democratic administration (1964–1970) strengthened agrarian reform laws, and over the course of the next decade, the implementation of agrarian reform upset what many have held as the historic compromise responsible for Chilean political stability.[26] Crudely presented, this compromise was seen as rightist party rule in the rural areas in exchange for progressive legislation, left-wing gains in Chile's cities, and a "three-thirds" balance in national electoral politics among the left, right, and center. The combination of such electoral and agrarian reforms encouraged the Socialist, Communist, and Christian Democrat Parties to wage intensive organizing and vote-getting campaigns throughout the Chilean countryside, and their efforts proved successful.

In this period of massive recruitment drives and mobilizations, political party loyalists, another of the cognitive ideal-types presented in this study, proved particularly important to their parties. Party loyalists sustained the party machines, organized at the base levels, and focused on battles in the universities, shop floors, and neighborhoods to win support. In an era that predated mass public opinion polling, the "sound bite," and technological expertise in attaining the right media image in Chile, party loyalists were politically invaluable.

The 1960s thus bore witness to an explosion in popular political participation, from dramatically increased voter participation to increased mobilization in both the cities and the countryside. Chilean left discourse was full of the revolutionary potential of *"el pueblo,"* "the people," the masses of workers and peasants, the urban and rural poor who possessed the capacity for mobilizing to demand transformation of the Chilean state and society. There was no real disaggregation of the popular sectors, in either sociological or politico-ideological terms.[27] In an enlightening essay on the evolution of the Chilean left, Chilean sociologist Tomás Moulián argues that by the mid-1960s, Marxist ideology had become a basic referent not only for left political parties but for many sectors of Chilean society.[28] Moulián bases this argument on the content of debates being waged in university classrooms, union halls, neighborhood meetings, and, importantly, in the Catholic Church. By the late 1960s, Moulián contends, Marxism had "expanded its influence among intellectuals and consolidated its position as a 'popularized philosophy.'"[29] The left dominated many of the country's leading civil society organizations, including the Chilean Labor Confederation (CUT), student federations, newly organized peasant unions, artist groups, housing movements, and other popular class- and community-based associations. The PSCH and the PCCH possessed lively presses and radio stations, all of which enjoyed wide circulation. Thus, while the 1970–1973 Popular Unity administration would reveal unwieldy internal differences in ideology and strategy within the governing left coalition, the Chilean left managed to maintain a powerful collective identity in Chilean society. This would be demonstrated in the electoral arena and elsewhere throughout the Popular Unity period.

The Chilean left was not immune to many of the world debates and struggles of the 1960s, from the civil rights and antiwar protests in the advanced capitalist countries, to revolutionary struggles in Algeria, Cuba, and Vietnam. Moreover, in spite of Khrushchev's revelations and in spite of the Soviet rollback of progressive movements in Hungary in 1956 and Czechoslovakia in 1968, the perception of rapid industrialization processes taking place in the Eastern bloc made state-planned, "real socialism" models appealing.[30] The strength and sophistication of mass movements for change imbued many sectors of the Chilean left with the sense that revolutionary transformation was a logical product of historical forces as well as a desired goal for the country.

Cuba drove home to the Chilean left a heightened sense of the "moral imperative" of revolutionary struggle. According to Moulián, much of the imagery surrounding the Cuban struggle, conceived in "epic" terms as the ultimate self-deliverance or sacrifice on behalf of the revolution, appealed to the deeply rooted Catholic sentiments that were so much a part of Latin American culture.[31] Cuba symbolized the weakness of capitalism on moral as well social or distribution grounds. The idea of Cuba as a moral imperative consistently surfaced in interviews with leaders of the Chilean left, from the Catholic to the secular left. Cuba and her leaders/heroes were the primary international referent for Chile's sixties left generation.

The combination of dramatic electoral and agrarian reforms, a strong left showing at the polls, and the perception of Cuba-inspired revolutionary movements spreading throughout the region visibly shook the Chilean right. To counter a potential Allende victory in the 1964 presidential elections, the right supported Christian Democrat Eduardo Frei. Yet the Chilean right was quickly disillusioned by the agrarian reform laws and other progressive legislation backed by the Frei administration. As many analysts have asserted, the 1960s marked an across-the-board ideologization of Chilean politics, a polarization of the political left, right, and center that ran from the country's political class to the Chilean voters, roughly a third of whom tended to vote for the right, a third for the center, and a third for the left.[32] It was a time when the right began to reformulate an offensive strategy, when the center attempted but failed to lead the country on a non-Marxist path toward social change and community harmony, and when the left was convinced that it was close to capturing the political power necessary to initiate revolutionary transformation. Capitalist ideology competed with the ideas of nationalization, redistribution of wealth, and workers' control of the state. While such ideas polarized society, it was far from clear that strategies for their implementation were defined or agreed upon by their proponents.

THE POPULAR UNITY VICTORY

In reflecting upon the September 4, 1970, electoral victory of Salvador Allende and the Popular Unity coalition, Moulián writes of a double meaning to the evening's celebration in the streets, a combination of carnival and drama that would serve as a metaphor for the three-year Popular Unity period:

> On the night of September 4, 1970, the crowd took over the major avenues to dance and shout, to hug one another and to share their triumphant hopes together. The human wave which engulfed The Alameda (the major avenue of Santiago) was not some amorphous mass, some heterogeneous collection of dispersed individuals, but a people, a community expressing its happiness: everyone reflected this in their faces. But they all knew that their act was not only an act of catharsis or a communal rite expressing happiness for a long-awaited triumph. They knew that happy and festive march was not only celebratory in character; it was also the first move in a battle mobilizing as an act of happiness but also as a demonstration of force.[33]

Allende was elected with 36.2 percent of the vote. He was not the first Chilean president elected with a minority of the popular vote (in 1958 Jorge Alessandri won with 31.5 percent, for example). Yet neither did this showing represent a clear mandate for revolutionary transformation, though the left claimed that it did, interpreting the vote for left Christian Democratic candidate Radomiro Tomic, who garnered 27.8 percent of the vote, as a vote for social change to be added to the Allende vote.

The largest political party members of the Popular Unity coalition were the Chilean Socialist and Chilean Communist parties, followed by the Radical Party (Chile's historic center party, which was replaced in size and significance in the 1960s by the Christian Democratic Party), the MAPU, and a handful of other small left groupings. In 1971 the IC also joined the Popular Unity coalition. In 1972 the MAPU divided into two parties, the MAPU and the MAPU–Worker Peasant Party (MAPU-OC), yet both remained in the Popular Unity coalition.

As Moulián suggests, from 1970 to 1973 battle lines would be drawn, lines defined by ideology and class—but not limited to left-right polarities. Rather, some of the most painful memories recounted in this study center upon internal left struggles, upon the incapacity of the left to formulate a cohesive program, upon sympathetic popular mobilizations that became combative against the opposition and escaped from the control of the political leadership, upon government paralysis in the face of rampant inflation, severe shortages, brawls in the streets, and vicious debate in the halls of Congress. The urgency, volatility, and immediacy of the political moment was reflected in several memories of the UP period, including those of current ambassador to Austria and former MIR militant Osvaldo Puccio:

> I remember having bought a pocket radio and having worked out my own system, so that I could tune into a frequency which allowed me to listen to the news every fifteen minutes. And it wasn't a personal neurosis, it was just that every fifteen minutes there was the possibility of listening, that no more than fifteen minutes would pass, and at least you *believed* you were listening.

Urgency also characterized the UP platform. The platform was, indeed, a revolutionary one, calling for a complete restructuring of the state and property relations.[34] The specific undertakings of the UP program, however, were necessarily vague, for, as indicated above, there were fundamental disagreements within the coalition over how such a program would be implemented and on what timetable. Allende himself saw his six years as preparing the ground for a subsequent transition to socialism.[35] In the simplest of terms, the splits can be seen in three general areas. First, recognizing that political mechanisms as they stood would be obstacles to the transformation of society, the UP platform called for an overhaul of the state. The official UP program, advocated by the radical sectors within the UP, endorsed creating such institutions as a unicameral legislature, to be known as the People's Assembly, the outcome of a democratization process that would incorporate the desires of mass social and workers' organizations at all levels. Moderate sectors within the UP, on the other hand, feared that such an assembly would quickly alienate centrist support within the state.

Second, the UP program outlined a reorganization of the economy. This involved a division of the economy into three productive areas: the Area of Social Property (APS), which included nationalization of natural resource enterprises, banking and insurance, public goods and services, foreign trade, strategic industrial monopolies, and those industries determined to be inefficiently run; the Area of Private Property, which would continue to make up the majority of all enterprise activity; and the Area of Mixed Property, which called for joint development in manufacturing and industry. A corollary to this program called for thorough implementation of the 1967 Agrarian Reform Law. The radical left of the UP supported the intensification of the APS and the immediate expropriation of large landholdings. The moderate wing, which included the Communist Party and Allende himself, favored gradual implementation of the APS and agrarian reform.

Third, the UP platform called for "the mobilization of the people of Chile toward the conquest of power."[36] This went to the heart of many of the divisions over class and party alliances. The moderate wing claimed it was suicidal not to engage concrete middle-class and national bourgeois support for the UP program; the revolutionary faction within the UP claimed that popular-class mobilization and incorporation into the UP program was the only path and that no distinction should be drawn between the national and the international bourgeoisie. The split within the Popular Unity coalition became, on the one side, a strategy favoring an alliance between the organized working class and a vaguely defined middle class, represented by the Christian Democratic Party, and on the other, a strategy favoring an uncompromising "popular power" alliance, also vaguely defined. The moderate wing was led by the president, a minority within the Socialist Party, the Communist Party, the Christian Left, and the MAPU-OC, while the radical wing was composed of the majority of the Socialist Party leadership, the MAPU, and the MIR (although the MIR was not officially a member of the Popular Unity coalition).

Internal divisions over the means of transformation irreparably crippled a government already opposed by powerful domestic and international interests. President Allende faced a Christian Democratic Party that would be successfully courted by the Chilean right and the United States government to block the Popular Unity platform. The United States engaged in what are now well-documented covert operations to devastate the Chilean economy and to contribute decisively to political disorder. Opposition to the Popular Unity government would turn for the first time in several decades "to the barracks" to end the Chilean democratic regime.

THE TRAUMA OF DEFEAT

It is almost impossible to overstate the impact of the September 11, 1973, military coup d'état on the Chilean left. In response to my request that interviewees reflect over the course of their lives and name the two or three strongest influences on their political evolution, the first response was unanimous: "the coup d'état." This nearly reflexive response served as shorthand for the array of meanings that individuals came to assign to the coup, from the immediate impact of the event on personal security and livelihood to the ways in which the coup ended a vast number of assumptions about what was possible for Chilean society.

The orchestration of the coup itself was violent and swift.[37] While there were pockets of resistance in a handful of factories, campuses, shantytowns, and in the presidential palace, La Moneda, itself, these were isolated struggles. On the night of the coup, as Eduardo Reyes and others have recounted, small groups of left militants ventured into the streets, armed with very little. Most quickly realized that such action was suicidal. Chileans were not to mount a defense of the Allende government.

Both leaders and militants of the Chilean left who had not been arrested went into hiding, and many began to plan for their escape from the country.[38] The large-scale repression and horror of the early years of the Pinochet regime are well known. The postauthoritarian government-appointed Truth and Reconciliation Commission and the government's subsequent National Corporation of Reparation and Reconciliation together documented 3,129 human rights violations resulting in death under the dictatorship.[39] In the first two years alone, an estimated one in every ten families experienced arrest, torture, and/or exile.[40] The meaning of the Popular Unity defeat represents perhaps the most critical dimension in this study of political identity formation and transformation. As the personal accounts provided and analyzed in this study will demonstrate, the very language that individuals employ to reconstruct Allende's death, the military coup, and the coup's immediate aftermath reveals a good deal about individual processes of defining political identity.

PINOCHET'S PROJECT

Chilean sociologist Manuel Antonio Garretón periodized the initial years of the Pinochet regime into two phases: the first, from 1973 to 1978, he termed the reactive phase; the second, from 1978 to 1982, the reorganizing phase, he termed the refounding of state and society.[41] In the reactive phase, the military regime unleashed a massive repression campaign, geared to render past structural relations between the state and society expressed through its political institutions nonexistent. On the economic front, after initial uncertainty, the military removed obstacles to the market in order to embark on a path to recovery and growth.[42] In the reorganizing phase, Pinochet reordered traditional Chilean social and political structures based upon an extreme neoliberal model of the economy. By drastically reducing public spending, lifting price subsidies and tariffs, liberalizing the financial system, and opening the economy to international capital and consumer goods, the regime transformed social conditions for most sectors of society, from the urban and rural poor to the national bourgeoisie.[43] While the neoliberal model was by no means monolithic through Pinochet's seventeen-year dictatorship, the model virtually deindustrialized the country, signifying the decline and impoverishment of Chile's working class.[44] Emphasis on capital-intensive agribusiness caused further pauperization of the Chilean peasantry. The model on the whole reconstituted the Chilean ruling class, primarily the financial sector.[45] Moreover, Pinochet's neoliberal model enjoyed the support of the international financial community, particularly financial sectors in the United States.

At the level of political institutions, the Pinochet regime oversaw the writing and implementation of the new 1980 constitution, granting legitimacy to the regime and to the military's intent to ensure a gradual transition to what was officially termed a "protected democracy," in which the military would retain a powerful tutelary role.[46] In essence, Pinochet dismantled social and political structures and institutions and their expressions in the state, relationships that had developed since the turn of the century. Furthermore, he replaced the legal and democratic institutions through which traditional political opposition had operated for decades with a new and highly restrictive set of labor codes, decrees, and an authoritarian constitution. For the political opposition to Pinochet, the new "legality" presented a particularly difficult set of questions and challenges.

As Chilean sociologist Pilar Vergara argues, underlying Pinochet's recrafting of the state was a fundamentally *technocratic* conception of power. Within this conception, the state is the embodiment of the general interests of the nation above the interests of distinct groups and classes, and the preauthoritarian, democratic period is judged as institutionally conducive to stagnation and economic crisis.[47] In this new official political culture, technocracy becomes a substitute for politics, eliminating those institutions and norms of a representative regime. The public-administrative space, argues Chilean sociologist José Joaquín Brunner, becomes characterized by a broad "regime of exclusions."[48] Sectoral interests are seen as interferences that pose obstacles to the coherent development of program. When coupled with a neoliberal economic model, private capitalist interests become equivalent to the public interest.[49] Pinochet championed a neoliberal authoritarian ideology, which through the control of such channels as mass communication and the educational system, penetrated the Chilean social fabric and appealed to authoritarian sentiments deeply embedded within the Chilean social structure. "It is clear," states Vergara, "that in the search for conformity or the passive consent of the popular sectors, coercive mechanisms played a dominant role, yet it is erroneous to assume that [conformity] has been based solely on the use of force."[50]

Such interpretations of lasting transformations in Chilean political culture did not easily translate into clear strategies for the Chilean left political party opposition, an opposition devastated by the repression. From 1973 to 1975 the military regime eliminated the leaders of three consecutive internal Chilean Socialist Party directorates. By 1976 military intelligence had decisively penetrated the internal organization of the Chilean Communist Party, and in that year seventy-eight of the more than one hundred Communist Party members killed were midlevel officials. From the end of 1976 until 1978 security forces almost eliminated the PCCH's internal leadership.[51] Left party militants who remained in the country struggled to regroup as best they could. Former Communist Youth leader Raúl Oliva, who remained in Chile until 1976, described clandestine PCCH operations:

We organized three to a cell, and those three could only have contact
with two additional militants. We would meet in private homes for
short periods to share information, commiserate. There was no real debate among us, just an attempt to follow party instructions if and when
we could. My wife, who was also a Communist Youth organizer, and I
didn't communicate with one another for eight months.

Before the coup, I would say that between the PCCH and the Communist Youth there were 280,000 members. In 1975, I remember that
there were more or less 5,000 of us.

Other left parties used similar cell structures, yet the Chilean security
forces rapidly penetrated them. Former Mirista leader Patricio Rivas described internal organization and the trauma of everyday life:

> [In the days following the coup] I began to live a kind of day-to-day
> internal drama. It is much more difficult to stay quiet and live this way
> than to do politics. It was like opening a Pandora's box where I wasn't
> sure what vermin would come out. And funny things would happen
> in all of this. We changed our identities so many times, we changed
> the way we looked and at times wouldn't recognize each other. . . .
> We changed houses. . . . We changed cars. . . . But the tension
> destroys you.
>
> I was really in charge of internal coordination. And we set up our
> cell structure modeled after the Bolsheviks, one person in charge of
> three people. We began to organize Resistance Committees, all of
> that. . . . And we really perfected our communications system, our cell
> structure . . . and we were fine, Bautista [van Showen, a top Mirista
> leader] was the only one who had fallen, until March [1974].

During the first years of the dictatorship, the majority of the Chilean left
continued to believe that the military regime would not endure. In its December 1974 message to party militants, the Communist Party leadership
wrote: "A little more than a year of dictatorship has been sufficient to make
clear that Pinochet and his cohorts cannot sustain themselves much
longer. The Military Junta is strictly transitory."[52]

Despite this overly optimistic prognosis, the PCCH experienced acute de-
moralization among those who continued to remain in the country. By
1976 the infiltration of Chilean intelligence officials into the Communist
Party had created a traumatic climate of paranoia and suspicion within the

party's ranks. In the words of Raúl Oliva and his wife, Alicia, "Either you were a traitor or a *desaparecido*":

> Given we knew someone was informing on us, it led us all into this sense that if you were caught you were either a traitor or you would soon be a *desaparecido*, and if you hadn't been caught, why weren't you caught yet? We were all so afraid, living under unreal circumstances, in addition to economic precariousness, and this traitor element was so strong. There was such uncertainty. It was a feeling we carried with us, a feeling that continued to drive us to questioning ourselves even after we had left Chile for exile.

Such trauma and doubt, even within the most organized clandestine left party, the PCCH, took an enormous toll on left organizers. Repression, including imprisonment and exile, proved a painful catalyst for individual political identity transformation.

PARTY ACTIVISTS IN EXILE

> One leaves with the idea of the (triumphant) return, each one of us swears it so on the border: if there were any doubt, leaving would be unbearable. We left *because* we will return, and that is the only way we can conceive of it. [It] is symbolized by Ulysses . . . : a Ulysses who after a thousand dangers returns to his native Ithaca to reassume his throne, his wife (who never stopped waiting for him), and even his old dog![53]

While it is difficult to estimate the number of Chileans who went into exile after the 1973 coup, reputable Chilean groups, such as the Chilean Commission for Human Rights, place the figure at between 200,000 and 250,000 political exiles and their families. Political exiles—whom I define as those who fled the country and who remained active in political activity abroad against the military regime[54]—were expelled from the country under various circumstances. Hundreds sought refuge in foreign embassies and were granted political asylum abroad, thousands crossed the Andes to Argentina and either remained there for some time or continued on to other countries. Between 1974 and 1978, through agreements between the military and the International Committee of the Red Cross, Decree Law 504, and a government amnesty, at least four thousand political prisoners had their sentences commuted to exile.[55] This meant that many of those people were subjected to the trauma of arrest and torture before arriving in exile.

Until the early to mid-1980s, Chilean left party support and sustenance would depend upon political party headquarters established in exile. In addition to the PSCH and the PCCH, this was also the case for the smaller but significant parties of Chile's New Left, including the IC, the MAPU, the MAPU-OC, and the MIR. While the parties attempted to maintain a dynamic balance in leadership between those inside the country and those in exile, the vast majority of the left political party leadership was in exile. The exiled political elite represented a global network of approximately three hundred political leaders.[56] The most important nuclei of the exiled Chilean party leadership were Rome, (former) East Berlin, Moscow, and Mexico City. Rome became the headquarters of Chile's most significant multiparty coalition and base of solidarity in exile, Chile-Democrático. It was also the party headquarters for the MAPU-OC. During the dictatorial period, thinkers and political entrepreneurs of the MAPU-OC would play a vanguard role in "renovating" Chilean socialist thought, and, ultimately, in formulating the positions of what would become the dominant faction of the Chilean Socialist Party. Several prominent PSCH and PCCH members also resided in exile in Rome.

The second nucleus involved groups who resided in Moscow and East Berlin. The former was the headquarters-in-exile for the Chilean Communist Party, and the latter served as the headquarters-in-exile for the Chilean Socialist Party and for an important group of Communist Party thinkers.

The third nucleus of exiled political leaders was in Mexico City. These politicians and intellectuals were either sent by their parties to Mexico or made a conscious decision to remain in Latin America. Chileans in Mexico founded the Secretariat of Solidarity for Latin America, which worked to provide support for the Chilean opposition and which promoted models of interregional cooperation in order to strengthen the institutional bases of economic and political democratization. In addition, some of its members established an institute to analyze formally the history of the United States and its relations with Latin America.

From as early as 1974 members of the Chilean left within Chile as well as abroad began to produce think pieces analyzing the Popular Unity period and advocating particular strategies of alliance and activity against the dictatorship.[57] In October 1973 a Socialist Party internal directorate had been constituted, composed of a handful of existing members of the Central Committee as well as new members co-opted from the party base and the Socialist Youth directorate (including Eduardo Reyes). In March 1974 the internal directorate released a document critiquing the party's failure to provide a coherent revolutionary project:

> The defeat of the people and the triumph of the counterrevolutionary alternative cannot be explained as the simple military defeat of the direct resistance to a coup. The political defeat of the popular movement was sealed before September 11, being determined by the degree of isolation of the working class and the absence of a real leading force capable of making use, with possibilities of triumph, of the latent revolutionary potential in the forces of the masses and in the instruments of institutional power within reach of the government.[58]

The internal directorate also criticized the PSCH for its inability to compromise with the Christian Democratic Party, recognizing that "tactical compromises are possible and necessary in a revolutionary policy."[59] Moreover, the directorate acknowledged that "all forms of struggle," including armed struggle, would be necessary to defeat the military regime. The directorate insisted that the PSCH become the true Leninist party it had professed to be, exercising hegemonic leadership and discipline while working to create a "broad anti-fascist front," including an alliance with the Christian Democrats against the dictatorship. The "March Document" proved quite similar to the analysis and proposed oppositional strategy that emerged from the Chilean Communist Party. The PCCH, which consistently presented a unified position, called for the party to build a mass antifascist movement against the dictatorship, a movement of alliances bridging parties from the center to the left. Interestingly enough, however, until the early 1980s, the Communist Party did not argue that armed struggle would be a necessary component to defeat the dictatorship.

The interpretation of the Popular Unity period by the Socialist Party internal directorate and that party's outline for a broad front strategy brought criticism from other shades of the ideological spectrum within the PSCH. To the "left" of the directorate were those who felt that the Popular Unity defeat was primarily a military defeat and that there could be no alliance with the Christian Democrats. To the "right" were those who felt that orthodox Leninism failed to distinguish the Socialist Party sufficiently from the Chilean Communist Party.

In contrast to the Chilean Socialist Party, the Chilean Communist Party consistently framed its 1970s proposals for a socialist Chile within the country's formal democratic institutions. Its initial analyses of the dictatorship claimed that Chileans could be divided between democrats and fascists, and in keeping with the Comintern position, the PCCH claimed that Chile had to return to democracy before it could become a socialist society.[60] The PCCH called upon the middle classes, the national bourgeoisie, and those "democratic elements" within the armed forces to join an antifascist front against the dictatorship.

Nevertheless, in an oddly paradoxical way, while Socialist Party and other socialist left intellectuals were beginning in the late 1970s to refute Leninism and to revalue the question of democracy, the Chilean Communist Party began quietly debating strategies that in 1980 would publicly move the party to a "popular rebellion" position, advocating armed struggle as a necessary component of its strategy against the dictatorship. The popular rebellion strategy sealed the PCCH's alienation from the political center.

The PCCH's shift was caused both by external conditions and events and by conditions within the party itself.[61] External conditions included first, the Cuban Communist Party's increasing influence within the Comintern and, therefore, within the PCCH; second, analyses of the 1970s struggles in Central America, which attributed a marginal role to the local Communist parties in those struggles; and third, the Christian Democrats' continuing refusal to ally themselves with the Communists. As an increasing number of party leaders and militants were assassinated and imprisoned, party members expressed frustration and the need for a reinvigorating of the party to respond to an entrenched military dictatorship. PCCH documents reveal a prolonged debate within the party over its pre-1973 position regarding the electoral road to socialism, questioning the party's emphasis on *la vía no armada*, or "the unarmed way" to socialist transformation.

Currents within the PCCH had begun to judge that the "objective conditions," including the immiseration of the Chilean majority and military repression, demanded Guevarist-inspired actions to incite a people's revolt. The intellectual leaders of this current were young Communist Party exiles in East Germany, and they became known as the Leipzig Group (explored in detail in chapter 5). Isolated from the concrete realities of life under the Pinochet dictatorship and ignited by Central American struggles, these thinkers proposed that the PCCH create an armed wing to combat the regime.

While the Chilean Communist Party was taking a marked turn to the left, sectors within the socialist left, including sectors of the PSCH, the MAPU, and the MAPU-OC, were moving toward an anti-Leninist stance in their analyses of the failure of the Popular Unity project, the necessary alliances to challenge the dictatorship, and proposals for a postauthoritarian Chile. These sectors led the process of socialist "renovation," which as Kenneth Roberts succinctly describes, involved a rethinking of political and class struggle and a revaluation of democracy:

> Ideologically, renovation entailed an explicit rejection of Leninism as a theoretical doctrine, and a "secularization" of Marxism to strip it of its quasi-religious dogmatism and open it to alternative theoretical perspectives both within and outside of the Marxian philosophical tradition. Intellectuals exiled in Italy discovered Gramsci and employed his concept of the *bloque histórico* to "overcome the schematism of class against class" concept of orthodox Leninism and create a new vision of an alternative hegemony for democratic transformation. . . . The process of renovation thus came to be associated with a rejection of authoritarian and bureaucratic models of socialism. . . .
>
> Strategically, the early proponents of renovation broke with the concept of revolution as an act of political conquest and replaced it with the Gramscian notion of developing an alternative hegemony. As such, they advocated a broad, Center-Left alliance to isolate the dictatorship and promote a *salida política* [political exit] from authoritarian rule. . . . [T]here was a broad consensus on the need to construct a more diverse, multi-class socio-political bloc that would supersede the traditional conception of the Socialist-Communist alliance and comprise a solid majority for democratic transformation. Consequently, socialism would not be imposed following a sudden conquest of power, but would be achieved through a gradual "deepening" or extension of democracy to new spheres of social and institutional relations.[62]

There were several variations on socialist renovation, some emphasizing the need for greater internal party democracy, others focusing on party and class compromise across broader shades of the political and social spectrum. What united the "renovationists" was a rejection of Leninist doctrine as inherently antidemocratic. In a damning critique of the "Leninization" of the Chilean left during the late 1960s, Moulián claims that the left increasingly divorced theory from "real politics," that is, from the multiplicity of reasons that Chilean citizens historically identified with the left and with left parties. Leninization represented an attempt, Moulián argues, to overcome what was seen as "bourgeois democracy," or "electoral illusionism."[63] Democracy had become perceived as an obstacle to transformation.[64]

Divisions within the Socialist Party leadership shifted from what might be termed a left-right divide to a horizontal one between Leninists and anti-Leninists. The Leninists were composed of a group nicknamed the *patrulla juvenil*, or "youth patrol," which had received political and military training in Eastern Europe and which exercised control over the Socialist Party inside Chile. The renovationists were both those influenced by their exile experiences in Western Europe, most notably Italy, and those who remained at Chile's Facultad Latinoamericano de Ciencias Sociales (FLACSO) think tank, supported by European governmental donors and by U.S. private agencies. In 1979 the Socialist Party formally split; it would not reunite until the close of the Pinochet dictatorship. The split symbolized an opposition unable to mount a successful, unified challenge to the dictatorship. Until 1983, the Chilean political party left could do little but organize solidarity campaigns abroad, debate with one another, and reflect on their failures of the past and their hopes for Chile's future. The dictatorship was deeply entrenched.

In 1980 Pinochet and his supporters scored a major victory in a government-manipulated plebiscite to approve an authoritarian constitution. The 1980 constitution declared Marxist parties to be illegal. It outlined what would be a gradual transition from military rule to a "protected democracy." This process would begin in 1988 with a national plebiscite to determine whether Pinochet would remain as president until the close of the century or would step aside to allow national elections in 1989 for a new president and Congress. The constitution granted broad powers to the executive and unprecedented autonomy for the military. For a political class that, despite its revolutionary rhetoric, was accustomed to operating within the legal bounds of its constitution, the passing of the 1980 constitution was a tremendous setback. Until 1983, left political parties seemed to be deflated.

Yet events within Chile in 1983 jolted the political party opposition back into action. Pinochet's neoliberal economic "miracle" of the late 1970s succumbed to its own rigidities and to the Latin American debt crisis of 1982. The country's unemployment rate soared to approximately 30 percent, while economic growth plummeted, falling approximately 14 percent, and the entire banking system virtually collapsed.[65] The breakdown of radical neoliberalism sent even its former supporters among the middle class into the opposition. In May 1983 the Confederation of Copper Workers called for a national day of protest, a call that would initiate a three-year period of popular mobilization against the dictatorship. The May 1983 protest surpassed the opposition's expectations, as businesses closed their offices and an estimated two hundred thousand citizens demonstrated in the streets. National Days of Protest became a monthly occurrence, a collective expression organized by a revitalized political party leadership, weakened yet capable unions, and the activism of party militants and others in an array of grassroots social organizations and movements.[66] Political party loyalists mobilized party bases, while political thinkers and entrepreneurs maneuvered to create alliances and negotiate strategies to topple the regime.

In a concessionary move, the Pinochet regime began to release lists of names of those exiles who would be allowed to return to Chile. Exiles began planning their return, some through "legal" channels with the appearances of their names on the military's lists, others clandestinely, and others still who returned publicly only to be arrested and immediately deported or held for trial. Many of the most well-known political exiles staged dramatic public returns and were greeted by party-organized welcomes at the airport.

Political party leaders scrambled to take advantage of the momentum by forming interparty alliances to coordinate opposition demands. Yet ideological and strategic differences continued to plague the left political class, reflected in the kinds of party alliances formed in the wake of the first protests. As Manuel Antonio Garretón argues, the party alliances represented distinct "ideological identities":

> Although the opposition re-entered public space and it became clear
> that many political parties had survived and had gained a significant
> presence, it did not agree on a transition formula, on the issues the
> group should face, or on the steps needed to form a multiparty coali-
> tion. Instead, there was a cluster of ideological blocs that were more
> concerned with the identity of those included or excluded than with the
> terms of a proposal for confronting the regime.[67]

The first alliances to emerge in Chile in 1983 were the Democratic Alliance (composed of small groups from the right of center, the Christian Democratic Party, other small center parties, and renovated Socialist Party factions); the Democratic Popular Movement (other Socialist Party factions, the Communist Party and the MIR); and the Socialist Bloc (an attempt by

Chilean socialist intellectuals to unite the socialist left). As Garretón states, from 1983 to 1986, these blocs all agreed on a general platform of " 'exit of Pinochet, provisional government and constituent assembly' and on 'a social mobilization strategy.'"[68] Yet there was little agreement on the specifics underlying the platform, and there were deep divisions between the Christian Democratic Party and the Communist Party, which had now adopted a "popular rebellion" position. This seeming impasse between the PDC and the PCCH tested the Socialist Party's past loyalties and identities, forcing socialist groups to choose between a party that had been a bitter former enemy and a party that had been a close ally. Rifts within the opposition, coupled with a resilient regime that managed to overcome economic and social crisis through tactical and strategic use of both coercion and co-optation, eroded the opposition's expectations of a "quick" defeat.[69]

The opposition's initial hopes of a collapse of the dictatorship eventually gave way to the belief among most that the transition would have to proceed by Pinochet's timetable for the transition, established in the 1980 constitution. In 1986, a year hailed by the left as the "decisive year," two events thwarted both oppositional unity and any hope of Pinochet's immediate downfall. First, the regime discovered an enormous arms cache belonging to the Manuel Rodríguez Patriotic Front (FPMR), the new military wing of the Communist Party. This lent credibility to the regime's claim that a violent communist threat was still afoot in the country. Second, the FPMR staged a dramatic assassination attempt of Pinochet, which failed. The two events led to increased repression against a broad sector of the opposition and ended several important attempts to unite political and social organizations. The military staged massive raids into the city's shantytowns, rounding up and holding overnight substantial numbers of the neighborhoods' male population. In addition, security forces arrested leading opposition figures and relegated union and other social activists to remote areas of the country. Such repressive actions exacerbated already widespread insecurity and fear, and the social mobilization through protest strategy proved no longer viable.

In 1987 the opposition abandoned its strategy for toppling the regime but still refused to accept Pinochet's timetable and plan for a 1988 plebiscite.[70] In January 1987 the Democratic Alliance and the Popular Democratic Movement called for "free elections" in place of the plebiscite. By midyear, several "free election" groupings had been established. Behind this call, however, the opposition remained deeply divided into roughly three camps, reflected by separate "free elections" committees. Christian

Democrats led one committee, moderate socialists another, and the groups from the socialist and communist left another. The divisions represented concerns within the ideological camps regarding postdictatorial politics, concerns that were all too reminiscent of predictatorial divides.

Pinochet refused to accept a proposal to replace the plebiscite with free elections, and the regime continued to operate according to the timetable of the 1980 constitution, establishing voter registration processes, electoral mechanisms, and other procedures to prepare for the plebiscite. The regime had begun to manufacture propaganda for the "Yes" vote, a vote supporting Pinochet as president of Chile until 1997. As 1987 passed month by month, the October 1988 plebiscite date loomed closer in the minds of opposition strategists. By mid-1987 non-Marxist parties had officially registered as outlined by the constitution. In December 1987 Socialist leader Ricardo Lagos announced the moderate socialists' decision to register the Party for Democracy, a "non-ideological" instrumentalist party invented to contest the regime in national elections without the Socialist Party's compromising its rejection of the regime's constitution and institutions.

In January 1988, Christian Democratic Party president Patricio Aylwin publicly announced that his party would participate in the plebiscite and would join any party in a campaign for the "No" vote against the regime. By the end of February, most opposition parties had signed on to a platform urging Chileans to vote "No" in the plebiscite—"No to Pinochet." Aylwin became the head of the Concertación Alliance for the No. This marked the beginning of an unprecedented center-left effort to beat the dictatorship at its own game, and it would be this same sixteen-party coalition that constituted the Concertación alliance for the 1989 Aylwin presidency.

Through a massive organizing effort, the "Campaign for the No" defeated Pinochet with 54 percent of the vote. The campaign urged Chileans to overcome their fear, to vote for a new and bright future for the country. The victory was a watershed for all who had worked for more than a decade to defeat the dictatorship, including those who had doubted the opposition strategy of participating in the Pinochet-orchestrated plebiscite until the day of the plebiscite itself.

The Chilean Communist Party remained ambivalent about whether it would encourage its members to vote until only shortly before the plebiscite, when it instructed them to vote "No." There was reason to be skeptical about the sincerity of the regime's intentions. The dictatorship had manipulated the 1980 plebiscite, which ushered in the authoritarian constitution, and it was unclear that the government would cooperate regarding such issues as transparency of the electoral rolls and vote counting. Raids continued in many of the poor neighborhoods, and severe repression against particular groups, including the Communist Party and the MIR, was still being conducted. In addition, it was unclear what would happen after the plebiscite in the context of an undemocratic constitution, which, among other things, proscribed Marxist parties, allowed Pinochet to appoint nine "designated" senators, gave the military supreme authority, and made it extremely difficult to amend the constitution itself.

Nevertheless, voter turnout for the plebiscite was well over 90 percent. While the 43 percent voter support for the "Yes" was troubling, the opposition was euphoric, and the experience of cooperation and consensus proved invaluable in preparation for the December 1989 elections for president and Congress. The opposition did manage to negotiate a series of approximately fifty constitutional reforms, approved by plebiscite in July 1989. These reforms included a shorter transitional presidential term (from eight to four years), an increase in the number of elected senators (from twenty-six to thirty-eight), and revision of the constitutional amendment procedure itself (reducing the percentage required for amendment from three-fifths to two-thirds in two consecutive congresses).[71] Presidential candidate Patricio Aylwin, the very man who had been president of the Christian Democratic Party during the Popular Unity government and who had staunchly supported the coup, was now a figure for unity against the Pinochet-supported candidate Hernán Buchi and right-wing neopopulist candidate Francisco Javier Errázuriz.

In March 1990 Pinochet handed the presidential sash to Aylwin. The Concertación alliance garnered approximately the same percentage of votes in the presidential elections as it had in the plebiscite. Aylwin won with 55 percent of the popular vote. The Concertación also won a majority in the Chilean House (70 of 120), though not in the Senate (22 of 47), but only because of the designated senators.

The left had a poorer showing than expected. Chilean socialists ran for the legislature in both the Concertación alliance and in a separate alliance, PAIS, composed of the Communist Party, a sector of the Socialist Party, a sector of the Christian Left, the MIR, and other left groupings. PAIS supported Aylwin for the presidency but ran its own candidates in several congressional electoral districts.

Through their instrumentalist party, the Party for Democracy, socialists won twenty-one congressional seats. An additional six candidates representing the "left" wing of the Socialist Party won congressional seats. Of the forty PAIS candidates who ran for the House and Senate, only two were elected. Not a single Communist Party candidate was elected.

The elections were perceived as a victory for the "center," those who supported moderate social reform and political stability. The Concertación government ran on a campaign promising policies that would combine growth with redistribution, maintain an open and competitive economy while beginning to address inequality and real wages that had fallen well below their 1974 level. Regarding human rights, Aylwin had campaigned promising to attempt to repeal the 1978 amnesty law exonerating human rights abusers who acted between 1973 and 1978, the worst years of repression. Yet he had also warned of the difficulty a new government would face in "seeking justice" as well as the truth regarding human rights violations. In the area of constitutional reform, the Concertación had great plans but decided it was prudent not to push for such reforms given the need to have a two-thirds or three-fifths majority to amend the constitution.

The Aylwin government pursued cautious policies in its four years as the country's transitional government. The Aylwin cabinet, composed half of Christian Democrats and half of ministers from the Socialist Party, the Party for Democracy, and the Radical Party, maintained a cohesive profile, publicly united in its politics of consensus with the right-wing opposition. The new regime became recognized as a Democracia de Acuerdos, or Democracy of Agreements. The 1980 constitution remains fundamentally intact, neoliberal economic policies largely mirror those of the last years of the Pinochet regime, and though the government has attempted to address the needs of the very poor, there has been little redistribution of wealth in a country that in Latin America now ranks second to Brazil in the disparity of income between rich and poor.

The Chilean left within the Concertación fully backed the Aylwin administration's approach to the polity and economy, as it did with Aylwin's 1994 presidential successor Christian Democrat Eduardo Frei Jr. Left leaders tended to adopt a pragmatic politics-of-consensus approach among the political elite, discouraging broad-based participation to support more extensive social reform. Political discourse was filled with a "modernizing" Chile that would avoid the "populist" patterns of its neighbors—"growth in the first year, inflation in the second, political trouble in the third."[72] Even in 1993, as the administration was drawing to a close and PPD–Socialist Party leader Ricardo Lagos launched a call for primaries within the Concertación between himself and leading Christian Democratic candidate Eduardo Frei Jr., there was no noticeable difference between the two candidates' economic platforms.

Yet ten years after the transition from military rule, cracks clearly surfaced in the alliance. Christian Democratic leader and president of the Senate Andrés Zaldívar challenged PPD–Socialist Party leader Lagos to represent the Concertación in the December 1999 presidential elections, forcing a primary vote. This public split between leading Christian Democrats and Socialists conjures up past images of bitter fighting between the two parties, and in his battle against Lagos, Zaldívar alluded to the Popular Unity government to resuscitate memories of the Socialist Party's disastrous record of governance.

The PPD and the Socialist Party (now two distinct parties that forbid "dual membership" for all except Ricardo Lagos) had a stronger showing in both the 1993 and the 1997 elections than expected, as did the Communist Party. In the December 1997 congressional elections, the combined votes of the PPD, the Socialist Party, and the Communist Party surpassed the vote percentage received by the Christian Democratic Party. The PDC fell from 27 percent in the 1993 elections to 23 percent in 1997. The Communist Party garnered 7.5 percent, a significant gain over the 4.98 percent it received in the 1993 elections. The PSCH remained steady at 11 percent, and the PPD made a modest increase to 12.5 percent.

Yet what proved most disconcerting about the 1997 elections was the dramatic decrease in voter participation. Between failure of the government and political society to recruit young, newly eligible voters to register and the abstention among those who were registered, approximately 38 percent of Chile's voting age population—a record high—chose not to participate.[73] Many analysts and politicians interpreted this unprecedented decrease in voting as a sign of generalized dissatisfaction with the political class. Echoing a classic vein of Western democratic political theory, others argued that some degree of abstention reflected mere political apathy and that political apathy is not a terrible thing for democratic stability.

Nevertheless, for both the Concertación government and the political left, voter nonregistration and abstention triggered a series of internal discussions regarding the need to reinvigorate the electorate. In mid-1998 prominent members of the center and the left released two distinct public documents, each signed by different leaders, attempting to lay out the Chilean government's accomplishments in the 1990s as well as its goals for the beginning of the twenty-first century. The documents reflected distinct emphases and positions regarding the Chilean modernization process. The first document, "Renovating the Concertación: The Force of Our Ideas," was signed by more than sixty prominent Socialist, PPD, and Christian Democratic leaders of the executive and the legislature. The document lauded the Concertación's achievements in returning society to the rule of law and alleviating the economic desperation of the poorest of the poor. It highlighted Chile's top ranking among less industrialized nations regarding standards of human development and political freedom. While the document recognized that social and economic inequality continued to plague the country, it affirmed the current neoliberal model.

In contrast to the self-congratulatory tone of the first document, the second document, "The People Are Right," was more critical of the Concertación in the areas of social and economic policy. Fundamentally, however, the second document focused on what it termed the exclusionary, elitist nature of Chilean politics, calling for greater citizen incorporation and empowerment. President Frei had instructed his cabinet to refrain from signing any second document, and "The People Are Right" was signed only by Socialist, PPD, and a handful of Christian Democratic thinkers and members of the Congress. Nevertheless, the two documents reflected distinct thrusts within the Concertación regarding the role of the state and the market as well as the relationship between the state and civil society.

In addition to these debates over modernization, social equity, and political participation, the issue continuing to loom large on the spectrum is human rights. While President Frei failed to champion reconciliation as his predecessor Aylwin had attempted to do, by mid-1998 politicians on the center and the left were beginning to perceive a new opportunity for truth-telling and reconciliation. Regarding the issue of the disappeared, for example, politicians on the right had begun to speak about the moral need for families to know "where the bodies were buried." Newly appointed Chilean archbishop Francisco Javier Errázuriz has taken a far more active stance than his predecessor on the need for former persecutors to come forward, and several bishops are initiating renewed data collection and investigation of the fate of the detained and disappeared.[74] Several leading politicians, including Ricardo Lagos, have suggested a second government-sponsored Truth and Reconciliation Commission.

One of the most important symbolic acts of 1998 regarding human rights and the past was the official decision, publicly supported by Pinochet himself, to end the celebration of September 11, the anniversary of the military coup d'état, as a national holiday. Instead, the Congress agreed to support a National Unity Day, to be held during the first week of September each year. The "Pinochet-blessed" decision seemed to lead to a flurry of popular media imagery and reports focused on the brutality of the coup and the first years of the dictatorship. For the first time, popular press, popular talk shows, and other media concentrated significantly on stories and debates about the nature of the repression itself, a discursive shift from a focus upon the chaos and disaster of the Popular Unity government. The arrest of Pinochet has furthered such debate. Questions now being raised include: What was life really like in those first years of the dictatorship? Was the degree of repression so necessary?

This shift in popular imagery and discourse has led to a decrease in the defensive character of significant sectors of the Chilean left political class. While strategy-making and personal political positioning dominated left politics over the past several years, Chile appears to be at a crossroads in its democratization process, and that may provide a window of opportunity for a new period of direction and vision from the left.

CHAPTER 3

THE BINDS AND BONDS
OF PARTY LOYALTY

■ Chapter 1 focused on how people form and sustain political identities, introducing the concept of individual cognitive orientations, grounded in the interplay among individuals' class, education, political party, and generational backgrounds, as well as in their own self-perceptions as political actors. Chapter 2 provided the historical context for the 1960s revolutionary generation of Chilean left leaders whose lives are the center of this study. Based primarily on interviews conducted over the past eight years, this and subsequent chapters will provide in-depth analyses of several leaders, examining the course of their lives, their understandings of politics, their contributions to politics, and their positions in the political process today. What these "autobiographies" reveal is that while the political climate changed dramatically from the 1960s to the 1990s, there is remarkable continuity across individual cognitive frameworks, across individuals' fundamental values and approaches to politics, from their early involvement in the politics of the 1960s to the present.

Moreover, as we explore the relationship between individual biographies and the larger political context, it becomes clear that particular political moments from the 1960s to today privilege particular kinds of individual political leadership. For example, the approaches of political party loyalists were far more valued in the 1960s, a period of extreme sectarian party mobilization, than in the 1990s, a period of extreme consensus politics. Nevertheless, as the 1990s decade draws to a close and sectarian politics reemerge with renewed force, I would argue that political party loyalists are also regaining prominence.

The political and social movements of the 1960s had a profound impact on the political identities of the Chilean left leadership of this period—indeed, on the entire youth-based 1960s generation.[1] Political party loyalists in particular retain a deep attachment to the hopes and vibrancy of the 1960s, in which young people as well as members of the working class ex-

perienced greater social solidarity and greater political mobility than had
been known before in Chile, and in which their political parties were at their
peak as mass, popular organizations. The predominance of left political parties within the union and student movements earned top political positions
for working-class and student leaders who were loyal to their parties.

Memories of 1960s events—even what might be termed 1960s discourse—continue to prevail today in the lives and ideas of political party loyalists. For example, Chilean Communist Party leader Jorge Insunza spent
the bulk of my interview with him retracing the 1960s battles within the
Chilean left over the means to move toward socialism.[2] His discourse on
revolution and the role of "the masses" is a language rarely heard in Chile
today. Former Mirista leader Patricio Rivas also employs discourse more
reminiscent of the sixties than of the present, a discourse he himself characterizes as "hippie-ish." The vast majority of the narratives of our interviews are devoted to their memories of that period. This is a stark contrast
to those who are described by the political entrepreneur orientation. While
political party loyalists refer constantly to their memories of 1960s politics
to empower their self-perceptions as political beings, political entrepreneurs
distance themselves from 1960s memories in order to align themselves
with political images that are dismissive of left politics of the past.

The narratives of political party loyalists also reveal distinct party cultures. As described in chapter 2, the Chilean political party system of the
1960s was composed of an array of traditional left and new left parties. The
Socialist Party (PSCH) and the Communist Party (PCCH) represented large,
established institutions with several hundred thousand members. The
MIR, MAPU, and Izquierda Cristiana had much less institutionalized traditions. Narratives of early political party militancy reflect the contrasts
among these political party cultures.[3]

Internal tendentiousness dominates the texts of PSCH members across
cognitive types, indicating that the relationships among leading ideological
currents on the left, PSCH doctrine, and party praxis were problematic at
best. For young Socialist Party leaders, the relationship between ideology
and party and that between ideology and praxis are confused, uncertain.
For example, Eduardo Reyes's text (examined at greater length in chapter
4) reveals a highly conflicted young militant, dismayed by the internal factionalism of the PSCH:

> When I entered the PSCH, I had read the PSCH statutes, but practically
> the day after joining I knew that the statutes didn't exist, you know

what I mean? Because the day after I joined there were people who, after a night's graffiti work while we were having a cup of coffee, were already hounding me with the question, "What tendency I belonged to within the PSCH?" and I said I didn't belong to any tendency, that I had just gotten there, and there were people who wanted to recruit me within the PSCH for the MIR.

Reyes's concern over what he views as the destructive aspects of PSCH factionalism is a constant theme of his text, from his accounts of early life with the Socialists, to the present period. His reference to the PSCH statutes alludes to the contrast between the Leninist, democratic centralist internal structure of the party as outlined in the party's statutes, which Reyes supported, and the reality of the competing factions within the PSCH.

In contrast, members of the Chilean Communist Party who participated in this study generally perceived their party to be the provider of a cohesive and all-encompassing program, of an ideology that guided their activism. Party conflict is not a theme for young Communist leaders of the pre-1973 period. Rather, as exemplified in the text of former congressman and ex-PCCH leader Luis Guastavino, religious metaphors pervade the PCCH accounts—faith in party doctrine, blind belief, militants as missionaries:

> I remember when I was first making contact with the party, how
> they invited me to the beach, then to play soccer, and then there was
> a session where we spoke. We went to the beach and there were some
> forty to fifty people, I didn't know them, and we play soccer, and we
> take a break, and we sit down and a voice begins to speak. It was
> Citriano, who was later a PCCH congressman, and he spoke, it was
> an underground meeting on the beach, and I felt a kind of euphoric
> symphony. He spoke of the Soviet Union, of a socialist world, of a
> new world, he spoke of Chile, of the struggle against the dictatorship
> of González Videla, the struggle of the working class, of the peasants.
> It was a beautiful thing! And I felt very linked, it was very strong for
> me. . . . The struggle was worth it, for we were winning, not only did
> we struggle, we knew we would win.

In spite of such contrasts and other differences between these two parties in terms of the relationships among party militants, organization, ideology, and praxis, the texts of this sixties generation of national PCCH and PSCH leaders suggest that they shared the belief that their parties held the keys to ideologies they would come to absorb, embrace, question, challenge, modify, rework, and, in many cases, abandon. While individually held ideologies would evolve a good deal over time, this early embeddedness within all-encompassing parties would have a deep and lasting influence on their core political identities—and for none so much as for the political party loyalists.

Political party loyalists represent those individuals whose identities are inextricably linked to collective organization, symbolized by their parties. Unlike other cognitive ideal-types whose members draw from networks outside their parties for their political sustenance and mobility, party loyalists rely on their parties and their tight relationships with them as their chief source of political identity.

What follows are selected narratives and analysis of four political party loyalists: Jorge Insunza, a former congressman and a top leader of the Chilean Communist Party; Isabel Allende, a congresswoman and Socialist Party leader; Adriana Muñoz, vice president of the House of Representatives and a leader of the Party for Democracy; and Patricio Rivas, a university professor and official within the Ministry of Education and a former leader of the Revolutionary Left Movement (MIR). Jorge Insunza represents a classic political party loyalist, whose narrative and behavior are intimately bound to the Communist Party. Isabel Allende and Adriana Muñoz are loyalists to the largest left parties within the governing alliance. Patricio Rivas remains loyal to a collective that has ceased to exist.

JORGE INSUNZA

The political identity of top Chilean Communist Party leader Jorge Insunza is inseparable from his attachment to the historical strength and past ideological grounding of his century-old party. Insunza's world is centered in party structure, organization, and activity. He is deeply concerned with party order.

Born to a lower-middle-class Catholic family, Insunza attended Catholic schools until college. The oldest subject in my study, he holds that priests and historic Chilean Communist Party leaders represent the most important influences in his life. He possesses a proselytizer's authority, bureaucratic expertise, a strong sense of organization and hierarchy, and a paternalistic attitude toward his listeners and followers. Painfully aware of the damning critiques and marginalization of his party today, Insunza frequently strikes a defensive posture. Our interviews often ran like a history lesson on the Communist Party's contribution to building and sustaining a democratic Chile.[4] The former congressman emphasized the primacy of historical tradition, party organization, and global reach:

> I joined the Communist Party in 1954. It was the year the United States invaded Guatemala. There was a great deal of student solidarity with the people of Guatemala. My first political participation was linked to that event.
>
> I joined the Young Communists—and not the Young Socialists— because they were the great young left force, the most organized, the most renown in the School of Engineering of the University of Chile where I was, they were the *only* force at that time.
>
> The Young Communists were extremely organized, structured. They possessed a vision that linked the international situation, the national situation, and the situation within the university movement to our tasks at hand. It could have contributed to a certain mechanicism, but really it kept us abreast of everything, we read a great deal, it was an extremely formative element for our preparation as the young vanguard, those in the struggle against fascism.

Insunza's text stresses the global ideological framework that the Communist Party provided. This framework, Insunza claimed throughout the course of the interviews, continues to be relevant in spite of the collapse of the socialist bloc, and he continues to hold firm to his belief in scientific socialism.

In his late teens, Insunza became a Communist Youth leader and was quickly absorbed by the Communist International. Insunza's text reveals a personal life meshed intimately with his political vocation.

> [In 1956] I was an elected member of the Central Committee of the Young Communists, then an Executive Committee member. Political activism became my life. In 1957 I left the country for the first time to attend the World Gathering of Youth in Moscow and for Europe, to be exposed to different cultures, societies, politics. This trip reinforced my convictions in contradictory ways. When I compared, for example, the level of development in the Soviet Union to that of advanced European capitalist societies, the contrasts were obvious. Yet the level of inequality in those societies, the disdain for basic values of social justice, seemed to me far more reason to reaffirm our convictions.

I graduated in 1959, and political activism absorbed my life. . . . I finished my thesis in 1962, I had married, I had a little girl, I worked in the university as a researcher but was chiefly focused on political activity. Then in 1964, with the new elections and Allende a candidate, we were convinced it was possible to achieve a victory.

Insunza concentrated on the late 1950s and 1960s debate within the left over the "peaceful road to socialism," on the use, not exclusively but primarily, of the electoral process to achieve real social change. He linked party loyalty, personal conduct, ethics, and values to the left's varying ideological stances on the means for achieving socialism.

The combination of the success of the Cuban Revolution and the electoral defeat of Allende led to a tendency to promote armed struggle as a viable avenue and to a real attack within the left on the PCCH. The PCCH was characterized as reformist, pacifist, et cetera.

It was a political period in which the PCCH was able to maintain and sustain a large popular following, maintaining its argument regarding the peaceful road, but it was also a time when we should have thought more deeply about the military question. . . . This is a period in which the influence of the Cuban Revolution was expressed also in a contradictory way—on the one hand, the process of social transformation taking place there, of basic relations within society was dramatic and was a positive influence, but on the other hand, the interpretation became that there was only one way, and during all this time, the 1960s, the whole discussion focused on the *paths* to revolution, to a point where we had to put everything into it, and this is a theme more false than Judas, because, finally, it was really an intransigent, academic debate, which nonetheless became the most impassioned, all-encompassing struggle. And those—and this is a point worth exploring for the historical record—those who were in the most ultra-left positions then are the biggest reformists today, and you can see this by first and last name! It is a political fact.

Q: And how would you explain this?

I think it's a manifestation, in the first place, of a fundamentally individualist conceptualization of the march of history, of the self affirmation of the role of the individual in history. Of course I believe in the importance of individuals, but if we are going to examine history as we should, as the struggle of masses, then this type of posturing should be handily dismissed. I also believe that the interpretation of history must have a scientific base, and must be treated as such. This may sound a bit dogmatic, but I think it is often difficult for those today to distinguish between a certain degree of dogmatism and the need for a sound theoretical base to analyze history and popular struggle.

Insunza's distinction between the individualists and his own understanding and approach to Chilean politics carries several meanings. First, it is a condemnation of those who place what he would term voluntarist, individual behavior before class-based, structural analysis. Second, it is an implicit condemnation of those whom Insunza views as power-hungry, self-interested politicians. Insunza consistently links individual leadership and activism to collective struggle led by a vanguard party, a party that had chosen to support Salvador Allende as the presidential figure.

Insunza contrasts his own ideological continuity with that of those who once berated the electoral road to socialism and who now, Insunza claims, are the ultra "reformists," who he regards as focused exclusively on the electoral dimension of democracy. Insunza hammered home the message of the PCCH's historic commitment to electoral democracy as the strategic key to the left's success:

> We [Communists] defended to the hilt the democratic path as the most viable, necessary road for the left to government. We defended the democratic government of Frei. . . . We then identified completely with Allende, with the commitment of the Popular Unity platform, with his path. . . .
>
> We worked from sunup to sunup, not sundown—sunup of the following day. We worked all day. The Political Commission of the PCCH met every day to go over economic plans, support for the government, everything. We worked like crazy. We had the absolute conviction that it was a process in which we could triumph. You know that Allende won with 36 percent of the vote. There was another round of elections six months later, the municipal elections, and the left took almost 50 percent of the vote. It was a political watershed. It meant that in six months of governing we had achieved something, we on the left. You know that in the parliamentary elections [in March 1973] we obtained 46 percent of the vote, only as the left. It proved that this three-thirds dilemma [in which a third of the Chilean vote tended to go to the left, a third to the center, and a third to the right] could be

overcome if we could prove to Chile that we were capable of managing
a successful economy. . . .

The right understood perfectly well after the March 1973 elections
that they had been defeated, and as history is a dialectical process, this
led to their decision to promote a coup. They realized that the only way
to defeat us was militarily. And we began to realize this was a strong
possibility, but we just didn't have the time to plan our defense. . . .
We began to work to build a mass capacity, including an armed
capacity. They weren't contradictory positions, but, of course, if there
had been an ability to build both capacities things might have been
different. . . .

Once the army had decided to support a coup, a coup was inevitable.
The other branches of the armed forces were secondary, but the army
was decisive. In terms of the small dramas of the time, anecdotes—we
had some ten thousand men who had some degree of military preparation, principally concentrated in the great industrial centers. [Allende
supporter, army general] Prats had some knowledge of this and was in
agreement that there should be some kind of containment of a coup
attempt. After the *tancazo*—the first coup attempt, though not institutional—in July, he designated Pinochet to help design a resistance plan
to a coup. So Pinochet knew exactly what little potential, or the most
significant potential that existed. It really adds a dose of hypocrisy to
the story, the great propaganda after the coup about the tremendous
resistance plan. The reality is there was little.

Insunza emphasized that the defeat of the Popular Unity government was
not historically determined, that had there been more focus on educating
and training "the masses," politically and militarily, "things might have
been different." He expressed remorse for the left's failure to develop a
military policy that incorporated both the armed forces and the popular
sectors. This emphasis in Insunza's text lends ideological continuity to his
defense of the PCCH's policy of armed rebellion in the 1980s. It is a conscious logic on Insunza's part. Yet this stress on failing to arm and train
the masses is ironic, given his strong criticism of the "ultra-leftists" earlier in his text.

Later Insunza alluded to the PCCH's internal critique of its own responsibility for the defeat of the Popular Unity government. In our predominantly open-ended interview, however, Insunza chose not to elaborate on
this self-critique:

I remained in Chile after the coup in clandestinity from 1973 to 1975.
At the end of 1975 I had to leave the country . . . to protect the leadership it was resolved we would leave. I remained in exile from 1976 to
1983, when I returned and remained underground until 1990. It was
a period of great political and theoretical reflection for all of us on
the left as we sorted out what the reasons were for our defeat. I was
focused very much on the question of power. I feel strongly that we
Communists engaged in a very serious and honorable reflection,
trying to get to the bottom of what our own responsibility was in
the defeat.

Insunza's subsequent description of his exile in the former German
Democratic Republic and in Moscow is another example of the continuity
in his identity between past and current ideological beliefs, a reflection of
how a party loyalist identity can tend toward ideological freezing rather
than ideological transformation:

I spent my exile in East Berlin from 1976 to 1980 and then in Moscow
from 1981 to 1986. I would not be honest if I didn't tell you that my experiences in the German Democratic Republic reaffirmed my conviction as a communist. First, because it was a society in which social
equality was highly valued, their handling of the questions of health,
of diet—I had never seen anywhere like it, certainly not in Chile, a
capitalist country. The attention we received freely, the social welfare
standards we enjoyed . . . I got to see how workers lived. . . .
    Nevertheless, I also recognized levels of division in German society,
which for us Chilean Communists were plainly undemocratic and
clashed with our value structures. Regarding certain forms of education, for example, there was a formalism that bothered me, a *dirigiste*
approach. I commented upon this to a German comrade, and his explanation was that to have this system function economically, socially, and
politically, a high degree of centralism was necessary. I did feel a good
degree of defensiveness. Yet in an important sense, this is justifiable.
You know, today, after the collapse, it is as if everything in the socialist
bloc had been terrible, everything bad, and there is a focus on its antidemocratic character. But these great theorists of capitalism fail to
mention in their great indignation with Stalinism that capitalist societies did everything in their power to prevent the possible democratization of these socialist societies. You cannot discuss democracy in these

societies out of the context of the Cold War. And that is why we communists didn't consider legitimate public criticism of the socialist countries for their incomplete transformations. . . .

Democracy comes from the historical development of a society. In Chile there is a long democratic tradition with the participation of the Chilean Communists, which the Chilean Communists have helped to construct! In Cuba, Cuba has never had a democratic tradition. Their capacity is extremely limited. They're confronting a major power that seeks their destruction. . . .

History has demonstrated that the Chilean Socialists have been largely noncritical of the nondemocratic socialist experiences around the world, that their criticisms have come out of their attempts to differentiate themselves from the Chilean Communists, that if you closely examine Chilean history you would have to arrive at the conclusion that it has been the Communists, not the Socialists, who have been the strongest promoters of democracy.

Insunza returned to the grounding of the PCCH in historic national movements for democratization, again contrasting the Communists' record with what he asserts is the Socialists' historic disregard for democracy. For Insunza, it is imperative that I understand that the PCCH is a party committed to democratic principles and that it is only adverse forces—in Chile and around the world—that have prevented socialist societies from democratizing. It is also ironic that his criticism of the PSCH's failure to criticize publicly the socialist bloc countries comes in his text after his own explanation for the PCCH's failure to do the same.

In the 1989, 1993, and 1997 national elections, Insunza ran unsuccessfully for Congress, though he and the PCCH gained slightly in support. He continues to assert the necessity of a democratic centralist party. Today Jorge Insunza is one of five members of the PCCH's Political Commission. His party remains the historic Chilean left force that publicly berates the neoliberal paradigm and that claims the model is reaching exhaustion:

Not only in Chile but throughout the world, the "drunken stupor" of neoliberalism is ending, and there is a returning to a search for alternatives to capitalism. This whole notion of "an end to ideology" is coming to a close. Chile is celebrated today around the world as a great success of the neoliberal model, and if one looks at this in terms of transnational capital interests as well as the interests of the national monopolies, it

is true that the model is a successful model. Yet I want to signal to you
three separate studies [a 1998 United Nations Development Program,
a World Health Organization study, and an International Labor Organization study], not conducted by our party, that suggest otherwise. . . .
And I think the results are a very strong accusation against the system,
against its essential inhumanity. If the great majority are found to be
so unhappy, it is a huge mark against the model, a model that favors
extreme social disparity and an increasing exclusion of large sectors of
the population, and for those of us inspired by Marxist analysis, not in
dogma, but in creating an authentic, meaningful politics, I found in
Marx's reflection a solid explanation: that capitalism, in its very core,
is incapable of creating a socioeconomic model that is sustainable as
a social, cultural basis for society.

Insunza does not claim that his party holds the alternative to Chile's current trajectory. Nevertheless, in a show of remarkable continuity, he appears to draw from an old Communist International position: that the productive forces will sooner or later reach their point of maturation and a
new stage will be inevitable.

So what is the reality? I can say to you that in the immediate future
there is little possibility of developing an alternative program here in
Chile based on the general social well-being, that we have not yet
reached that phase. And for the forces on the left, the weight of defeat
is still very profound. The forces of the left were not liquidated, much
to the chagrin of the Pinochet regime, nor were they peacefully liquidated as many capitalists had hoped to have happen through the
media, psychologically, even democratically, if you will. This did not
happen. Clearly today there is a restoration process going on, not just
within the PC. As a powerful symbol of this I would point out that ten
days ago [in May 1998] the Chilean Socialist Party, in their congress in
Concepción, decided to retake the position that their party has roots inspired in Marxism, something they had abandoned three years ago, and
now they return to a position they had assumed around 1943, that
Marxism is an instrument of analysis that is useful, as is secular hu-
manism and liberation theology–based Christianity. This is very important, given the role of the PSCH in the Concertación over the last several
years, their wholehearted adoption of neoliberalism, and now the
PSCH's own reaction.

Insunza struggles to reassert the PCCH as the true representative of Chile's popular sectors, the party that can lay claim to concern for Chile's popular tradition. The definition of the "popular sectors" has shifted, however, to encompass all whose chief concerns and identities are politically marginalized, including ecologists and certain feminist sectors, as well as the poor majority:

> So we're optimistic, not over the immediate term, we're not kidding ourselves, but we do think conditions are being laid down for there to be an alternative, an anti-neoliberal alternative, and we believe that social sectors are in a phase where they are deciding to be in favor [of] or against neoliberalism, and that their articulation, in their multiple ways, is essentially a rejection of neoliberalism. For example, the ecologists don't really have the notion today that the system itself has to change, rather they protest against specific manifestations of the system, but we believe that if they're serious, that this green banner they wave will eventually combine with a red one, not that there will be a hegemonic takeover, but rather an alliance to work together. Among feminist circles as well, though I use this carefully, for not all feminist strands lend themselves to this course of action, but from within some feminist sectors are struggles against the structure that favor fundamental change. . . .
>
> We see a struggle for a socialist ethic, not because every sector has a revolutionary bent, but because they are challenging things like corruption, egoism, the rupture of solidaristic links, and they join us in believing these should not be sustained in our society.

Insunza's text calls for a collective sense of struggle championed by his party. In his text, in his discourse, Insunza uses the first person plural, "we," far more often than the first person singular, "I." Other political party loyalists echo this discursive pattern, a pattern not shared by the political thinker and entrepreneur cognitive orientations of this study. The "we" bonds Insunza to his party. As a true political party loyalist, he processes and expresses his politics through the lens of the party itself. Insunza's political identity is inseparable from his party.

ISABEL ALLENDE

Like Jorge Insunza, political party loyalist Isabel Allende, daughter of the late president, maintains a political identity intimately linked to the past.[5]

Isabel Allende is a torchbearer, a keeper of the flame, whose political behavior is tightly bound up with her representation of past traditions and symbols. The family name of Allende is inseparable from the Chilean political class, and it has been the defining institution of her life. The family as referent dominates Allende's text, not only as she discusses her personal life but also as she puts forth her politics. Allende's political identity and public persona rely on the memory of her late father. Yet unlike the personal loyalists of the next chapter, Allende uses her family name to build and strengthen the Socialist Party. In contrast to the "Allendistas" of chapter 4, who are inherently critical of the Socialist Party and who are often more loyal to the memory of the leader than to his party, Isabel Allende uses her family credibility to enhance her party's image.

> My best memories are of our times in [our beach house in] Algarrobo, in terms of family, leaving behind so much of what our daily life was, as you can imagine, just the relaxation, the swimming, the sharing of our lives together was very important. . . . The other side of our lives was here [in Santiago], in this house where you and I sit, the house where we have lived since I was seven years old, the activities of this home. And my father would leave in the morning, but he would always, almost always, return home for lunch, and rarely did we eat alone. Even as little girls [my sisters and I] were there joining in the conversations, listening to the conversations—conversations that were usually about international affairs, Chile—with Latin Americans from all over, Europeans, incredible dialogues, always.
>
> My father—my father, he believed that the lunch hour was a time for meeting, not just within our family, but with other families. It was always a family atmosphere, but with a great deal of conversation. So from early on I realized, when I went off to school, that I was from a very different kind of family.
>
> I began in a very small school, and then I was sent to an English school, which I never liked. My father believed a great deal in being able to speak other languages—this was very important to him, communication—and I would say it was one of the only undemocratic decisions made in the family. We switched schools without being asked if we wanted to or not.
>
> And I repeat, this question of conversations in the home, it separated me from my girlfriends. Politics was a part of my daily life from very early on. I breathed it always. It wasn't that I was a party militant

early on, no, I was in a private school. . . . It was more how I perceived things differently from my schoolmates. . . .

I was never a *real* party militant, never was. I had dramatic experiences during the campaign. From early on in my childhood, the two most influential phenomena politically were the conversations at lunch, and when I accompanied my father on campaign trips, to hear how people conversed about things. The campaigns were difficult, the effort exerted, the organization, and, of course, facing the defeats. These influenced me quite deeply. The senatorial campaigns. I remember in 1961 for three months during the summer, going door to door in Viña, Valparaíso, with our pamphlets, house to house, and I witnessed a great deal, the poverty, . . . an old woman without water, without basic services. A very powerful experience conversing with people this way.

In 1961, at sixteen, I went on my first trip abroad, with my parents, to Cuba. It made a huge impression on me. It was the beginning of the revolution. We were so *influenced* by Cuba. It was a beautiful sight, what was going on, speaking with the peasants, with workers, with housewives, what was going on in terms of education, health—which particularly impressed my father as a physician, everything just beginning, very impressive. Returning to private school that year was like a douse of cold water, I was so enthusiastic about Cuba, my girlfriends about the next party. . . .

In 1963 I traveled with my family again, to China and to the Soviet Union, and I had to admit that from Chile, one didn't perceive the incredible differences, the Sino-Soviet struggles, so it was quite eye-opening for me. . . . In China the communes, the collective system. The USSR I also found extremely interesting, we went to the theaters, cultural events, and I was amazed by the lines, the *lines* to get into the movies, the theater, people could afford to go and enjoy cultural events. We went to Romania, Bulgaria, Czechoslovakia. Then we jumped to Western Europe, where we went to Italy and England. Our objective at that time was to look for support for the 1964 campaign.

Unfortunately the 1964 campaign was so . . . aggressive, the campaign of the PDC, of the Socialists, and it distanced a lot of people who were once friends . . .

Well, returning to this trip, it was a six-month trip. I was seventeen. It influenced me a great deal. We then ended up in Mexico, which we loved, and to which we returned, once immediately before the coup, and a week later, on the twelfth to thirteenth [of September 1973].

Throughout Allende's text, politics and family are intertwined. Allende recognizes how her life experiences, from her immersion in her father's campaigns to her world travels, set her apart from others. There is a great deal of nostalgia in her voice, particularly in her memories of the summer house and in the daily conversations at the family table. It is a nostalgia magnified by her continuing to reside in the very house she lived in as a child.

Since her early militancy in the Socialist Party, Allende, like her father, has been tied to the more moderate wing within the party. It is a wing that has carefully sought to differentiate the party from the centrist Christian Democratic Party by drawing from the Socialists' historic progressive nationalist program and by using a collectivist rhetoric in defense of human dignity and social justice. This differentiation has become more pronounced over the issue of Chile's position regarding the arrest of Pinochet. On behalf of human rights and dignity, Isabel Allende led the Socialist Party's support of the former dictator's arrest. The leaders of this tendency include Minister of Government Jorge Arrate and Senator Ricardo Nuñez, both of whom were close friends and colleagues of Isabel Allende's in the pre-1973 period.

> I joined the Socialist Party in the university, this is when I began my career as a militant. Life in the university was normal, intense, it was the 1960s, so Cuba was very much alive, we protested in the streets, we were beaten up. . . . We felt it was a moral imperative to defend Cuba, the Cuba thing, the most important phenomenon in Latin America at that time. I feel very defined by that period. And obviously, in '68 we felt very much that big changes were ahead. This was the period of struggle over university reform. . . .
>
> The Socialist Youth was very tied to *lo popular*, to folklore, guitars, the *peñas* [coffeehouses], the shantytowns. It was the generation of black stockings, the ponchos, the guitars, the *kemas* [indigenous musical instruments]. It was a period of liberation.
>
> My group in the university was Ricardo Nuñez, Armando Arancibia, Luis Alvarado, Enzo Faletto, Germán Correa [all of whom are important Socialist leaders and thinkers and (with the exception of Faletto) have served as congressmen or cabinet ministers in the postdictatorial period]. . . .
>
> Then came 1970 and all of that. In March of 1970 I began to work in the National Library. I have to say that leading up to this period it

was a personal search for me, that I wasn't incredibly defined in terms of my own direction, a search without a great deal of clarity. Beginning in the National Library was an extremely important period in my life. I was there from January of 1970 to 1973. It meant, in essence, that in the midst of those years I was able to remain calmly in the National Library. . . .

It was an important formative period for me there in the library, for I rose to direct a program. It was the first time I had to deal with a staff, in a way which was, let's say, which was to try not to politicize work conditions in what was such a politically charged national climate. We functioned in an extremely merit-based way, we devoted a good deal to training, it was really quite a beautiful experience. And I am convinced that I was chosen to direct the program not because I was the daughter but because they felt I was capable of directing it in the way necessary, which I did. People perceived I had real leadership capacity, not for my last name, but because of who I was. And that was very empowering. . . .

I also participated in a very reflective socialist study group, an exceptional group, really, composed of Jorge Arrate, at the time executive secretary of Codelco, the Central Bank president, the foreign minister Clodomiro Almeyda, a group of highly connected government people, respected intellectuals. It was a way for me, who was not in the government, to stay abreast of what was going on, to *observe* the debates going on. It was a nucleus that actually functioned for about fifteen years. We would meet once a week, at one person's house, at another's house. Obviously, the themes of the group were the national questions, policies, the critical political junctures.

Allende's nostalgic tone continued through her discussion of the pre-1973 years. Her recounting of her position in the National Library as an important formative experience in her life was meant to call attention to her belief that it was the one activity of her life that was free of family association. Nevertheless, Allende's participation in a top-level Socialist Party nucleus, despite her lack of a formal political position, is testimony to the privileged position her name grants her in Chilean politics.

Upon the invitation of Mexican president Luis Echeverría, whose family was very close to the Allende family, Isabel Allende and her mother became exiles in Mexico. Allende's discussion of life in Mexico reflected the relative ease that her family experienced there. Her text also revealed how she came to personify the image of her father as she spoke out against the Chilean dictatorship in trips throughout Mexico and other countries.

> So much of my time before 1980 was spent traveling on solidarity campaigns, all over the world, at great personal costs, abandoning my children, great personal costs, although upon reflection I think it was inevitable. After 1978, while I clearly sympathized with the Altamirano, Arrate, Nuñez camp, I distanced myself from the party for a period, to become a student again, dedicating myself to books, this time from a clearly different outlook in Mexico. It was a way of opening myself up, it was very important to me. This was roughly from 1980 to 1982.
>
> I began to travel again in 1982. This was also a period of break with the Communist Party, which had changed so radically. We began to focus so much on the basic question of democracy, democracy, it was distinct in its framework from socialist agendas of the past, this deliberate focus, emphasis.
>
> And our comrades began returning, first Nuñez, then others, the period of the return, of more and more contact with Chilean reality. . . .
>
> And I continued on solidarity trips, not as a party militant, but increasingly close to this.

In this text, Allende portrays her role as "the daughter" as virtually inescapable in terms of her responsibilities to the Socialist Party and to the struggle against the Pinochet regime. Though she "distanced" herself from her party, it was only for two years. Allende claims her renewed political involvement was "inevitable."

> In terms of my own return [to Chile], in 1986 I was encouraged to join a group returning but who had to negotiate with Pinochet, and I absolutely refused this. I finally was able to return in 1988, a month before the plebiscite. . . .
>
> It was quite emotional, a shock to return, to fly over the snowcapped Andes, to go to the Plaza de Armas, to see La Moneda presidential palace, where Salvador Allende died. What helped was the enormous generosity, the people in the streets warmly welcoming my return, the incredible generosity. The impact on me was tremendous. It is an important memory I retain, the first few days of the return.
>
> Yes, there have been important changes in Chile. The first thing I felt was this very competitive spirit. Less solidarity. A capacity, not to

look deeply at much, not to remember much, to take the most comfortable, easiest path, a generalized egoism. The stratification. The world
of poverty, marginality distant from this other world. . . . And here it
affected me to see this visual separation, not what I remember of 1973.
I can now circulate within the world I live in and work and not really
see what's happening! This whole sense of community we once possessed seems somehow lost. Now the message is not to butt your nose
into others' business. There are real changes, real changes. I think
there is still a generalized lack of trust among members of our society.
The kind of transition was very complex, slow, behind closed doors in
a sense, mystical. . . .

The notion of the loss of community is echoed throughout the texts of the
political party loyalists. It contrasts sharply with the tenor and description
of the past recounted by other types in this study. Chilean political entrepreneur Clarisa Hardy, for example, who also spent her exile years in Mexico, claims that her years in Mexico enabled her to see Chilean class stratification and the lack of solidarity of the pre-1973 period all the more clearly
(see chapter 6). Such contrasts suggest a tendency toward romanticization
of the past on the part of the party loyalists.

In discussing the 1990s transition period, Allende was unafraid of expressing her frustration on several fronts: first, with what she terms a failure to "re-create" a solidaristic social fabric to combat inequality; second,
with what she views as the extreme consensus politics of Chile's political
class; and third, with an incapacity to address a basic sense of insecurity
among Chileans regarding their future:

This has clearly been a process of transition, with its advances and its
setbacks. Perhaps the major disappointment has been that we thought
we would have reached a point by now where we were firmly establishing a limit, an end to the continued trajectory of inequality, a level of inequality Chileans did not know in the past. This has not happened. . . .
We have failed to re-create an integrative sense within society, a common bonding. When everyone celebrated the Chile-Italy game and went
to the Plaza Italia last night [June 1998] it was one of the very few times
we could see different sectors of society banding together.

Another of the many themes weighing upon us is how these elaborate processes of establishing political agreements in order to advance a
legislative measure are interpreted by society. We are clearly viewed as

the political class of consensus. It has created a real distance between the political class and society. Ironically, this sense that we must avoid mobilization, disagreement, has begun to cause mobilization within society against perceptions of this great consensus within the political class. It has been a process that has impeded participation from the population, that in turn has created a demand to be heard. I think we have reached a point where we need less politics of agreement and more differentiation, more participation, more mobilization to distinguish among ourselves, an end to the blocking of important social gains by the right, against labor reform, for example. This has been a transition that has been substantially blocked, frozen. . . .

Another theme which is important to discuss is what this whole model of modernization has signified for the citizenry, and that is that citizens are terrified, are insecure, it is this subjective dimension. Before, people in Chile were used to labor stability, for example, that they could be secure in one job, in their career, that they would live and die in the same career. Today in this globalization process, et cetera, et cetera, the process requires more flexibility. Everyone talks about labor flexibility, but the difference is there are no protective measures accompanying this flexibility. Entire careers disappear, or they require new technological training, or there is a lag time between the training for new demands and the ability to work in them. And here we are failing. The subjective element is as important as the objective one. People feel subjectively unprotected, and, for that matter, objectively as well. The labor situation is not at all clear, and we have not been able to resolve the question of assuring the very basic needs of a family.

Allende continues to accept and to nourish her identity, firmly embedded in family and in the Chilean Socialist Party. She has attempted, unsuccessfully, to head the Socialist Party. In 1993, however, she was elected to the Chilean Congress. She is now also vice president of the PSCH. Like other Socialist Party and Party for Democracy leaders, Allende is very concerned about the recent insinuation from within the Christian Democratic Party that the socialists have not proven to possess governance capacity. As the daughter of the last socialist president, Allende is increasingly assuming the delicate role as her father's defender on behalf of the credibility of her party:

There are still very real fears. And anything that appears as conflict is something seen as very worrisome. In principle, all of us want to avoid conflict, but there are times when trying to avoid conflict will only create more conflict. Today we are in absolute denial of conflict, which creates a kind of consensus that in part is superficial. There is a very real part of the population that remains traumatized. The whole theme of conflict, violence, is very worrisome for them. But on the other hand there is a kind of vulgarization of politics, on one side from the right, and from the other side [the Christian Democratic Party], in a move that is quite wrong, to try to profile itself as the party that guarantees stability.[6] We have the same abilities, the same interests, the same capacities. So our challenge at this moment is how as the Concertación to move forward toward the next presidency united but getting rid of this tendency to create scary ghosts. . . . We have to break this pattern.

In part for this reason the Salvador Allende Foundation is planning a great homage to Allende on the twenty-fifth anniversary of his death, a great act that will take place in the National Stadium, with international participation. And I feel a great need to do this, a great homage in all its senses. And why is this necessary? I think it is absolutely necessary to recapture, reappropriate the symbol of Allende if we want to move forward, we must dispel the ghosts. I can understand this strategy coming from the right, as a strategy. Not from the Christian Democrats. They do this because there is clearly a certain part of the population that has hesitated to define itself.

We will carry out this homage as a major cultural event but also as a recognition of what democracy stands for, what Allende stood for, that democracy is also related to social justice, in favor of social justice, he favored a revolutionary process through democratic channels, "opening steps toward change in pure freedom." . . . a testimony in its many forms. And I feel doing such a homage to Allende, to resuscitating a memory, implies not being a prisoner of that memory. We're in another period, this will be opening a space. We are still in a very constricted, restricted democracy . . . and yet we as the left are not divided and we are united in the Concertación. This is where the PDC is wrong and we must come up with a solution for the presidential candidacy that will not reinflict wounds. Otherwise we will be on a dangerous path, which I really believe we can avoid. We have learned something from the past—the PDC could not govern alone in the 1960s, we could not govern alone in 1970.

As sectarian politics return to the fore, party loyalist Allende's identity increases in prominence, as she works to remobilize important sectors within Chilean society toward the party. Together with Congressman Juan Pablo Letelier (a son of former Chilean ambassador to the United States Orlando Letelier, who was assassinated in Washington, D.C., by Chilean government mercenaries in 1976) and other Socialist Party members of the Chilean Congress, Isabel Allende traveled to London to voice strong support for the British arrest and pending extradition decision against Pinochet. Letelier and Allende have become the most visible Socialist Party leaders in their stance against the Chilean executive's argument that Pinochet should be released immediately and returned to Chile. Drawing upon the continued reverence within the popular sectors for Salvador Allende, Isabel Allende is concentrating her efforts on championing a Socialist Party message of human rights and dignity, as well as a call to the party's fellow militants and to Chilean citizens to support a Ricardo Lagos presidency.

ADRIANA MUÑOZ

Like Isabel Allende, Adriana Muñoz is a torchbearer, first for the Chilean Socialist Party and now for the Party for Democracy.[7] Muñoz is the first vice president of the Chilean House of Representatives. The text of this congresswoman and party loyalist emphasizes her socialization in collectivities, namely, her neighborhood community, her generation, and her party. It is an attempt to relay a continuity between her past roots and the communities she was publicly elected to represent.

Nevertheless, unlike Isabel Allende, Adriana Muñoz is a feminist.[8] The contrast between Isabel Allende's and Adriana Muñoz's texts reveals the gendered dimension of individual political identity arrived at in this study. Not once in our three-session, five-hour series of interviews did Allende discuss what it was like to be a woman in a male-dominated party and politics. Like her male counterparts interviewed for this study, she kept a notable *silence* regarding the possible influence of intimate personal companions and relationships on their political thinking and behavior. The one exception to this was Patricio Rivas (below), who consistently discussed his personal relationships and their influences on his political behavior and ideological evolution over the course of his life.

Feminism and party loyalty have often represented competing forces within Muñoz's political identity. In a country morally shadowed by a conservative Catholic Church hierarchy, Muñoz's outspoken stances in favor of a divorce law (which Chile does not have) and of the right to an abortion in extreme cases cast her as a threat to "family" and to Chilean tradition. They are positions that her party has failed to champion.

In recounting her youth, Muñoz stressed her bonds to community life:

> In the period that I was born, well, I was born in 1948, I'm a Libra and I come from a Christian family, a mother who was a housewife and a father who was a store owner. I'm the oldest of five children, and I was born in a neighborhood known as Recoleta, and my young life revolved around the community-oriented neighborhood, the collective. Later I studied in a parochial school run by nuns. All of us studied in religious schools, from kindergarten through high school. . . .
>
> Collective life in a neighborhood is a beautiful thing. It's something that deeply influenced me, my friends during that period, neighbors who to this day are my friends even though they've left the neighborhood and I've stayed, our games in the street, games that mobilized the whole block, we were twenty or thirty kids in the street . . . and there was a strong sense of solidarity, of equality, because there were middle-class sectors in my neighborhood, but there were also poor sectors and I remember having grown up with poor children who were at the same level as I, we were very equal, we all felt we belonged to the same neighborhood. We all went in different directions—those of us who were from the middle class became professionals, those who were poorer, well, many ended up alcoholics, others, well, it's a life that stamped you with a kind of seal of community . . . we were from the same generation and we were very together.

Like other political party loyalists, Muñoz is nostalgic about community life growing up in the 1950s and 1960s. In her reflections, nevertheless, she reveals how class differences led to contrasting life trajectories. Muñoz's emphasis on organic ties to Chilean communities fits her public persona as a congresswoman and her focus on grassroots loyalties and recruitment.

Muñoz's political career began in the university student movement. Muñoz was a sociology major at the University of Chile "in the most politicized years, '66, '67, '68." The university represented her first exposure to coeducational, secular education.

I began to participate in discussions at levels I had never known before. The arrival of all the foreign professors, the arrival of Brazilians, Argentines, Uruguayans [to Chile] marked the development of sociology as a science in Latin America in that period, and, well, our positions became more politicized. We had professors like Clodomiro Almeyda [Chilean Socialist Party leader], a Marxist, and I intellectually became a Marxist, I began to find that Marxism made sense, and already in 1966, 1967, I began to want to become a militant, and I became a militant of the Communist Party (PCCH), because my closest friends were PCCH members, but then I became frightened. I had the sense that if I got my PCCH card I would somehow lose my freedom, I had the sense that it would be entering a party where I couldn't leave on my own will, and so I didn't join officially, and later I met people from the Socialist Party (PSCH) and I became a militant in the Chilean Socialist Party.

Q: *In 1967?*

I joined the PSCH before the end of 1966, because in 1967 they gave me my card.

For Muñoz there was little temporal separation between her initial exposure to left ideological currents and the decision to become a political party militant. She "intellectually became a Marxist" and explored both the PCCH and the PSCH in the same year. This represents a common pattern of individual political identity formation in this study, where ideological conviction quickly leads to joining a party, and the party is seen as the locus for defining theory and praxis.

It is unclear from Muñoz's narrative why she was afraid of the PCCH. Perhaps anti-Communist sentiment while growing up in a right-wing Catholic family, coupled with parochial school from kindergarten through high school, had affected her "sense" of the Communist Party, but it is impossible to judge from her text.[9] It was also not uncommon in this highly charged political atmosphere for students to have a negative experience with one party and to decide to join another. In any case, Muñoz quickly became a leader within the National Federation of Students of the University of Chile (FECH) as a political secretary and later as a Socialist Party delegate. She completed her degree in rural sociology, and as a PSCH militant and rural sociologist, she became an undersecretary in the Allende administration's Department of Agriculture. She was twenty-two years old. Muñoz's narrative captures how consuming militant life proved to be.

> As militants we were in nuclei. I belonged to one that included professionals and functionaries of central Santiago, and we were extremely active although ideologically divided, and I was in the more hard-line tendency. . . . I became a Trotskyist at twenty. In 1969 I traveled to Cuba, where I was exposed to the whole bureaucracy of being socialized in a socialist state . . . and I returned to work hard for the revolution. . . . We were a group trying to extend and further the kinds of changes afoot. Perhaps in this sense we contributed to the chaos, yet we were trying to radicalize the party from within, and I worked in a peasant union, and it was a period of a lot of rage, as I was able to reflect on it somewhat once I was in exile. We were trying to redistribute the wealth, and of course we were, we were the generation imbued with the great paradigms, with the great revolutionary models and tendencies, the Bolshevik, the Cuban, the Chinese, the PLO, and we were trying to apply these models to the Chilean case. . . . And when we had time to reflect in exile on how out of touch we were with the sense of security Chileans cherish and how threatened they felt by our great schemes. . . . I was so swallowed up by my militancy, by the internal struggles within the party and by our struggles with the right. We were completely oblivious to the risks. We were mainly young people, a period led by young people. I was twenty-four when we left the country.

This sense of being "swallowed up" in the intensity of party militancy continues to be the defining feature of Muñoz's cognitive political orientation. From her early political involvement, Muñoz's political behavior, like that of other political party loyalists, has been that of a dedicated party "workhorse." This behavior is consistent throughout Muñoz's political career, an unflagging loyalty in spite of the difficult personal and political moments in her life.

Muñoz and her five-month-old child followed her husband into exile in Austria. After a year of living with "their bags packed" in hopes that the dictatorship would be short-lived, Muñoz and her husband began their gradual assimilation into Austrian life. Muñoz began postgraduate work at the University of Vienna, where she completed a master's degree in political science. For four years she worked at a university international relations institute, where she focused on Latin America, and she began a doctoral program. Yet, as was common among exiles, Muñoz's marriage fell apart, and she gave up her studies to return to Chile and to Chilean politics:

> I began the doctoral program in political science and sociology but then abandoned it to return to Chile because I entered an extremely strong family crisis period and I separated from my husband and I was also feeling, let's say, I had always felt that in spite of all my effort to fit into this new reality, this new society, for my personal characteristics I couldn't do it. I began to feel each day that life had less meaning. Then I had a strong conflict with my son, who felt completely Austrian, who was very happy in school. . . . I just felt that I couldn't go any further in Austria, that I couldn't develop a personal project that satisfied me . . . and I felt this strong urge to return. Many people were going back and forth during this period and spoke to me about Chile. My mother came to visit, my father wasn't well, and in 1982 I managed to return without any problems of getting in.
>
> The return was a real struggle. I had no work. I spent almost two years selling signs at my brother's store . . . and finally I was able to get an investigative project approved by a Chilean NGO to establish my professional life again.

After a number of difficult years of reestablishing herself, Muñoz became a visible figure in the Chilean feminist movement and in the Chilean Socialist Party.

> [In 1985 and 1986] I began to work with Ricardo Nuñez in his efforts to reconstruct the Socialist Party. In 1986 we socialist women held a national conference of women from throughout the country. More than eight hundred women came, and we reconstituted the Federation of Socialist Women, which had been formed in 1966. It was a very interesting project where we women who were returning from exile had really become feminists, and we socialists managed to incorporate the feminist question into the party. It was an incredible fight against some of the most traditional sectors, the old-timers, but it was a real victory. . . . I played an active role in this, my militancy increased, I returned in a sense to my old militancy, and we women pushed to establish a presence in the Political Commission [of the PSCH], in the Central Committee. I was chosen to represent the feminist federation on the Political Com-

mission . . . and later I was proposed by the federation again to be a congressional candidate.

In this text we see Muñoz push the boundaries of her political party loyalty to struggle for a women's agenda. As a feminist, she remained within the Socialist Party at a time when many feminists abandoned party politics out of frustration and disgust.[10] Muñoz attempted to incorporate gender issues through party machine politics.

Muñoz continued to champion a feminist platform as a congresswoman, certain that while the PSCH did not match her visibility on the issue, the party stood behind her. However, Muñoz's promotion of legislation to protect domestic employees, to establish a divorce law, and, most controversially, to legalize abortion in extreme circumstances did prove to be a test for her own party as well as for the Chilean legislature.

Like other congressmen and congresswomen in this study, Muñoz is sketchy regarding a new set of visions to guide her politics and identity:

> We have an enormous task today, and that is somehow to reconstruct, reformulate, or formulate better a new and genuine idea of socialism. Given today's times we have little time to think, at least for those of us doing politics, and we hope that other comrades are reflecting and discussing all this. . . . We have to make people believe that we socialists have renovated, and that it is reflected in our way of carrying out politics. . . . We need a vision for the year 2000. We need a utopian vision, because I believe that a party without utopia, without proposals—I don't think we have to return to parties of dogmas, but we do need ideas. I am afraid that in the parties' attempts to advance, ideas are displaced, the party becomes an instrument of power, the concentration of power in few hands to serve personal interests and society loses out. . . .
>
> On the other hand, we also depend in important ways on our base, on those with ties in the community who win support for the party through their battles to deliver concrete goods to the community, on their service to their communities, not because of their political discourse but because of their abilities to tackle concrete daily problems, for those without homes, without employment. . . . And I spend much of my time fighting for concrete projects, working with a range of social community leaders to solve the problems of the people. And after these fights everyone wants to be in the party of the congress-

woman, it really is like that, without my asking for it. Like right now
there is a squatter settlement where sixty families are living in absolute
misery, and, well, because of my work, they all want to be in the party
of the congresswoman without my having delivered a single speech.

In her December 1993 run for reelection, Muñoz lost. Opinion was split
on why she was defeated. Many hold that she failed to have the necessary
financial and moral support of her party. Others, including Muñoz herself,
asserted immediately after her defeat that the Chilean right and the
Catholic Church ran a U.S.-style propaganda campaign to portray her as a
virtual baby killer and that her opponents employed scare tactics among
her former supporters from Santiago's shantytowns. In our June 1998 interview, however, as Muñoz reflected on her defeat, she asserted that her
1993 loss had more to do with her own failure to communicate well with
her constituency, to engage more closely with her district's needs. Muñoz
does not blame the PSCH leadership, so central to orchestrating party campaigns and electoral lists.

From 1993 to 1997, Muñoz served under PSCH minister of government
José Joaquín Brunner as the Socialist Party's liaison between the executive
and the Congress. By mutual agreement between the PSCH and the PPD,
Muñoz publicly renounced her PSCH membership to become a leader of
the Party for Democracy (PPD), which, in contrast to the PSCH that erected
it, has recently made a strong effort to recruit women for high-level positions.[11] In 1997 Muñoz ran again for public office, this time under the PPD
banner in a different district. As a party loyalist, she continues to organize
for the PPD, focusing on recruiting shantytown women in mobilizations for
just wages and protections.

When asked to reflect on her life and name the most important influences, Muñoz cited collective, generational experiences, rather than a specific person or figure in shaping her political identity:

> I've never had particular people who have been amazing influences
> on me, rather collective moments, and more than anything, my time
> in the university, my revolutionary generation, which held a powerful
> conviction for change. It was a great period of confusion but also one
> where we felt we had to change things, so it was my friends, my
> friends on the left who made me feel part of a revolutionary left move-
> ment to change society, in all its good senses. The idea that everything
> is possible, everything can be changed for the better. I think this has

marked me more than anything else, to be part of a generation euphoric for change.

PATRICIO RIVAS

"My closest friends are in the Rettig Report," said Patricio Rivas, referring to the Aylwin-commissioned investigation of gross human rights violations on the dead and disappeared under the Pinochet dictatorship.[12] Rivas was only twelve when the Revolutionary Left Movement (MIR), was founded, and he joined the group shortly thereafter. By the age of nineteen, Rivas had become a major party organizer.

Patricio Rivas was born into a middle-class, half-Basque, half-Jewish family in the capital. Their home was in a vibrant neighborhood bordering the Plaza Italia, close to downtown Santiago, and the neighborhood represented a central focus of Rivas's early life.

> In my neighborhood we had an unusual and beautiful thing going. We started a kind of debating society. On the one side was a kind of Mills, humanist perspective, on the other, Trotsky. All of the Christian types ended up in the MIR. Every Saturday we would get together, and we were theoretically very competitive. We would read from the Frankfurt School, Adorno, Marcuse. Even our parties were boring, we were so focused on this. Five from this group are disappeared today.

The theme of the disappeared and dead was the central referent of Rivas's text. Of approximately forty persons specifically alluded to in Rivas's recollections, more than thirty were killed or disappeared. Rarely did Rivas mention a name or describe an individual without referring to whether the individual was alive or dead. The story of Rivas's life was inseparable from the stories of others' deaths. Rivas is a torchbearer for his dead comrades.

The death of the other becomes all the more present (and haunting) in the text because of Rivas's emphasis on the collective—on bonds to the party, on collective responsibility to fellow militants, on the importance of work with "the masses."

> In school I met a group of young Miristas. I liked them all. I found them intelligent, responsible. And they took things very seriously. This was no longer our Saturday discussion group. We were very moral,

humanist. We read things like "Moral Force," by an Argentine revolutionary. Works of Che linking ethics, morality, and revolution. The Cuban Revolution—Martí. I started to feel part of a grand process. It was a kind of intercontinental identity. . . .

. . . I remember how we all felt around the time of Allende's election. It was a difficult decision within the MIR to decide to vote for Allende, but ultimately that is the decision we made. . . . I remember a group of us gathering in the morning of Allende's victory at the Plaza Engaña, we had established an entire system of communications in case anything were to happen, you have to understand. We thought that what was coming was either socialism or a coup! (He laughs.) . . .

. . . and later that evening, when Allende's victory was pretty assured, driving around in a small car, five of us squeezed in, observing everything. And we passed the Cerro Santa Lucia and there were masses and masses of people! And I remember we began to sing. Do you know the work of Elias Canetti? He has a passage in the introduction to one of his books about what it is like to feel part of a mass of people, standing skin touching skin, losing one's individual identity to become part of a collective identity, that is so much what it was like. . . .

. . . in terms of the Allende period, it had to be the most beautiful in all senses, in individual terms, in terms of the collective, culturally.

In this excerpt, Rivas refers consistently to the notion of individuals "as part of a collective identity," "a kind of intercontinental identity." He associates this collective identity with revolutionary commitment, whether it is belief in Che's model of the ethical, moral, guerrilla revolutionary or support for Salvador Allende. Rivas's recounting of Allende's victory is full of an elated imagery—the sights, sounds, and senses ("skin touching skin") of a collective moment.

Rivas depicted a tight-knit, highly organized revolutionary party, which he claimed remained united from its founding in 1965 to the first major split in 1979. He emphasized what he termed the MIR's moral and ethical influences on the Chilean left.

I went from being in charge of the community commandos, the industrial cordons, being connected to the masses, I felt so close to the workers movement!—I also realized that the MIR was far more organized than I knew, that it infiltrated many areas, that many had traveled to Cuba for training. The other thing about the MIR I realized

was its moral and theoretical influence on the Chilean left, on the
Socialist Party, that Miguel Henriquez (MIR leader) met with Allende
every week. You realize that you are involved in a serious group . . . this
includes the Christian Democrats, too, conversing. So I realized I was
involved in work at the mass level, and that the MIR was greater and
more organized than I had imagined.

Rivas thus felt that he was a part of the vanguard of an effective and highly influential ideological movement.

The majority of the Mirista militants were underground from 1965 to
1970. In 1970 the MIR made the decision to have most of its militants sur-
face publicly, although by 1972 much of the leadership and chief organizers had returned underground in anticipation of a military coup. When the
coup occurred, Rivas had already been moving from house to house with
false identification for several weeks. All were armed. Yet until the coup,
Rivas claimed, he had not committed a violent act in his life.

> And the coup came . . . And [my ex-wife] Alexandra and I agreed on
> a communications system, that we would be in touch every five days,
> indirectly through the family, and my son was crying, because children
> are so acutely aware of stress situations. And I left. When the coup
> came, everything changed, everything, everything, your way of seeing
> the other, everything.
>
> One of our biggest problems was the lack of gasoline. So, someone
> made a decision, it was a decision only a Central American could think
> up because we're too rational (ha, ha). We called her Ms. Moneypenny
> because she always had secret information, we teased her a lot. She was
> enchanting. Very clandestine because she was another nationality, she
> was a singer. Very cultured. . . . Moneypenny said, "But the street is full
> of cars." And we said, "So?" And she said, "But you have a gun, and
> one has to do what one has to do." I said, "What, go take one from
> somebody?" She said, "In Chile I learned that if you desire to do some-
> thing, you do it. But in Central America I learned that one can't always
> do something in the way one wants." For me this was the first exercise
> of violence. And we went. She and I go out in the street in her car, and
> we pass this Fiat 125, and she says, "This is a good car." And I said,
> "At the light stop, and I'll get out," and I really had no idea what I was
> doing. This was a whole new ball game. Everything was different from
> what we had formulated. So I got out and I said the most ridiculous,

stupid thing in the world, I said, "Get out of this car in the name of the people!" The guy looked at me, could see I wasn't comfortable, and said, "But why should I?" And I said again, "In the name of the people." So we begin this argument. And you know what saved this situation? He had a girl in the car who so angered me, she said, "*Terrorista marxista!*" And this made the guy more indignant, and I hit him. I knocked him to the ground, and I realized I had done something against all the rules in the manual, something you shouldn't do when you have a pistol, but I didn't fire at him. I got in the car and drove off. The car was full of gasoline. And we went through the car and found a revolver and in the glove box, $3,800 in dollars. Pure coincidence. Pure coincidence. And we drove around in that car all day until we ran out of gas. Carrying people to and from places, connecting people, carrying people to the factories.

I also lived the most important deception of that morning. I went to a factory in Vicuña Mackenna where we had really organized for this [coup possibility], at least somewhat, and I meet up with a comrade, someone who today is in the PSCH, and we meet car to car, because there weren't many cars in the street there, and I told him it would be good for him to go to San Bernardo where there was a mobilization I heard about on the radio. And he said, "No, I'm going to seek asylum." And I said, "But how?" And he said, "This doesn't have any future, no future." He said, "I want to be frank with you, I could have invented something." And in this sense he was very honest. "I'm going to get my family and I'm leaving. I can leave you my car. I just have to arrive at the Embassy where I'm getting asylum. I'll hide the keys in my car." He gave me all his money. He began to cry. He hugged me, and he left.

So when we ran out of gas this time I knew how to rob a car. None of this waiting at the light, the name of the people, nothing. I went right up to a guy and ordered him to give up his car. And the guy looked at me, a guy about forty years old, and he said, "Here. Now resist," and he left. Then I discovered it was a CORFO [Chilean state agency] car. But in any case, he gave me the car, he just gave it to me. The keys, the papers.

And for the first time, on the eleventh and the twelfth, we resisted. We were living what the Tupamaros had described to us, the Argentines who arrived in Chile, those who had been Peronist guerrillas, these "*terceristas*" who we would later be with in Central America, in Nicaragua. We were in combat. But it was a very unorganized strategy.

Yet at the same time the coup instigators were also unsure of us. So it was very chaotic, *very* chaotic. And twice we had direct confrontations with troop columns. Once, at five in the afternoon, and it was the MIR leadership. If there is one thing about the MIR, one must recognize that the leadership itself was out there resisting. At six, seven o'clock we're all resisting in the industrial zones, some unorganized, others more coordinated.

Then at midnight there is a change of house, and we're carrying a radio set from one house to another, and one comrade was shot and died, and that was my first experience with the death of a comrade at my side. I had him in my arms while we searched for another comrade, a woman who was a doctor, and I was scared, and he didn't move. Yet there was kind of a mystique around our resisting. The comrade who died was the child of a Spanish émigré from the Civil War. So somehow, it was very clear, this whole situation. My first encounter with death.

We fought on the twelfth, until there were many wounded by gunshots, we didn't have any gasoline, nothing. Until at noon, we made the decision to stop. It was hard to convince several, but we were also quite disciplined, so if the decision was to stop, we stopped. But we were all worried we would be surrounded. But at seven that evening, we could see workers walking through the streets, lines and lines of workers going home. It was a complete contrast to what we had imagined, a complete contrast.

This uninterrupted passage of Rivas's memories of his activities on the day of the coup is a rich and multilayered text, and it is worth close analysis.

The passage intimately links the personal—his leaving his ex-wife and his son, who is crying—with the political. The coup would change "everything, everything," his most intimate relations, his way of seeing the other.

The story of Rivas's first armed robbery is telling in its illustration of the abyss between revolutionary theory and discourse, on the one hand, and the reality of launching a concrete revolutionary struggle, on the other. The MIR's message of those years was armed struggle, and many of the party's militants went through military training in Cuba. In addition, during the late 1960s, discrete groups of Miristas had been involved in crimes "in the name of the people," including bank robberies. Yet here was a head organizer who reveals a level of naiveté probably not uncharacteristic of his comrades, many of whom would die violently in the years to come.

Rivas's encounter with a Mirista fleeing the country challenges his identification with the MIR as a committed collective, united to face the coup as the party determined. For Rivas, the act of ignoring orders by the MIR leadership to remain in the country was unthinkable. His individual political identity was intimately intertwined with MIR ideology and strategy, and it was not until his years in exile, from 1976 to 1984, that such links would be transformed.

Rivas's sense of identity to the collective was shaken but not shattered by his comrade's decision to flee Chile. He coolly robbed another car, this time from someone sympathetic to his perceived actions. His account of resistance on the eleventh and twelfth not only recovers his belief in the MIR, particularly its leadership, but links the MIR's resistance to what he sees as the historic resistance movements of the Southern Cone and to the defenders of the Second Spanish Republic. He momentarily creates the sense of a great "mystique" around those combating the military.

Yet the final passage represents a Mirista's revolutionary idealism coming to terms with the realities of the immediate situation, namely, that Chilean working people were not rising en masse to challenge the coup.

From the day of the military overthrow until June 1974, when he was arrested by Chilean Air Force Intelligence (SIFA), Rivas remained in Chile clandestinely, changing his appearance and his identity several times, making contacts, channeling information and resources. His memory of that eight-month period is vivid, and he virtually recounted it week by week. Perhaps the most interesting aspect of his recollections of that period is his perception that the MIR was highly organized, successfully building itself to face the dictatorship.

> About a week before Christmas I made contact with [a comrade]. She looked terrible, and I couldn't understand it, because it was a period when we were more confident, were recuperating, organizing big things, feeling almost untouchable, impossible to catch. We had false documents from the PSCH, from the PCCH, everybody. She said, "Bautista [van Showen, one of the top three Miristas leaders,] disappeared." . . .
>
> So the MIR reorganized, and I was really in charge of internal coordination. We modeled our cell structures on the Bolsheviks, one person in charge of three people. We began to organize Resistance Committees, all of that. . . .
>
> And we really perfected our communications systems, our cell structure, all our letters were written on cigar paper, which was terrible, and

we dressed very elegantly and walked with packages of spaghetti in our hands [to identify ourselves for rendezvous], and they had letters in them. . . . And we were fine, Bautista was the only one who had fallen, until March. . . .

And this is important, because I began arguing over a series of issues with [our head of military operations], and I want to be fair to his side, he's dead now, and I love him very much, but over how quickly to implement our offensive strategy, and we weren't really clear about the parameters within which we were working offensively and defensively, and I said, "But everyone is scared to death! It can be a war between us and them, but not between the government and the people!" It was a very, very difficult discussion, for me particularly. He was much older than I, had much more political experience than I, but we loved each other a lot. And one day we were arguing in a Citroen . . . and we were fighting a lot, and I got out of the car and he followed me in the Citroen, saying, "Get back in, get back in!" It's like we were a married couple (he said, laughing). Finally we made up. . . .

And a close friend arrived from Concepción . . . and through the summer a lot of our clandestine scheme broke down. I was out in the street, meeting with people, but it was okay because they were to be trusted. But at the end of the summer, beginning of March, our national committee organizer Roberto Moreno was captured, as well as another comrade on the political commission. The air force got them. So this was a big blow, but not so big because we had shown the capacity to recuperate fairly rapidly from something like this.

Throughout this passage, Rivas insists on the ability of his party to reorganize and "perfect" itself, even in the face of the disappearance of one leader and the arrests of several others. Yet the fact that several of the leadership fell by March, and that Rivas himself was arrested in a setup in June, would suggest that the MIR was *not* so organized as Rivas perceived. The argument that Rivas recalls between himself and the head of Mirista military strategy was not over whether the MIR could successfully challenge the military, for both of them assumed that the MIR could and should do so. Rivas was head of internal coordination, which may explain his insistence that the MIR was highly organized. Yet the intensity of Rivas's memories of this relatively short period may also cause him to perceive that the MIR resisted for a far longer time than was actually the case.

In prison, ideological resistance assumed new meaning, namely, that of physical and psychological survival. Rivas recounted the various "phases" of his imprisonment with the SIFA, from the first nine months he spent incommunicado, blindfolded on a bed, to his "discussion sessions" with SIFA officials regarding theoretical and strategic differences within the left. He also described an intra–armed forces struggle between air force intelligence (SIFA) and army intelligence (DINA) over his custody, in which the air force agreed to hand him over for a brief period with the stipulation that he be returned. By the end of his incarceration, Rivas had suffered permanent damage to his spine. Mirista resistance had now come to mean managing to stay alive:

> And one day I receive the possibility of a visa and grant to Belgium, and I'm able to commute my sentence from prison to exile, so it happened like this: One day I was taken hooded and I was hooded all the way to the plane! From there to Europe. Very strange. And in Europe I meet up with my friends, the mother of my son, and there's a party. I arrived in Europe extremely sad to be exiled from my country, but I arrived, too, with the sensation, with the total conviction, "I'm alive! I was not defeated!" Am I explaining myself okay?
>
> I remember saying to an old Communist comrade, when he asked me about the MIR, "We're fine. We're alive, which is a statistical error because we should all be dead!" This was one of the greatest errors of the dictatorship, because it made us all the more committed to our cause.

Rivas's major exile experiences from 1977 to 1984 were in Mexico, Central America, and Colombia, where he spent a good deal of time with guerrilla leaders. In perhaps a counterintuitive way, these experiences, Rivas claimed, contributed to his contention that the MIR leadership's 1979 decision to return militants as guerrillas to Chile was wrong, was suicidal. It was a decision made by a vote of three to two, and Rivas was one of the two on the losing side.

In 1984 Rivas returned clandestinely to Chile, still committed to the MIR. By this time, many Mirista militants had died in raids, captures, and shoot-outs with the military. Rivas could not escape the tremendous sense of responsibility he felt for being a part of such a fatal strategy.

> . . . a girl, my aide, who I adored, who was eighteen, nineteen years old . . . and we're still not clear what happened, but I will tell you. She got involved in a group, and she was part of my communications sys-

tem, my assistant, and they detect her, and I don't have time to tell
her because I had a clandestine group in my house, and they kill her.
And this was like reliving my past. But the question is responsibility,
and I had direct responsibility for her. And it meant my rethinking
everything and a serious set of discussions with my comrades, and
because I didn't know where the blow came from, I decided to get
everyone out of the country I was responsible for, everyone. Which
meant getting the resources, the money together, a huge nightmare.

In the final analysis, while there were divisions within the MIR regarding a number of theoretical and strategic positions, Rivas implies that the
MIR division fundamentally had to do with whether to continue to risk lives
in the name of resistance to defeat the dictatorship. In an important sense,
the MIR leadership was creating new forms of embeddedness for its militants that could mean their death.

The most difficult thing for me to talk about is the MIR division.
We tried to take division as a constructive way to revive the party. As
for the leadership, we concluded that there was no possible way to
correct the great error we had made [of returning militants in 1979].
And I remember spending nights and nights and nights arguing over
whether we should divide or not, this was the atmosphere. And the
second factor in all of this was how to begin *saving* lives, even if it were
[only] two or three. Of course, politics continued, our political discussions, but this other [dimension] was operating strongly, our mistake,
our responsibility. Imagine. We sent people to Chile without contacts
for their own security, with few resources, few safe houses, and the
dictatorship called this the great Soviet-backed terrorist attack they were
combating, but we had nothing, nothing of real substance. . . . And we
divided, and this was extremely painful, these were people I love very
much, and we separated. . . .

Then I experienced an acute physical crisis because of my back,
from the torture, one day I can't walk, and I have to get help. I had
problems with my spine, and they had to operate, and I felt from the
MIR as if I were betraying them, leaving them because I had to be operated on—I was operated on in Mexico. And the division was classic,
those internationally with those in the historic MIR against those in
Chile on the ground. And when I was being operated on they killed

one of my closest friends in Chile. They killed him. And I began to realize that the whole picture was so fragile. It was evident.

> . . . we fought, we fought, we fought so much, and I would arrive
> home and I would think, "But we're fighting and we're how many, three
> hundred, five hundred?" It was a difficult, difficult period. And on top of
> all this, with all the discipline of the party. It was schizophrenic.

This passage blends several layers of pain and trauma—the experiences of
party division, comrades dying, collective responsibility, intense physical
agony from past torture, and the irony of feeling the traitor because of the
personal need to leave (if only momentarily) the morass. The issues of life
and death that divided the MIR also kept Rivas clinging to it for several
years. In April 1992, however, he publicly resigned as head of the MIR-
Politico and announced his decision to join the newly founded and short-
lived Autonomous Union Movement (MAS). A party somewhat styled after
the Brazilian Workers' Party, the MAS represented an eclectic coming together of several small traditional and New Left factions. Rivas's decision
to join the MAS was in stark contrast to the decisions of several of his former comrades, many of whom joined the PSCH and now hold high-level
government and party posts.[13]

In terms of his cognitive framework, Rivas has strongly identified
throughout his life with what he perceives as a collective ideological left. In
his early years of activism, Rivas links himself with what he views as a
mass movement, a collective of students, workers, and intellectuals in
Chile. He sees the Chilean movement as part of an intercontinental movement of Latin American revolutionaries. With the fall of the Allende government, Rivas's sense of the collective narrows to focus intensely on his
fellow Mirista comrades and on the revolutionary left leaders with whom
he comes into contact in exile.

While the MIR represented the central form of institutional embeddedness for Rivas, one that molded his early commitment to revolutionary
struggle, his relationship with the MIR proved extremely dynamic, marked
by dramatic internal conflict and the loss of intimate fellow leaders and
militants. As a Mirista leader, Rivas came to know other Latin American
revolutionaries who would have a dialectical effect on his political thinking
and action.

In his return to Chile, Rivas's identification with a collective expands
once more, though it is tempered by his exile experiences, new realities in

Chile, the fragmentation of traditional social movements, a sense of fear of the real power of the military and its supporters, and the recognition that important sectors of the Chilean left were moving toward negotiation rather than confrontation with the regime.

Rivas possesses a self-awareness atypical of the other party loyalists of this study. He is an intellectual, and in a sense he bridges the typology of loyalist and thinker. From 1992 to 1993, Rivas headed a small group of former Miristas and other former revolutionaries who were attempting to build a movement inspired by the structure and evolution of the Workers Party of Brazil (PT). It fizzled. Today Rivas searches for a collective sense through his university teaching and his work with the cultural division of the Ministry of Education.

> This country is strange, I don't even know how to explain it. The left is in a very profound crisis. Really the word "crisis" is too soft. It is like a loss of identity, an inability to confront itself. But at the same time, over the last two years I have found, teaching in the university, that while it is clear people are living with pain, a sadness about everything that happened, there is also a generation of people emerging not tied to this pain. But they are not thinking in political terms. It is in cultural terms—music, rock, literature, poetry, film. There is some kind of change occurring from below, something distinct. So I think this cycle of pain is closing. A very long period, this Catholic sense of pain, long, long. It's a very Catholic pain.
>
> Given politics is so disreputable today in Chile, the change is coming through culture. If you look at student movements, you can find that in the 1920s, 1930s, something similar occurred, where there was this need to recognize the other, to know oneself. And I feel that within a few years there will be a very radical social-cultural movement here. If you look at the last university election in the Catholic University, the left won, in the University of Chile, the left won, in the University of Santiago, the left won. So you ask yourself, how is it that the left does this? People are not drawn to the formally political. For me the political class today is made up of these professional men who do politics, things are frozen.

What continues to dominate Rivas's political identity is his deep embeddedness in the revolutionary generation of the 1960s and in the MIR, and his political discourse and behavior continue to reflect this connection, though couched today in what might be described as poststructuralist terms:

> Why am I still a leftist? I will tell you in the most simple terms in the world. Because it is not at all certain that what exists today is the best possible world it can be. And because it is not the best it can be, I try to do two things: I try to think about the maximum possible change that will cause the minimal human damage. This is one theme, almost an epistemological one. How to accomplish the most change with least suffering, when what in fact has been happening is maximum suffering with the least change. And the second theme is to think absolutely collectively, with everyone. People of different religions, skin colors, identities, how everyone can feel part of the same humanity. This is my aesthetic understanding of what it means to be on the left.
>
> In terms of those I admire, Miguel Henriquez [a founder of the MIR who was killed]—not out of nostalgia, out of pure love. Che. Not out of nostalgia either. Because I love him. Clearly the Beatles. Maybe the Rolling Stones, too. And Michel Foucault. And now what I tell you will seem strange, for he's a complex character. Of those living, I admire Marcos, in Chiapas. Marcos because he was able to create a sense of humor, and I love that. Marcos is a very impressive thing. I feel that the challenge for the left is to achieve social meaning where capitalism as it exists is simply an episode in a completely transformative project for humanity.
>
> Why am I not in the PSCH or the PCCH? Well, the PCCH bores me. And the PSCH I am very distanced from. To create a true force for change, an alternative collective, it might require any number of people. In the U.S. Revolutionary War, it required some ten million. To create the Cuban Revolution, let's say, four hundred thousand. You need some number, but one never knows what the number should be. If you want to take a trip, to explore a place, to change a piece of the world, you don't do it alone, but maybe you don't need so many. It is not purely arithmetic, it is moral, it is a force, of impulses, energy, of believing in yourself. In terms of numbers, if you identify all those who consider themselves socialists in Latin America, the number is very large, but they don't do anything. The PCCH in Chile is very small, but is large compared to the situation of other communists of the world, and the PCCH continues to do a lot being very small. . . . How can a group move a people? If there is no passion, there is no politics of the left.

We can sit here and discuss different logics, Gramsci, et cetera, but our greatest challenge is to bring many people together on this very small planet, and if we don't, we are condemned, if not to extinction, to ever greater crises.

Why am I a leftist? I'll tell you very simply. Because capitalism is for shit. But what is the alternative? I don't know, I can't sit here and tell you, I don't know. The first great attempts have failed, failed miserably . . . and I have no shame for what I did. It's my life, and I won't come out with some ridiculous claim, like if it happened now I would do it differently. One does what one knows. And that's what I knew, and I'm very proud of what I did. Very proud. . . . And I continue to believe that you, me, all of us are the last monkeys, but the first man has yet to appear. The man who is profoundly humane has not yet appeared. And this world will end with us if we are not capable of producing certain changes. . . .

Many times I have felt guilt for being alive. Because I am a statistical error. But I don't know why, it's chance, so I have this responsibility to history and to my history to continue thinking with the same courage. I can't accede to this hug of death, because it is the death hug of power. I can't renounce everything I've done, I've believed, not because I'm a fanatic, I'm not a fanatic because I do try to understand others, to understand why they think and act the way they do. We're at the very beginning of a long process to create human beings. . . . And we have accomplished little things that are so important, the creation of the word, for example, communication. And we feel tenderness, love.

LOYALISTS COMPARED

For the political party loyalists of this study, the political party as a collective enterprise looms as the dominant referent of their individual political identities. From their first participation in politics to the present, party loyalists have dedicated their lives to organizing and activity within the confines of their parties. Unlike political entrepreneurs, who draw from several organizational networks for their political identities, party loyalists rely on one.

Political party loyalists of this study are also marked more strongly than other types by their embeddedness in the 1960s generation. While all those of this study can be defined as members of that generation, the party loyalists have been more attached to the political, social, and cultural movements and expressions that characterized the period. This is reflected in the discourse and ideological sentiments of party loyalists, from their voiced nostalgia about the period to their use of 1960s events as constant referents for their current activism. Others in this study, such as the thinkers and the political entrepreneurs, spend far less time discussing the 1960s, or they "repackage" the 1960s in their current discourse on modernization and neoliberalism. Party loyalists' narratives often seem to be frozen in the discourse of the 1960s or at least clearly adapted from the cultural and political expressions of that period.

Of the party loyalists examined in this study, Jorge Insunza best illustrates the type. He holds fast to the Leninist roots and the past glory of the Chilean Communist Party. He remains dedicated to retrieving the importance of his party in Chilean politics. Rather than sacrifice the PCCH for a political organization more reflective of current political tendencies—a characteristic behavior of the political entrepreneurs of this study—Insunza remains with the PCCH. He continues to place tremendous value on effective organizing of his party's bases, of those militants who represent support and mobilization networks for party promotions and campaigns. As a party loyalist, Insunza derives political meaning from his ability to recruit members, to attract militants to the party. Such a role overall was particularly valued within political parties in the 1960s, in a period of mass mobilizations and movements.

Throughout the 1990s transition period, as the means for securing political support changed, where public opinion polling, focus groups, and media campaigns dominate political party attention, political parties placed far less value on militant recruitment. In the age of the sound bite and the demobilization of Chilean society, party loyalist Insunza became "old-fashioned." He is embedded in 1960s-generation imagery and in nostalgic representations of their political parties. Given the dynamics of the Chilean transition and the state of international communism, this holding on to such past representations politically marginalized the former congressman.

In contrast to Insunza, loyalist Isabel Allende is integrally linked to a left party that has sought to reinvent itself. Allende has cautiously supported this reinvention, though her discourse and identity continue to represent the Socialist Party's old, albeit moderate, guard.

For Adriana Muñoz, political action is today a more deliberative, conflictive process than in her past, as she is torn by the dual identity of loyalist and feminist. Yet Muñoz has not privileged her feminism over her loyalty to the party, a behavior that would be characteristic of the thinkers of this study.

Patricio Rivas's attachment to past revolutionary ideals and the comrades who died for them continues to overshadow his current political decision making. He searches, unsuccessfully, for what he perceives to be a sense of social solidarity and meaning infused in the MIR in a new political collectivity.

Chapter 4 will examine the second cognitive orientation of this study, the personal loyalist. Like political party loyalists, personal loyalists are party organizers and recruiters. Yet unlike party loyalists, personal loyalists privilege particular individuals whom they hold as heroic, and their identification with those heroes represents the primary referent in their lives.

PERSONAL LOYALISTS AND
THE MEANING OF ALLENDISMO

■ Images and memories of Salvador Allende are woven in complex ways into the political and cultural fabric of contemporary Chile. Throughout the 1990s postauthoritarian period, for example, the Chilean political right has periodically invoked Allende as a disastrous president who brought chaos and the specter of communism to an otherwise peace-loving, Christian, capitalist society. The Chilean Communist Party, today on the margins of mainstream politics, has championed Allende in its pamphlets and magazines, convinced that among current and potential supporters, the figure of Allende is remembered with admiration and affection. Allende's own party, the Chilean Socialist Party, today appears to be the most reticent to call upon the memory of Allende, as associations of tensions and the party's betrayal of Allende are among the most negative collective memories of the Popular Unity period.

Interestingly enough, through the 1990s, the figure of Allende has enjoyed more visibility on the cultural plane than on the political one, particularly among Chilean youth and within the Chilean grassroots. In poor neighborhoods, streets and communal associations are often named after Salvador Allende. Popular-sector soccer clubs are named for Allende. In a June 1998 encounter with representatives from a hundred-thousand-member youth soccer federation, the representatives claimed James Dean, Che Guevara, and Salvador Allende to be their idols. When asked why Allende, members said, "Because he was serious, he stood for something, he died for what he believed in."[1] Among these youth, Salvador Allende earns far more respect than current political leaders.

Salvador Allende and the idea of Allendismo have represented the central referent in the political lives of the three individuals upon whom this chapter will focus. Like those in Chile's poor neighborhoods today, the three were born into Chile's popular classes—Hernán Del Canto the son of a Santiago working-class family; Aníbal Palma, of an Argentine immigrant working-class mother; and Eduardo Reyes, of an agrarian proletariat family in the Chilean provinces. Early in their political lives, the three identified Salvador Allende as the man who most inspired their political beliefs and actions, and in the texts of Del Canto and Palma, particularly, Allende appears as a virtual father figure. As personal loyalists, Hernán Del Canto, Aníbal Palma, and Eduardo Reyes define their political ideologies and roles by tightly linking themselves to Allende as an individual political leader. These loyalists to Allende define their ideologies in terms of "Allendismo," which they interpret as progressive nationalist sentiment and a commitment to formal democratic institutions. They view themselves as preservers of Allende's vision, which they attempt to champion in their political party.

In contrast to the political party loyalists of the previous chapter, personal loyalists identify with a political leader to an extent that outweighs any loyalty they harbor for a political party. Attachments to individual leaders can both elevate and alienate personal loyalists within their parties. This chapter will explore how, through their identification with Allende, personal loyalists attempt to transcend negative public perceptions of the Socialist Party in order to preserve their individual political integrity and self-worth.

It is a *memory* of the association with Allende that is reflected in the texts of personal loyalists, a memory that they depend on to define their present identities. Indeed, as is emphasized throughout this book, memory is central to the concept of identity. How individuals remember and recount the memories of their pasts says a great deal about how they perceive themselves, how they fit in their communities and polities. In the words of social historian Alessandro Portelli, "Memory is not a passive depository of facts, but an active process of creation of meanings."[2] Historians such as Portelli and Luisa Passerini have emphasized the meshing through memory of what is termed an "all-ready memory," that is, the popular or generalized view of the world, with the subjective, individual sense of identity, the "consciousness of oneself."[3] This chapter will illustrate how strongly individual memories can be shaped by popular conceptions of past events and protagonists, and how, in turn, individuals latch on to those conceptions as they reformulate their own political identities.

Memories are also critical to collective identities. As Robert Bellah and his colleagues have argued, entire communities are bound by shared memories:

> Communities . . . have a history—in an important sense they are
> constituted by their past—and for this reason we can speak of a real
> community as a "community of memory," one that does not forget its
> past. In order not to forget that past, a community is involved in re-
> telling its story, its constitutive narrative, and in so doing, it offers
> examples of the men and women who have embodied and exemplified
> the meaning of the community. These stories of collective history and
> exemplary individuals are an important part of the tradition that is so
> central to a community of memory.[4]

This chapter will begin by examining the uneasy memory that the Chilean
Socialist Party sustains of its former leader Allende. On occasion, current
PSCH leaders have attempted to utilize the image and beliefs of Allende to try
to overcome the negative images of the party's own past, to preserve a crucial element of political party identity as its collective identity, and to appeal
to the party's historic militancy and constituency. In an important sense, Allendismo has come to symbolize an intellectual strand that can be represented as ideological continuity within the party, even as the PSCH attempts
today to project a fresh, modern image to the Chilean polity and society.

Individual leaders and activists whose lives were dedicated to revolutionary change rely on self-referents that contribute to a positively framed
continuity in their lives, even if this means shifting the memories of their
pasts in order to preserve their present political identities. The Socialists
recognize the contrasting images that Chileans hold of Allende and the
party, and many have adjusted or reprioritized their past associations and
beliefs to reflect these distinctions. For personal loyalists, Allendismo has
lent an ideological continuity to their political identities, representing a
kind of haven within a party historically plagued by serious internal friction
and division. In contrast to political party loyalist Isabel Allende, who has
used her family name to secure her attachment to the Socialist Party, personal loyalists rely on the memory of their associations with Allende in
order to detach themselves from the party.

After a discussion of Allende and the Socialist Party, this chapter will explore how through the recounting of their associations with Allende, three
individuals have struggled to preserve their own political identities despite
bitter individual setbacks and the painful repiecing together of their political
lives. The three individuals are former cabinet ministers under Allende and
current PSCH Central Committee members Hernán Del Canto and Aníbal

Palma, and former PSCH youth leader and current PSCH Central Committee member Eduardo Reyes. For Del Canto and Palma, memories of close contact with and admiration for Allende continue as dominant forces in their public images as well as their political identities. For Reyes, who is ten years younger than Del Canto and Palma, memories of Allende's leadership and vision continue to inspire his own attempts to infuse the PSCH with a solidaristic commitment to Chile's working classes.

ALLENDE AND THE SOCIALIST PARTY

Drawing a distinction between Allende and his party, the Chilean Socialist Party, was quite common among those interviewed, among both socialists and nonsocialists. On the one hand, this distinction reflects a broader political history, in which a handful of national leaders transcended their parties in an appeal to a peculiar kind of populism in Chilean politics.[5] On the other hand, studies such as those of Carlos Huneeus also show that historically Chileans have drawn a clear distinction between presidents and their administrations.[6] In the case of Salvador Allende and the Popular Unity government (1970–1973), opinion polls taken in 1972 and in March 1973 illustrate that Chileans sympathetic to the Popular Unity administration tended to be more positive about Allende himself than about his government (see table 4.1).

Since 1973 the analytical and symbolic separation between Salvador Allende and his party has been drawn all the more sharply. Leading scholarly analyses of the breakdown of the Chilean democratic regime have portrayed the Socialist Party as a thorn in the side of a president attempting to transform Chilean society through the country's democratic institutional channels.[7] Such analyses focus on the high degree of factionalization within the PSCH and on the increasing prominence within the party of an "ultra-left" faction, which eschewed attempts to appease opposition to revolutionary change in Chile.

Further, a number of Socialist Party thinkers have produced works that critically examine the role of the Socialist Party in the 1960s and in the Popular Unity period.[8] While they tend to be less damning of the party per se, they are serious critiques of those factions and parties of the left that supported extra-institutional means of achieving socialism. Such works have contributed to universal condemnation of the majority of the pre-1973 Socialist Party leadership.

Table 4.1

Polls of Support for President Salvador Allende and His Government

| | 1972 | | March 1973 | |
	Allende	*Gov't*	*Allende*	*Gov't*
Excellent	16.8	7.3	12.3	4.6
Very Good	12.3	5.6	8.1	5.3
Good	35.0	31.0	29.5	23.8
Okay	24.4	37.8	23.4	30.7
Bad	6.1	10.0	13.5	18.5
Very Bad	3.3	5.7	8.1	14.7
No Comment	2.1	2.6	5.1	2.4
	100.00	100.0	100.0	100.0
	N=881		N=753	

Source: Eduardo Hamuy 1972, 1973. Cited in Carlos Huneeus, *Los chilenos y la política* (Santiago: CERC, 1987),85.

Yet perhaps more important than scholarly and political tracts critiquing the PSCH are the memories and symbols held by Chileans themselves of the Popular Unity period and of the role of the Socialist Party during those conflict-ridden years. Filtered through the lens of seventeen years of dictatorship, these memories include societal polarization, large mobilizations and countermobilizations, street brawls, food and gasoline shortages, and general instability.

The Pinochet regime reinforced such memories, primarily through state-controlled television. This was best demonstrated in the 1988 plebiscite campaign, when government propaganda focused on the dangers of a return to the problems of the Popular Unity years should the government be defeated. According to textual transcriptions from government-produced commercials, Chile's Popular Unity period was characterized by "extremist violence, shortages," and "inflation, infant mortality, illiteracy, lack of housing, lack of hope, of feminine dignity, of peace, of a future, poverty, helplessness, hunger, unemployment, uncertainty."[9] The dictatorship played on the memories of conflict and turmoil to improve its own image as one of order and stability.[10]

As Bellah et al. argue, "exemplary individuals" often come to personify sentiments about the past for an entire community. Perhaps the ultimate negative symbol of the Popular Unity period's Socialist Party leadership has become that of former PSCH secretary-general Carlos Altamirano. Accused of promoting sedition within the navy, Altamirano was the last Chilean exile to receive permission to return to Chile.[11] Altamirano's September 9, 1973, speech in Santiago's main stadium is etched in the Chilean collective political memory. The tenor of it was aggressive and combative, calling on Chileans to defend, with arms if necessary, what appeared to be an inevitable military coup d'état:

> The conspiracy of the Right—our Party thinks—can only be crushed with the invincible force of the people united with soldiers, classes, non-commissioned officers and officers loyal to the constituted government.
>
> Know: the Socialist Party will not allow itself to be crushed by an oligarchic and seditious minority. . . .
>
> Never will we submit ourselves to the force of an illegitimate power.
>
> We are a party, the vanguard of the working class, with forty years of tradition in the proletarian struggle, resolved to resist whatever coup attempt.
>
> Chile will be transformed into a new heroic Vietnam if the sedition dreams of planting itself in our country. . . .
>
> The coup cannot be combated with dialogue. The coup can be crushed by the force of the workers, with the force of the people, with the organization of the working class, with the community commands, with the industrial belts, with the peasant councils. . . .
>
> Comrade Allende will not betray us, comrades, he will give his life if necessary in the defense of this process.[12]

Altamirano has been styled as the "black beast" of Chilean politics, "the most hated," "the worst enemy of the Allende government."[13] In an interview with leading Chilean journalist Patricia Politzer, Altamirano recognized the symbol he became: "As long as I am held as the guilty party for Allende's failure, everyone else can sleep peacefully."[14]

In contrast to Altamirano's speech as a symbol is the death of Allende himself. How Allende died—whether he was killed or committed suicide—in La Moneda palace was a matter of controversy until 1991, when his family had his body exhumed and concluded that the death was a suicide. Nevertheless, in death Allende became a martyr, a man who died for his convictions.[15]

For Chileans who identify themselves on the left, the separation between Allende and the PSCH represents a common tendency, that is, the positive presentation of an Allende who was ultimately betrayed by the brazen ambition and horrendous errors of his party. While respect for Allende varies widely across contemporary Chilean society, most Chileans share a negative view of the role of the PSCH during that period. To be considered a major player in the Socialist Party from 1970 to 1973 is to be viewed today with suspicion and mistrust.

The Socialist Party leadership has been acutely aware of such sentiments. In 1987 Socialist Party thinker and former PSCH secretary-general Gonzalo Martner linked Allende to the Socialists' search for a left agenda uniting democracy and socialism, challenging his party to reassume Allende's legacy:

> In spite of more than a decade of intimidating propaganda from the junta and servants of the regime, few dare to deny the immense moral value of the example of President Allende, who paid with his life for his opting for democratic institutionality and socialism. But has such a fertile legacy been abandoned? Have the conditions been created for his future projection? We must focus on . . . the relationship between democracy and socialism, . . . one of the key elements of the reconstitution of the credibility of the socialist and communist left. . . .
>
> Once in government, Allende clearly formulated his Chilean road to socialism as that which fights "to assure social liberties through the exercise of political liberties." With that pledge, and without ever obtaining the resolute support of his party to govern, he died combating the military in defense of democratic institutions.[16]

For the past several years, in monographs, organized debates, and party journals, the PSCH has consciously explored the many facets of Allende, of Allende's relationship to the party, and of his relationship to Chilean society as a whole.[17] In these explorations, Socialists have attempted to strengthen the party's collective identity through invoking the memory of Allende and Allendismo. It is an attempt to renovate or modernize the party while maintaining historical continuity and a sense of the party's contribution to historic progressive Chilean politics.

This is not to suggest, however, that the Socialists have invoked Allende in purely laudatory terms. In a 1988 forum organized on the relationship between Allende and socialist renovation, for example, socialist thinkers analyzed both the contradictions in Allende's positions and his under-standing of the meaning of democracy and socialism. Former PSCH president Jorge Arrate criticized Allende's notion of uniting workers through political parties narrowly defined as workers' parties, as well as his failure to devote more attention to constructing the Socialist Party in ways more conducive to his project.[18] Socialist thinker and ambassador to Austria Osvaldo Puccio emphasized Allende's own insistence on defining himself as a Marxist-Leninist who conceived of democracy as the overcoming of capitalism and the breaking of links with imperialism and who claimed that reactionary violence had to be met with revolutionary violence.[19]

Despite these other facets of Allende's thought and discourse, the Socialist Party today emphasizes his commitment to Chile and to a national project of social transformation through the country's democratic institutions. Former MAPU leader Oscar Guillermo Garretón argued that the basis for today's Socialist renovation should be recapturing the virtual "love affair" that Allende enjoyed with Chilean citizens sympathetic to the left. This love affair, according to Garretón, was the result of the citizens' identification with Allende's profound, progressive nationalist commitment to Chile.[20]

On April 19, 1990, Senator and PSCH leader Ricardo Nuñez addressed the Chilean Senate in a speech marking the fifty-seventh anniversary of the Socialist Party. In this speech, Nuñez linked the memory of Allende with the principles espoused by the PSCH today:

> After this long dictatorship we Socialists have been vigorously reborn in Chile. . . . Some of our truths have remained in the air. Others, we are constructing through honest efforts to renovate our basic ideals. In this effort, the figure and the example of the best of us holds special validity: the president martyr Salvador Allende.
>
> He was the best achieved synthesis of the fundamental values of socialism. That is, in Allende the idea of freedom as the full realization of the person materialized; the idea of justice, as the end to all discrimination on the basis of race, sex, or social condition; the idea of equality, as a value dignifying the human condition; the idea of solidarity, which identifies us with the victims of injustice and puts in practice the aspiration for a better humanity; all those principles and values by which socialism considers the historic and moral sense of democracy, as the full realization of human rights.[21]

In the postauthoritarian period, the Socialist Party has somewhat fitfully attempted to reinterpret and incorporate strands of Allendismo into its on-going formulation of a renovated collective identity.[22] Fearful of the contin-uing effects of negative societal associations, PSCH invocations of Allende appear to be directed toward the party's historic militancy and constituency, rather than toward Chilean society at large. It is a recognition that none holds tighter to an inspired memory of Allende than those of the party base, whom the PSCH relies upon for day-to-day work and support. Allendismo resonates with individual party organizers such as Aníbal Palma, Hernán Del Canto, and Eduardo Reyes, all of whom have constructed their current political identities and ideologies from their early associations with Allende.

HERNÁN DEL CANTO

"I was so young and inexperienced," Hernán Del Canto repeated as he traced the course of his political life.[23] Del Canto was born in 1940 into a working-class family in Santiago, the son of a metalworker. His first po-litical memories come from the method that his father employed to teach him to read. From the age of nine, Del Canto would labor through *El Siglo*, the Communist Party daily newspaper, reading out loud to his father. Though his father was not a member of the Communist Party, he expect-ed his son to grow up to be one.

At fifteen, Del Canto began as a metalworker at the Phillips plant in San-tiago. He attended night school for his high school diploma. At sixteen, in-fluenced by a group of friends at work, Del Canto joined the Young Social-ists (JS), and he became an active member of the union rank and file. Del Canto laughed when he remembered his father's reaction to the news he had joined the Young Socialists instead of the Communist Party, with which his father had always sympathized:

> When I entered the JS my father thought I would enter the Jota [the Young Communists]. This would have been his ideal. I entered the JS, and he said that was fine, that it seemed like a positive move because it was like a step for me on my way to entering the Jota. It didn't happen like that.

Del Canto's memories of the late 1950s and 1960s are filtered through the lens of a young Socialist Party militant and labor leader. At seventeen,

Del Canto became the president of a local youth branch of the FRAP, the Socialist-Communist alliance for the 1958 presidential elections. He recalled his first public speeches:

> The first time I had to speak was when I had to say something before a big group of four or five thousand people in a rally we organized for Allende in the Simón Bolívar Plaza. . . . I don't think I spoke for more than three or four minutes and it reflected my own lack of formation in many ways, the lack of a capacity to speak in public, the very nervousness I felt before the microphones then, and the second time was in a cemetery at the burial of a comrade who was a member of the Central Committee of the JS, who died in a train accident on the campaign trail with Allende.

Del Canto remembers that his first efforts at public speaking were directly linked to his work for Allende. He launched into a description of the general political climate of the country, of the excitement and turmoil around the presidential campaigns, of the frustration and bitterness of electoral defeat and of the efforts to reconstruct, rebuild, and recuperate after each campaign. Approximately 60 percent of Del Canto's text is in the collective "*nosotros*," or "we," reflecting a life inseparable from Allende, the Socialist Party, and the union movement. He also recalled the strategies and objectives of organized labor as if he were reciting a union position paper chapter and verse.

At twenty-four, Hernán Del Canto became secretary-general of the Young Socialists. At twenty-seven, he was elected second-in-command of the CUT, the country's leading union confederation. At thirty-one, Del Canto became Salvador Allende's minister of the interior.

Del Canto's political trajectory, which carried him from union organizer in an automobile plant to a cabinet post, is highly unusual for Chile. In a society that is markedly class-stratified, the Allende years represented a moment of political mobility for the Chilean organized working class.[24] Del Canto's two primary networks—the Socialist Party and the trade union movement—placed him in the seat of left political power.

Del Canto's text focuses extensively on the Popular Unity period, the period in which he played his largest roles in the PSCH, the union movement, and in the government itself. He emphasized his close relationship with Allende as well as his commitment to Allende's positions.

In the [PSCH] Congress of La Serena in 1971, where Carlos Altamirano was elected secretary-general, it was a very new, renovated Central Committee, renovated from the generational point of view. More than half of the PSCH Central Committee were people between twenty-five and thirty years of age . . . and I was the commissar of that congress . . . and afterwards I was elected to the Political Commission . . . and on that commission I was very prominent, as they say now, because I got the highest number of votes from the Central Committee. . . . I was a person that provoked a certain unity internally in the PSCH for one reason. First because I was a person very *unlinked* to the internal groups, and second because I had a very high rank in the union movement. . . . So, we acted in the Political Commission, I was one of the two or three people who had relations with President Allende. . . .

What we [the Popular Unity government] were really experiencing between 1972 and 1973 was an organized insurrection that brought the military into action in 1973, so that what I can say is that in that period we lived *very* intensively in a great linking with President Allende, a close collaboration. I had a very frank, very cordial, very fraternal relationship with him in spite of the fact that naturally we had a big age difference, he was double my age. I had a close friendship with President Allende's daughters, and I would say that together we lived with great intensity what for me has been the most important period of my life, a period that gave me great satisfaction, although I also learned some big lessons about what politics is, what confrontation is, what irrationality is. . . .

Inside the Popular Unity government there were two political projects, one that felt the process should be more moderate, greater agreements with the opposition, greater understanding, a search for the legal channels to get away from the problems we were confronted with, and the other sector that supported greater political, economic, and social radicalization, including those that at one point were disposed to stop supporting the president. In our own party in which we were leaders, there was a division within the leadership, in the Central Committee, almost half and half, in which one sector sustained that the government was veering off its revolutionary course. . . . there were those in favor of creating a parallel government. And there was the other sector, which felt the party had the *obligation* to support the government, that our *responsibility* was to continue, that was the commitment we had

made to the country, a democratic path, of plurality and liberty . . . And
we had many internal confrontations, many differences, I considered
myself always a part of those who were supporting President Allende.

In this excerpt Del Canto portrays himself as a kind of political mediator
in a party polarized virtually in half. Del Canto was a member of the highest echelon of the party, the Political Commission, a commission that favored a more rapid radicalization than the president did. He allies himself clearly with the Allende position, which he holds ideologically as
loyalty to Chile and a commitment to formal democratic institutions. Del
Canto blames youth and inexperience for his own shortcomings as a politician, as well as for the errors of the Socialist Party. As he describes the
basic division within the PSCH, Del Canto never questions Allende's politics and leadership.

Throughout the five-hour interview, Del Canto emphasized his commitment to Allende, to the Allende family, and to Allende's vision of a democratic road to socialism. In a manner that parallels the PSCH's projection of
continuity within its own renovation, including its emphasis on democracy
and compromise, Allende serves as the inspiration for Del Canto.

When asked what were the three most important events in his life, Del
Canto answered, first, becoming secretary-general of the CUT; second, his
appointment as minister of the interior; and third, the final minutes and
death of Allende in the presidential palace.

> I would say that the third event has most affected my life, hit me in
> a very complex way psychologically. On the eleventh I was sent to La
> Moneda by the Political Commission of the Socialist Party. I entered
> when he was fully engaged in giving instructions to the people who
> were there to carry out a defense of La Moneda palace. I had to wait for
> him to speak [his final radio address] in order to speak with him and to
> transmit to him the Socialist Party opinion regarding the events taking
> place that morning. I listened at his side, practically at the same dis-
> tance that you and I are here, to the last speech he made. I said to
> Augusto Olivares, a well-known journalist and close friend of Allende's,
> that it was clearly his farewell speech, that there was nothing more to
> do after that speech. I waited for him, I spoke with him, I had a short
> conversation, well, I, and that had a huge impact on me given that I
> saw him with an enormous integrity, disposed to remain there until
> the final consequences [Allende's death].

I went on behalf of the PSCH to tell him that we considered that his attempt, at this point, that this coup attempt was pretty invincible, and that, therefore, his immolation in the palace didn't make much sense. This was the position that the Political Commission adopted, and it sent me, to carry the decision, to transmit this decision. I was the only one that went to La Moneda that day to express this to the president. Books have been written, very deformed versions of this event, including versions from others and not from me. I am now giving you my confirmation of the final conversation I had with Allende.

I entered La Moneda when there was still a palace guard, police who were with him, and when I left they were already against him, and a rifle was put to my chest and they didn't let me leave! But I managed to get out anyway . . . and the bombardment came, and the closing of Parliament, and the *bandos*[25] for us, and the sacking of our homes, including the harassing of my wife, who had our year-and-a-half-old child at home, and the robbing of everything in my home, well, these are naturally things that have a big impact on one's life, then leaving Chile— But I can't complain.

As Del Canto indicates, the way he remembers this moment is quite distinct from a number of popularized accounts of his last conversation with Allende. The "deformed version" Del Canto is probably referring to appears in the book *El día en que murió Allende*, written by the highly respected Chilean journalist Ignacio González Camus. Now in its third edition, González's book is considered an authoritative journalistic account of the major events that took place on September 11, 1973, the day of the coup. In one passage, González recounts Hernán Del Canto's final exchange with Allende:

Allende observed Hernán Del Canto with hostility. At his side was Joan Garcés.

Del Canto said to him that he had arrived at La Moneda representing the Socialist Party leadership to ask him what he wanted the leaders to do; what should their action or their help be at that moment.

The sum of the discrepancies between the President and his party, those which had occurred during his government and especially in the final months, and his own frustration at having been cast into the scenario he was now living, led to a very acid response. He spoke briefly, in a short tone.

He said to Del Canto that it was strange to him that, after so much time of not having taken his opinion into account, that the leaders would bother to ask. He added that, at the same time, the party leaders surely knew very well what to do. And that he, for his part, knew very well what his duty was.

Del Canto stood alone, diminished, in a certain sense scorned by the attitude and words of the President.

"After he spoke with Allende, it gave him a crisis of nerves," remembers detective David Garrido, drinking his coffee and smoking a cigarette.

Garrido had the rough voice of a smoker. His wife circled around him, calling him "*papi*." Garrido strikes one as a man of action, some-one who knows what he wants.

"He cried desperately," Garrido continues, referring to Del Canto. "'They're going to kill us, they're going to kill us,' he said. He had to be asked to leave so he wouldn't create a crisis or collective hysteria. Allende's bodyguards had to remove him from there."[26]

In González's third edition, the author includes an addendum relaying the version that Del Canto reported to him in 1988. The account closely resembles his account to me in 1991.

The purpose of presenting these contrasting texts is not to decide which is right and which is wrong. Rather, it is to explore how one individual remembers and recounts his past to preserve his identity in the face of pending tragedy and his own powerlessness to prevent it. Erik Erikson argues that when memories are painful, "they at least recover from the defeats of the past the stragglers of unlived potentials." "All confessions," Erikson writes, "seek to settle a (big or small) curse."[27] For Del Canto, the exchange between himself and Allende is perhaps the most important of his life. In today's context, in which the former Political Commission of the PSCH is considered treasonous, Del Canto holds tightly to his close association with the president.

In an account of an Italian worker's experience with the death of a comrade, Alessandro Portelli analyzes how memory attempts to heal the wounds of humiliation and powerlessness.[28] Portelli's worker recalls action rather than inaction, shrewd observance rather than uncertainty or fear. As Portelli states, "Oral sources tell us not just what people did, but what they wanted to do, what they believed they were doing, and what they now think they did."[29]

After the coup, the PSCH directed Del Canto to leave the country. He sought political asylum in the Colombian embassy, spent six months in Bogotá, and then moved with his family to East Berlin, headquarters of the PSCH's External Secretariat. There he was placed in charge of international relations for the PSCH, a position he held for a decade. Del Canto spent fourteen years in exile, and yet had it not been for persistent questioning, he would have spent no time discussing it. For Del Canto, the fourteen years based in East Berlin were little more than a "parenthesis" in his life.[30]

Del Canto returned to Chile in 1988. Today he is still an elected member of the PSCH Central Committee, and he holds a midlevel position in the Ministry of the Presidency. This post is but a shadow of the governmental positions that he occupied twenty years ago. Unlike Aníbal Palma, below, for whom university education and training gained him slightly greater access to contacts and opportunities both in exile and upon return, Del Canto found that his class and labor background and subsequent structure of opportunities limited his possibilities in the transformed political moment.

The Popular Unity government represented the pinnacle of Hernán Del Canto's political career. Despite a number of painful memories from that period, Del Canto's memories of both personal political prominence and his sense of self-worth are far more elevated then than at any other moment in his life. Such prominence, Del Canto believes, was linked to his loyalty to Allende over and above any loyalty to the party. Del Canto's narrative fits Portelli's description of individuals who have been transfixed by particular life experiences:

> We may . . . come across narrators whose consciousness seems to have been arrested at climactic moments of their personal experience: certain Resistance fighters, or war veterans; and perhaps certain student militants of the 1960s. Often, these individuals are wholly absorbed by the totality of the historical event of which they were part, and their account assumes the cadences and working of *epic*.[31]

As the PSCH attempts to modernize, as political party leaders and organizers tend to downplay the once deeply penetrating role of the party in civil society, Hernán Del Canto remains frozen in his memories of the past and his loyalty to Allende. He relies on his early association with Allende in a vague profession of hope for the party's return to past ideals. His text reveals a contradictory, conflictive stance on the question, for example, of the relationship between the party and organizations in civil society. On the one hand, Del Canto proclaims his support for the autonomy of civil society organizations, for their freedom from control of the parties as was common in the past. On the other hand, when asked about his visions of the role of the party in society, Del Canto berates what he terms an *"internista"* or *"inward-focused"* culture in today's PSCH, in which the party appears to show little interest in playing a visible role in crucial organizations of civil society:

> There's a certain *internista* culture within the party in the sense that
> they believe that the party functions well when they meet, arrive at
> certain accords, pay their dues, read the act, and they're through,
> they're happy with this. We have to put an end to this behavior. We
> have to ensure that the problems of the people, the problems of the
> people in the neighborhood organization where I live, the problems in
> the sports organizations, in the struggle for cleaner air, in blocking the
> cutting down of trees because it negatively affects the environment, of
> assuring that sporting events function properly . . . these are the prob-
> lems of the people, and we have to have an answer for them, gather
> their proposals and transform them into program and *push through
> our agenda at the neighborhood level* and not allow our party to become
> a kind of closed parish, where people are unsure if the party exists
> or doesn't.

Del Canto is embedded in the Socialist Party yet alienated from much of its current leadership. Historically the other most important network for Del Canto, the trade union movement, is no longer the working-class political and social force it once represented. Wrenching, traumatic experiences have caused Del Canto to grip the political identity of his past, an identity that has been more idealized over the decades.

ANÍBAL PALMA

The cover design of *Un sólo norte*, a collection of speeches, essays, and interviews that Aníbal Palma had released for his unsuccessful 1989 Senate race, consists of a large head shot of Palma in the foreground, linked to a portrait of Allende receding in the background.[32] It is the perfect symbol for Palma, a man who has been a committed Allendista since his first political activism as a young student leader and militant of the Radical Party in the 1950s.

Like Hernán Del Canto, Aníbal Palma was born in 1940 to a poor Santiago family. Palma's father died when he was four. His mother, an Argentine social worker, believed strongly in education, and Palma sought refuge in his studies. He excelled in high school and entered the University of Chile Law School, where he earned the highest distinctions. The university also proved the catalyst and training ground for Palma's entry into politics. He entered the Radical Party, for it was the party of his closest friends, including Jorge Arrate and Ricardo Lagos, both cabinet ministers in the postauthoritarian period, leaders of the Chilean socialists, and the latter a potential future Chilean president. In 1957, as a leader of the Young Radicals, Palma became secretary-general of the FECH, the most important university student confederation in the country. It was then, at the age of twenty, that Palma met and was profoundly taken with presidential candidate Salvador Allende.

Founded in 1886, the Radical Party had historically played the pivotal role of Chile's centrist party, carrying candidates to the presidency based on alternating alliances with right and left parties.[33] Yet by the late 1950s and early 1960s, the Radical Party's position as the center party had begun to be eclipsed by the increasingly popular Christian Democratic Party and its charismatic leader, Eduardo Frei Sr. For Palma, the Radical Party "had always been defined as a socialist party, of the people, of the left, a party with a socialist program." It was the one Chilean political party that was a member of the Socialist International. Nevertheless, in the ideologized atmosphere and hotly contested presidential elections of 1964, the Radical Party refused to support Socialist Party presidential candidate Salvador Allende and ran its own candidate, Julio Durán. Aníbal Palma resigned from the party. Palma worked on the Allende campaign, accompanying Allende to campaign rallies and speeches across the country.

After Allende's 1964 loss, Palma officially sat out of public politics and established a small law firm. Palma reentered the Radical Party when the Radicals joined the Popular Unity coalition, formed in 1969. In 1971 he was reelected to the party's national executive committee.

In September 1972 Allende appointed Palma undersecretary to Minister of Foreign Relations Clodomiro Almeyda. Shortly thereafter, Palma became Allende's minister of education. It was Palma's ministry that proposed one of the most controversial reforms of the Allende administration—an overhaul of the educational system. The proposal was modeled on many European systems and had been supported in large part by previous administrations. Yet, as Palma himself recognized in retrospect, the presentation of the proposal was "unfortunate" and ill-timed. The opening lines of the written and published proposal for a United National School (ENU) stated that the project's objective was to "assure the formation of the new socialist man."[34] This opening sounded yet another alarm to the Popular Unity government's opposition and proved to be a centerpiece for mobilization against the administration.

As described briefly in chapter 1, Palma recounted the personal anguish he suffered as education minister, as opposition students protested against him, as student supporters of the government stood up in his defense, as demonstrations became increasingly violent in universities and high schools in Chile's major cities.

> It wasn't just the demonstrations. *High school students* were taking over high school buildings. While such tactics had been used by university students, this was something new at the high school level. Other students would then go in and try to remove those students who had taken over the buildings, so there were very difficult confrontations, and impending danger. The opposition students took over the buildings, then students on the left who supported the government would take justice into their own hands to remove and launch a virtual assault on the building, and this resulted in very violent situations. I had to witness some of those episodes. . . .
>
> Imagine, my [two] children were students and I minister of education, and moreover, I lived in a sector of Santiago where the left didn't exactly dominate, so I lived a kind of curious coexistence with my neighbors. I can tell you as an anecdote that at that time there were a series of robberies in the neighborhood and a delegation of neighbors came to my house to say, "Why don't you have police protection, because that would serve the whole neighborhood, it would bring more peace to the neighborhood," et cetera, and I replied that I hadn't wanted protection because I had seen how in each demonstration [against the government] my neighbors went into the streets, banging their pots and pans, and that if there were a policeman there he would have to intervene and that I didn't want conflicts in the neighborhood. So we agreed that I would request a policeman for the neighborhood and they wouldn't have any more demonstrations in our streets.

Palma's text shows the tensions and ironies in this uneasy resolution of the public and private spheres of his life. Ideology—the larger vision of what is necessary for the common good—disappeared into the day-to-day tactical responses to vehement opposition. For Palma, the Popular Unity period was a traumatic political experience. Its effect was to bind Palma more closely to the president.

After his stint as education minister, Palma ran as a senatorial candidate for Santiago in the March 1973 elections, the last parliamentary elections to take place until 1989. Palma lost by a close vote, and Allende appointed him minister of government:

> I served in this position from March to August of 1973, basically the entire preparatory period for the coup, and I had one of the most complex and difficult positions that existed in this country, it is the ministry most at the side of the president, the one that has to manage information, be the face of the government, the voice, so that this wasn't an easy period, either . . . You know that all of this, in my opinion, is a period that is very difficult to judge if you didn't live through it, so strong was the motivation of those sectors [of the opposition], because depending on how one looks at the situation, in those times we faced a period of shortages as a product of many factors, of government policy, of international pressure, the boycott, et cetera, but finally the fact was there were shortages, lines to get goods you couldn't find, a black market, et cetera, et cetera. I was a senatorial candidate in a period in which I remember having arrived in poor neighborhoods to see immense lines of people waiting to be able to buy one item, and I as a government candidate, my position was very difficult, and some people wouldn't approach me, they would whistle derogatorily, but others would say, it's all right, comrade, it's the fault of the *momios*.[35]

This sense of personal anguish and personal responsibility resonates throughout Palma's text, matched by his political behavior at several points throughout his life. On the day of the coup, Palma, no longer a government minister, chose to go to La Moneda palace to be with his president. Together with several prominent cabinet officials, Palma was arrested. He spent the next three years in Chilean concentration camps before his sentence was commuted to exile. Palma would behave similarly in his decision to return to Chile. In 1985, facing certain arrest on charges issued by the dictatorship, he returned to the country. Upon his arrival at the airport, he was placed under arrest. After thirty days in prison, Palma was acquitted and released.

Invited to teach law and philosophy in the university, and at the behest of the Radical Party, Palma spent his exile years in West Germany. He represented the party's European regional organization, and as its representative, had contact with the most important leaders of the Socialist International, including Willy Brandt, Felipe González, and François Mitterand. Through his legal training and contacts that he had developed over the years with German professionals, Palma has been able to return to Chile to establish a professional practice that focuses on business with Germany.

Together with Del Canto, Palma served in the mid-1990s as co-secretary-general of the Socialist Party, and he draws on the figure and memory of Allende as his chief source of ideological reformulation. Unlike Del Canto, however, Palma, through his university education, was exposed early on to a different set of opportunities, and today he is Chile's ambassador to Colombia. Nevertheless, Allende represents the thread of continuity in Palma's political trajectory, in his continuing search for identity within the formal framework of the Socialist Party.

EDUARDO REYES

Eduardo Reyes had never before been interviewed.[36] A soft-spoken, gentle man, he is a member of the PSCH Central Committee. Reyes was born in 1951 in the village of Mulchén, an agricultural community in the central valley province of Bio Bio. His father was a poor agricultural worker.

> My father worked from sunup to sundown and didn't know an eight-hour day until [the 1964–1970 presidency of Eduardo] Frei. On my father's payday the family would buy a hundred-pound bag of flour at least, and this meant we had bread for sure. We never knew hunger, but we never ate well, either. . . .
>
> My dad couldn't read or write, but he was pretty smart, and I remember well that when I first started learning to read, he would pick up all the flyers there were and we would go to the meetings and protests. My father wasn't a political person, but he was very conscious of his rights, and I heard him say many times, "Sure, if you try to claim your rights, they call you a communist," and I believe he was an Allendista.

Reyes's narrative reflects his self-perception as an Allendista by instinct, from early childhood. It is an identity he also projects onto his father, of whom he speaks in only the most reverent tones. At thirteen, Eduardo and his father went to a neighboring town to hear Salvador Allende speak. He remembers that event as having made a profound impression on him.

> When I was a little boy I saw Allende. Allende came through all the towns, and in the small town plazas there is a kind of grandstand, one was installed in a small neighboring town and there Allende came to speak, and I remember that I went. I don't remember what he said, but I do remember that I sat on the grandstand, and I listened to Allende. I suppose he said things that interested me because I behaved well and I sat there and listened to his entire speech, which is a difficult thing for little kids to do. . . . So this had a decisive influence on what was my later life.

During the 1964 elections, Eduardo began disseminating propaganda for Allende in Mulchén, inscribing the letter "V" for "Viva Allende" on walls throughout the village.

Despite his early sympathies for Allende, Reyes also remembers that he was not equally taken with the Socialist Party, whose officials in his town "were not very good." The local PSCH officials, Reyes explained, were in large part to blame for his community's failure to support Allende—not, as conventional wisdom might hold, the fact that until the 1960s voting in the agrarian provinces was heavily controlled by the landed oligarchy.[37] This distinction between Allende and his party representatives parallels such distinctions during the Popular Unity period.

Reyes and another boy from Mulchén were the only ones from their rural elementary school to go on to high school. Education was important to Reyes, and he arrived in Santiago in 1967 in order to continue his studies. From a small rural school, Reyes landed in the Valentín Letelier High School, boasting a student body of two to three thousand working-class and lower-middle-class teenagers. Reyes recounts the tremendous sense of solidarity he gained at the high school, joining in large secondary school protests in the late 1960s, first against obligatory military service, then in solidarity with educational workers. He recalled that these demonstrations were largely unorganized, that they were often spontaneous, triggered by rallies and protests in other sectors of Chilean society. Reyes consistently re-created images of a mass movement in Chile in the late 1960s, of a highly participatory society.

He became friends with a group of young people in high school who attempted to decide collectively upon the political party they would join. According to Reyes, the choice was among the Young Communists (the Jota), the Young Socialists, and the newly formed Movimiento de la Izquierda Revolucionaria (MIR). Because of an unpleasant organizing experience with the Jota, Reyes claimed, he and his friends decided against the Communists. The group then divided their allegiances between the Young Socialists and the MIR. "I decided, even though I was aware that the PSCH was a mess, that for me it was important to have the right to an opinion, to say what you wanted, and, what did I know? I found this to be the case in the Socialist Party."

> I joined the PSCH in '69, already as a community leader linking our high school and the community of Recoleta. . . . and when we joined we began to work basically on the Allende campaign. At that time regarding the Socialist youth as such, it was difficult to convince the youth to work on the campaign because their leaders were not of this tendency, so the youth were only convinced some six months before, when the campaign was already launched, and they would argue over whether to go to the Sierra, or whatever. I didn't have this crisis, we had decided among ourselves immediately to work for Allende, I had *no* doubt in that regard.
>
> Meanwhile something very strange happened to me. The Miristas took me to a meeting to ask me to join the MIR, and they began to talk to me about the Tupamaros,[38] that Allende was a reformist, and I remember clearly that I said to them the Tupamaros don't interest me, I don't know them, I don't know *who* the Tupamaros are and I am an *Allendista*, so we have nothing to talk about.

Throughout the interview it was clear that the specter of the MIR both plagued and intrigued Reyes. He had a great deal of contact with Miristas, who "were arguing about going to the Sierra" and wanted him to join armed struggle. He referred several times to Miristas within the Socialist Party who were attempting to edge the PSCH toward more radicalized positions. Reyes had a strong connection with the Miristas, yet he felt uncomfortable with such strategies as the formation of *focos*,[39] and in talking about that he juxtaposed such a strategy with his emphasis on "participation of the masses." Reyes appeared to be torn between admiration of the Mirista militants of his generation who were wholly committed to action and revolutionary change and fear of the Miristas' physical and intellectual isolation from the Chilean majority.

Reyes is far more interested in action than in ideological debate. He talked at length of his respect for the Vietnamese revolutionary movement, for its ability, as he perceived it, to form alliances. In particular, Reyes spoke of the "modesty," or humility, of the Vietnamese, of their concern for the everyday person, of their incorporation of the Vietnamese peasantry. At several points in the interview, Reyes signaled his resistance to abstract intellectual debate within the party, preferring to discuss concrete revolutionary processes, such as the Russian Revolution, which he admired and had the opportunity to study in depth in a two-month trip to the USSR in late 1972. Throughout the interview, Reyes wrestled with the seeming contradiction between his desire for mass participation and the right to voice dissent, and his equally strong desire for internal party discipline, order, and clarity.

For Reyes, demonstrating his consistent faith in Allende has become an answer to this internal dilemma. He associates Allende with mass participation in electoral campaigns, the ability to form alliances, and with strong leadership. It is an association that bridges Reyes's past and present political identity.

It was extremely important to Reyes that he get across the notion that the profound divisions within the PSCH during the Popular Unity period did not translate into PSCH corruption or graft.

> It was the time I ate the worst, the time of Allende. . . . you can accuse us of many things, of errors with respect to the economy, et cetera, but you cannot accuse us of having robbed the people. . . . The popular sectors never had more possibilities than during that time. I also believe that the person who had the clearest picture of what had to be done was Allende.

As a leader of the Young Socialists, Reyes was sent in 1971 to organize in the mining region of Antofagasta. The PSCH head of the region was Carlos Lorca, a leading thinker for the party who is a *desaparecido*. Reyes took classes with Lorca and with Martha Harneker, classes that focused on the teachings of Lenin. He also made a brief trip to Europe and the Soviet Union for additional training. In Antofagasta, Reyes was named secretary of the Young Socialists for the northern region.

After the coup, Reyes formed part of the PSCH Political Commission's Direccion Interior underground until he was detained in 1975 by Chilean security forces, the DINA. Reyes was held incommunicado in the Cuatro

Alamos concentration camp for four months, a period that he did not wish to discuss, other than to say that he developed close bonds with a number of fellow Socialists while in prison. In early 1977, Reyes, like Palma, had his prison sentence commuted to exile. He was sent to East Germany, where he lived until his return to Chile in 1982.

Today Eduardo Reyes plays an organizing role closely identified with the psch base. In the cases of Del Canto and Reyes, neither the Socialist Party leadership nor the two men consider themselves "thinkers." Reyes claimed he had little taste for abstract postulating. "I never felt any great love for either Eurocommunism or for Gramsci ideologically. My vision was much closer to the processes of the Russian Revolution than to those processes that took place much later, like the Cuban Revolution."

The greatest political preoccupation for Reyes, Del Canto, and Palma is the lack of internal party unity, which in their view destroyed Allende's transformational project and will prevent the party from leading the country again. To these three men, Allende and Allendismo represent ways of linking leadership and militancy, a militancy that has tended to be skeptical of new directions in the party. Common to these personal loyalists is the immediacy of memories of the Allende period, detailed memories of victories and defeats that occurred more than a quarter of a century ago.[40] Vivid memories of the Allende administration find their way into the discourse and explanations of these personal loyalists' current politics far more frequently than is the case for other political leaders.

Yet there is a contrast between Hernán Del Canto, on the one hand, and Eduardo Reyes and Aníbal Palma, on the other. For Reyes, who is some eleven years younger than Del Canto, Allendismo appears to be a way to resolve past inner conflict while allowing for personal political progression or development as a party organizer.

> I feel I have evolved a great deal with time. I've read, I've rethought Allende. I have always been an Allendista and I think that Allende was the precursor who was capable of marrying democracy and socialism, who wanted socialism "à la chilena" with "red wine and empanadas." This symbolizes the problem of autonomy and the idiosyncrasies or peculiarities of what Chile was. Allende never wanted to break what had been a long democratic process, although it is clear that what we mean by democracy today is not the same as it was before the dictatorship, nor was our evaluation of human rights. And one thing is clear, at that time we spoke of the electoral process in somewhat pejorative

terms, as an instrument. I would say that today there is no other system, as imperfect as it is. Voting shouldn't be all there is to democracy,
but it is clear that it is the only instrument that controls power and
establishes a democratic coexistence with one another.

Reyes forms an active part of a group of thinkers and activists within the
PSCH trying to mesh historic party principles with contemporary concerns
and strategies.

> I continue to serve as a member of the Central Committee of the
> Socialist Party and to be very active in advancing the party. It is a
> difficult struggle, as this country, Chile, is moved today by the market.
> It is a society that lives for the market, and for an individualism that is
> alienating us from one another, and within the party as well, and I
> struggle to continue to contribute to a solidaristic sense, to a sense
> of the common good.

During the first five years of the Concertación administration, Reyes
served in the Ministry of Government as one of several important liaisons
between the administration and grassroots community groups. In 1996 he
shifted within the ministry to join a team dedicated to an experimental
drug-use-prevention outreach program, and Reyes oversees pilot projects
around the country. Reyes's younger years and new professional embeddedness in a government agency attempting to forge new relations between the state and civil society have strengthened his political commitment to a participatory society:

> It is an error to assume that simply with advances in social terms, in
> social policy, that people are not interested in participating in politics.
> It is a real problem that the poor majority feel excluded from politics,
> because of things like the binomial system, designated senators, politi-
> cal problems that offend society itself. It has contributed to a real disre-
> spect for the system, for people don't understand how such policies can
> be a part of the democratic process. This is very, very fundamental, and
> it weakens the Concertación, the government.

The cognitive ideal-types described in this study are meant to help us pre-
dict the dynamics of how individual political identities respond to major

political traumas and play particular roles during specific political moments. Faced with broadly similar kinds of traumatic political experiences,
the types provide a way to hypothesize about the dynamics of political identity transformations for a range of political leaders. For personal loyalists,
like the political party loyalists before them, wrenching political experiences cause them to hold tight to a central referent—in this case the referent is Salvador Allende.

Unlike the political party loyalists, however, these personal loyalists appear to be more influenced by collective memories or popular perceptions
of the Socialist Party as negative and of Salvador Allende as a democratic
martyr. This is especially important to Hernán Del Canto and Aníbal
Palma, whose political careers reached their pinnacle during the Allende
presidency. The personal loyalists of this study thus seek haven in their attachment to Allende in efforts to rise above their perceptions of the ideological polarization and antidemocratic sentiments within the Chilean left
of that period. It is not clear, however, that the Chilean public accepts the
distinction the two make: as ministers in the Allende cabinet, Del Canto
and Palma are associated with a failed political project. Palma has managed
to carve out an ambassadorship, but Del Canto has been unable to secure
a high-level public office in the postauthoritarian period.[41]

Like other cognitive types of this study, the Allende personal loyalists attempt to portray a continuity between the ideologies and political roles that
they assumed in the past and the present. Their allying themselves closely
with Allende tends to relegate them to a past era. Nevertheless, it is highly
likely that the personal loyalist cognitive type benefits Chilean political actors who are loyal to other prominent individual leaders. While the subjects
of this study are Allende loyalists, it is conceivable that there is a range of
personal loyalists in today's Chilean political class whose close identities
with other leaders, such as Eduardo Frei Jr. or Augusto Pinochet, privilege
their political roles.

CHAPTER 5

EXILE
AND THE THINKERS

*Dante said that the bread of exile tastes salty, but he also said that he
could gaze upon the face of the sun and the stars anywhere and could
contemplate under any sky the most precious truths. . . . Detachment is
necessary to recognize any truth; but it is a mental rather than a physical
process. One may travel around the world and return as provincial in his
tastes and judgments as when he departed. One may stay all his life in the
town where he was born and yet be a humanist. . . . [Yet] we should not
fail to note that emigration offers a chance to experience more vividly
and therefore to rethink more easily the most precious truths.*

—Hans Speier (1952)[1]

■ German intellectual and former exile Hans Speier is among
the many scholars who have contemplated the influence of the traumatic experience of forced "detachment" on their own thinking and political judgment.[2] As Speier indicates, it is impossible to generalize about the effects of
the exile experience on one's politics and understandings. The conditions of
exile vary enormously, and, perhaps more important, individual men and
women bring to their exile distinct identity-forming life experiences and
mentalities. Nevertheless, for leading thinkers of the Chilean left, exile as a
traumatic political experience played a transformative role in redefining their
ideological directions. This chapter will examine the lives and texts of those
whom I term political thinkers through the lens of their exile, a period for
deep reflection, debate, and ideological transformation. The "political thinker" cognitive type represents individuals who have consistently focused on
ideas and intellectual debates, who have tended to privilege ideas over political party program or self-interest. In addition, in the case of several of the
individual thinkers, such as Antonio Leal, below, the exile experience shaped
their political roles in the Chilean transition from authoritarian rule.[3]

In contrast to the political party loyalists, for whom exile was virtually an extension of party politics conducted in another fashion, exile experiences marked the thinkers in profound ways. For party loyalists, the party served as their "stepfamily" in exile, their "home away from home." The traumatic experience of exile seemed to have had little effect on their political ideologies. Party loyalists tended to immerse themselves in internal party politics at the expense of forming ties with other political and social groups and institutional networks abroad. A similar pattern can be found among two of the three personal loyalists in exile. Personal loyalists Eduardo Reyes and Hernán Del Canto spent more than a decade in exile in East Germany dedicated to the Chilean solidarity movement and to championing the name of Allende as a martyr of the Chilean socialist struggle. The two lived in a "ghetto" of the Chilean exile community. Neither learned German. University-trained personal loyalist Aníbal Palma did learn German in his place of exile, and he made important contacts in exile, which he later utilized upon his return to Chile. Nevertheless, Palma did not engage in the intense intellectual immersion characteristic of the political thinkers of this study.

For the thinkers, exile allowed them to reflect a good deal on past positions and to be engaged in networks of international debate that lent distance and perspective to the Allende period, to internal party politics, and to socialism as theory and praxis. While thinkers also engaged in party politics, they placed tremendous value on the exchange of ideas across intellectual networks. Important debates included the meaning of democracy and democracy's relationship to socialism, the role of the state, and the role of the political party and of the individual in transforming society. The thinkers presented in this chapter are Chilean ambassador to Mexico and PSCH leader Luis Maira, PPD congressman Antonio Leal, and Fernando Contreras. Leal and Contreras were former Chilean Communist Party leaders who took radically distinct intellectual paths both during their exile and during the postauthoritarian period.

Exile transformed these men from public leaders immersed in a grand project, to strangers in a strange land. Exile redefined these individuals' "sense of place,"[4] and it redefined that balance between the public and private spheres in their lives. As Diane Kay in her study of Chilean exiles in Scotland has asserted, such a transformation meant an extreme contraction of the public sphere of these individuals' lives, and, therefore, a dramatic expansion of the private sphere, a coming to terms with relationships and conditions within the home and family.[5]

While this expansion of the private sphere was a shared experience of all the exiles in this study, a significant element that differed from one to another of them was the place and condition of exile. These differences created distinct opportunity structures regarding such issues as financial security, employment, study, travel, and access to information, and these different opportunities had important ramifications for the exiles.

The terms of intellectual debate were different in different places. For many of the men and women of this study, exile represented, through its imposed exclusion from the day-to-day struggles in which political activists were enmeshed at home, a forum for serious and reflective engagement in intellectual debate. While ideas are in and of themselves unbounded and therefore unrestricted to one place of residence over another, it is clear that the parameters of intellectual debate—even the very nature of discourse— were different in a number of important ways, from exile circles in Rome, to East Berlin, to Mexico City. As exile circles rejoin, reconfigure, both periodically outside of Chile, and, ultimately, in the return home, ideas and discourse are reformulated, rejected, and translated into local debates.

How these ideas circulate and move from an elite level of abstraction to more concrete use in everyday political discourse and behavior has to do in large part with institutional embeddedness.[6] In his study of nineteenth-century Russian intellectuals, Robert Brym argues that by analyzing the shifting social ties of intellectuals to a range of groups in society it is possible to explain ideological production.[7] Similarly, I have found that ideological transformation among the thinkers of this study can be advanced by examining their ties to specific institutions in exile, particularly to host governmental and nongovernmental institutions, including political parties of the host country.[8]

By examining the relationships among distinct opportunity structures, the realm and flow of ideas, and the institutions in which these individuals and their ideas are embedded in distinct places of exile, I suggest in this chapter that there are, indeed, patterns in the transformation of individual political identity that relate closely to place of exile. Nevertheless, I also suggest that in granting the space for greater reflection, exile affirmed the cognitive framework—that of the thinker—of the Chilean leaders discussed here. As a traumatic political experience, exile proved to be a catalyst for ideological transformation and for the redefining of individuals' political roles.

Today the thinkers of this study occupy leading intellectual and political roles in their parties and in government. In contrast to the political party loyalists and the personal loyalists, the thinkers are breaking new ground in the public sphere in reformulating left visions of democracy and participation, the role of the state, and the role of the party in society. This has not necessarily meant, however, that their ideas have found an organizational expression. The thinkers are consistently hampered by both the limiting roles or possibilities of their offices and by their own lack of sustained interest in organizational questions.

LUIS MAIRA

Socialist Party leader Luis Maira is considered among the most brilliant contemporary left political thinkers in Chile.[9] His national political prominence began early in life. At twenty-six, as a Christian Democratic Youth leader, Maira was elected to the House, where he became the youngest person ever to serve in the Chilean Congress. Maira was seen as a protégé of President Eduardo Frei Sr., and it was widely believed that someday Maira himself would become president of the country. Rather than conform to such expectations, however, Maira broke from the Christian Democrat mold and his mentor to pursue his vision of a Christian socialist transformation of society.

By the late 1960s, Maira had grown increasingly dismayed by the lack of commitment within the Christian Democratic Party to a revolutionary program for Chile. In 1971, when his party failed to support President Allende's Popular Unity agenda, Maira resigned from the PDC and, together with several other young Christian Democratic dissenters, founded the Christian Left (IC). The primary ideological difference between the Christian Democratic Party and the new Christian Left was the IC's principal objective of "contributing to the construction of socialism in Chile." Understood as a process of "popular liberation," socialism would be achieved by "the definitive overcoming of the capitalist structure" and by "the progressive transfer of authority to those bases responsible for production and for the generation of goods and services." To do this, the IC argued, presupposed "a cultural change in society's values, behavior and personal habits." The process required a gradual convergence of Christians and Marxists.[10]

Maira described his vision of the Izquierda Cristiana as a movement that would represent the aspirations of the vast Christian popular sector of Chile:

> The party was a project we had imagined would become much stronger than it ever did. I remember writing once, "The Christian Left, a major-

ity being born." In the early 1970s there was this great vision that the left was growing, that the world was being drawn toward socialism, that that was where history was marching, and among Christians there was an enormous internal commotion to be a part, to be actors in this search for the socialist society, while maintaining Christian values and an appropriate spiritual understanding of man. In that sense I would say that Christianity added a great richness to the socialist project.

The discourse and logic of Marxism was a discourse of the masses, of a collective actor, an impersonal one, where the profiles of real human beings, the central, spiritual dimension of human dignity, [were] missing. On the other hand, the Christian vision was built from the search for a new man and options of a more personal sort in a more just society. Humanization of society was a more central element, and we felt that we offered socialism a decisive complementary element, and given the high levels of Christian sensitivity in the country, Christianity was such an important part of the culture of the Chilean popular movement, where a democratic popular tradition among Christian popular sectors was quite significant and we felt that the IC could be a faithful representative of this great current of thought, that it would represent the third great culture of the popular movement, next to advanced secular rationalism and Marxist thought.

This conception of the IC represents a vision of the party as a kind of social movement. There is a strong sense of mission on behalf of a spiritual man. Yet as the above passage illustrates, Maira conceived of the IC primarily as an intellectual current, and in essence, it is at this level that the IC remained during the Popular Unity period. As Maira recognizes, his vision of the protagonistic role of the IC would not come to fruition. His last public speech in the parliament would come on August 28, 1973, in defense of yet another Allende project to be flatly rejected in Congress. "That was like giving the green light to the coup," Maira recounted.

In an interview he gave to journalist Faride Zerán regarding his life from the moment of the coup until his escape to the Mexican Embassy in Santiago one month later, Maira recalled his first thoughts on the public/private dichotomy that his political trajectory had represented:

After the coup one was forced to reflect deeply on, for example, in my family life, was it worth it to be so detached? Did it make sense to put affection aside, allow your little girls to grow up alone, to initiate what seemed an inevitable process of "*desamor*," not taking the time to support and caress the relationship with your wife? These were the first existentialist questions we all asked ourselves, I think. Periods of persecution are periods of tremendous solitude, for those who shelter you don't really communicate with you, it's a bit like they have you but they must divorce themselves from you except to feed you and see to your material needs, announcing, "The bathroom's free," or "Good night, sleep well," or they bring you a plate of food to the room you're sleeping in because you can't endanger the children by eating with the family. . . .

So you are alone with yourself and you have a great deal of time to think. In the middle of the pain, more than the pain, in the middle of a world that has collapsed.[11]

For Maira, this questioning of the balance in his life between the public and the private was very much in keeping with his constant questioning of the role of political man in advancing the common good. His decision to leave the Christian Democratic Party, where he had earned national recognition and the backing of a powerful party structure, reflected an option to advance a revolutionary Christian vision at the expense, perhaps, of personal political mobility. His cognitive structure consistently links ruminations on the private with his intellectual concerns regarding the public. The defeat of the UP government would give Maira and others an opportunity, as unwelcome as it was, to develop their identities as thinkers.

Maira's world had, indeed, collapsed, and he was now wanted by the military junta. At the insistence of his party and family, Maira arranged to leave the country. He chose Mexico because he desired to remain in Latin America, and at that time Mexico seemed to be politically the most stable environment for him. As a congressman, Maira had visited Mexico and had lectured at several Mexican universities. He would be able to teach and to continue his work for Chile in a supportive atmosphere. After eight months in the Mexican Embassy, Maira was granted political asylum in Mexico.

Chilean exiles arrived in Mexico during the years of President Luis Echeverría, a man who styled himself a champion of the assertion of Third World movements and concerns upon the international stage. The Mexican government was among the first to condemn adamantly the military coup in Chile, and the country offered haven to the Allende family and to prominent members of the Popular Unity coalition. In addition, Mexico's rich tradition of providing political asylum to revolutionaries and antifascists, most notably the Spanish Republicans, made the country a likely site for Chileans in the immediate post-coup period.[12]

In Mexico City, far from the public eye that accompanied the post of congressman, Maira was based at the prominent think tank Centro de Investigación y Docencia Económicas (CIDE). He proved to be a prolific writer and investigative analyst. His intellectual work focused on the questions of Latin American regionalization, comparative studies of Latin American nationalization processes, and United States–Latin American relations.[13] The Mexican government provided resources for Chilean professionals and academics, who, working under elaborate systems with Chileans who remained in Chile, produced a range of studies, tracts, and monographs on Chile. "There were never so many studies of Chilean social reality as there were under the dictatorship," Maira laughed.

In reflecting on the influence of place of exile upon the Chilean political elite, Maira felt that in general the "Mexican experience" made the Chilean left appreciate the importance of a massive bureaucratic system, in which "the management of the system appears more important than ideas." This seemed paradoxical to Maira, who felt that his colleagues in Italy and France, for example, benefited from the intense intellectual debates that went on in those places of exile, to which he, in Mexico, was less exposed.

For Chilean party leaders in exile in Latin America, Maira claimed, it was contact with the nationalist, populist, moderate political parties of the region, such as the Mexican Partido Revolucionario Institucional (PRI), Venezuela's Acción Democrática, and the Alianza Popular Revolucionaria Americana (APRA) of Peru, rather than the Eurocommunist movements, that influenced their thinking on party structure and program, and it made those in Latin America a bit wary of "transposing" the European social democratic experience onto the Latin American cultural fabric.[14] These large, historic political parties of Latin America, Maira argued, have a grasp of the economic and political realities of the region, including heightened social inequality, delicate civil-military relations, and vast numbers of disenfranchised poor, all of which informed the parties' collectivist and comparatively statist discourse. The parties were not calling for a great retreat of the state from the economy. "There isn't a doubt," Maira said, "that those Chileans who have assumed more liberal visions are those who were in European countries."

This commitment to historic socialist positions, particularly the recognition of a major role for the state in the economy, has, until recently, cost Maira political power and mobility. In 1989 he chose to run as a senatorial candidate for PAIS, a left party coalition with far less promise for success than the Concertación coalition, which also welcomed Maira. In making this choice, Maira sacrificed his chances for victory to defend a traditional left political tradition.

Maira's vision of the role of the party is in keeping, he insists, with his early vision of the role of parties in the polity and society:

> We never saw the party as a vanguard party that embodies the project and the interests of the new class or new man. Rather, we saw the party as an efficient and necessary instrument for promoting societal projects and program. We never glorified or sanctified the party, we did not convert it into some infallible entity, we did not give it total power, we had a much more relative vision of the role of what it means to be a militant, to be politically committed, and in this sense we are closer to those from whom we were quite distant in the past.

While it is true that the Christian Left was never a Leninist party, it did advance a project calling for a Christian socialist man who would be the basis for the "liquidation of the antihuman structures of capitalism" and the construction of a socialist society.[15] A 1990 decision to abandon the Christian Left and join the Chilean Socialist Party demonstrated that Maira has clearly moderated his revolutionary aspirations of the past.

Maira insisted that there is a great deal of ideological continuity between his pre-exile period and the present. He claimed that what has changed are the dominant "orthodoxies" from the pre- and postauthoritarian periods, which have now placed his positions on socialism and the role of the state in a consistently defensive posture:

> I think, curiously enough, that my concept of socialism today is very similar to what it was in the mid-sixties, in the sense that we always took a socialist option outside of the world of Marxism, that we believed that socialism had to be a process married to democracy, that socialism represented the possibility of deepening democracy . . . and we also saw socialism as a profoundly decentralized process, our first idea, which we called the noncapitalist road to development, was the notion of reinforcing workers' communities, self-governing communities, regional enterprises, with a strong public sector, but as an alternative to the idea of forced planning. . . . We always envisioned a popular economy, not a state economy.

The concept of market and state were seen as complementary, we always supported the logic of a mixed economy. . . . I continue to see the state in the same way I saw it in the sixties. . . . It's not the market that will regulate the defense of natural resources, nor the market that will develop science and technology. Companies purchase this technology from other places. They are the same beliefs I held in the sixties, but today I am a person who appears as the defender of the state, whereas in the sixties I appeared against the type of statism in vogue. . . . So I feel we are in the best position to confront the neoliberal logic, and we don't face that devastating process so many have been through when your vision of the world is completely destroyed.

It is true that Maira's presentation of his vision of socialism and the state is not remarkably different from past visions that he supported. His experiences in Mexico appeared to affirm his belief in a continued central role for the state in the transformation of a capitalist society. Maira's text alludes to the overwhelming presence of the Mexican state and his appreciation for managerial competency in the public sector. In 1994, President Frei appointed Maira minister of Ministerio de Planificación y Cooperación (MIDE-PLAN), the research branch of the government. Maira was forced to confront several trade-offs, including the question of whether "system management is more important than ideas." In 1996, plagued by charges that members of his staff (though never he himself) were involved in corruption within the ministry and that there was general managerial incompetency, Maira was forced to resign. Shortly thereafter, he accepted the Chilean ambassadorial post in Mexico City. While he continues to be active in the Socialist Party leadership, Maira has somewhat distanced himself from the center of day-to-day party politics, allowing himself more time for writing and reflection.

ANTONIO LEAL

There is perhaps no Chilean political intellectual in Chile more obviously influenced by his exile experience than Antonio Leal.[16] A former Communist, Leal cofounded the Democratic Left Party, a short-lived party modeled closely after the transformed Italian Communist Party. He is also Chile's leading authority on Antonio Gramsci. Leal's dedication to ideas is what distinguishes him as a thinker, though this dedication is now limited by his 1997 election to the Chilean House. Leal is a PPD congressman representing a poor mining district in northern Chile.

Antonio Leal's mother was a primary school teacher and his father was an economist. Though the Leals were a middle-class family, they chose to live in the Santiago shantytown where Leal's mother taught. While his parents were not political party members, they were Allende supporters. Leal joined the Young Communists at fourteen. His four younger brothers and sisters were soon to follow.

In his reflections on his upbringing and early education, Leal emphasized his immersion as a boy in Chilean popular culture, in what he termed *"el medio popular."* This emphasis on *"lo popular"* carries politico-ideological as well as sociological meaning.[17] For Leal, it expresses exposure to the Chilean poor and working class and to their aspirations for a more just society.

> The 1960s were very unusual years, setbacks for the popular world, yet it was also the world of Che, the Cuban Revolution, and I, from very young, was a liberal progressive. . . .
>
> I entered the PCCH possibly by pure coincidence. I was arrested at a pro-Cuba demonstration, and the man who came to set us free was a Communist congressman, and we had a long conversation, and this was my first contact with the PCCH. And it was by chance. My father was a socialist, after all. I think it was attractive for its sense of organization, consistency, visibility in the country, its seriousness. International politics also fascinated me, and the PCCH had a clear link.
>
> I entered the Jota's Central Committee at sixteen, and at seventeen I was on the Executive Committee of the Jota. I was in the Jota until I was thirty, through my exile. I was a leader of the Popular Unity coalition for the youth up until my arrest on September 11, 1973, when I then spent two years in a concentration camp. . . .
>
> As a young person I wasn't sectarian, I was dogmatic, full of the mythology of the PCCH, but not sectarian. . . . It was a time of the emergence of poor urban grassroots activists, through the Neighborhood Committees, and of the peasantry, through the reforms, which were quite striking. . . .
>
> In 1965 the party sent me to study at the School for the Formation of Cadres in East Germany. I was there studying for almost two years, studying Marx, Lenin, it was a difficult period because I was so young [fourteen years old]. A school with the rigidity of Germans and the rigidity of socialists. For security reasons, we couldn't leave the school. We lived a very limited life. Very dogmatic teaching. Work with the classics. You couldn't even find Althusser, Gramsci, Luxemburg. And I

knew this then. You have to understand that in contrast to this generation of youth, where the expression "*Yo no soy ni allí*" is the dominant
expression, we were "*en todo.*"[18] At thirteen, fourteen years of age, we
had reading groups going. We would meet to read political literature,
poetry, we knew Althusser, Gramsci, Lukacs. So for me it was shocking
to arrive in Germany. Yet the school was crucial in disciplining me. It
gave me, more than anything else, grounding in method. A discipline
for work, for study.

In 1968 I was in a Paris seminar that coincided with the May
revolution. The student explosion happened at the same time as Czechoslovakia. I could hear the reflections of the Italian, French Communist
parties there, and when I arrived in Chile it was painful for me to have
to support the PCCH. I lived through this great explosion of freedom—
anarchists, semianarchists, exposed to the first feminist movements, I'm
convinced of the need and the emergence in the twenty-first century of
feminist movements to the foreground—in Europe, and it influenced me
profoundly. . . . It was a politics very inspired by values. There were great
ruptures with taboos and the status quo. I spent six months in Paris, in
the best of all worlds, experiencing this great cultural revolution.

This text confirms the impact of early exposure to left political culture and
the intellectual debates of the 1960s. Leal's reflections about his youth
blend domestic and global struggles, day-to-day culture, and politics with
immersion in heady theoretical work. At a very young age, Leal had already
been exposed to a set of dramatic and contrasting international experiences.
In each, he had absorbed distinct intellectual lessons and influences.

I arrived in Italy when I was twenty-three years old. I went there because it had been decided to make the UP-youth wing an international
body, and they asked that I remain as head, and that it would be set up
with Chile-Democrático in Rome. It was a decision of the party. I was
there with Guastavino every day for fifteen years, organizing events,
world conferences, attempts to get back in Chile. I arrived in 1975. I
began to travel around the world. I was in approximately sixty different
countries during my exile. Good part of Africa, Asia, Europe, Latin
America. The United States less, only in New York, because the two
times I was given a visa it was only to attend the UN General Assembly.

I got to know a range of characters, well-known artists, intellectuals,
writers—from Jane Fonda to Gunther Grass—people who were young

activists then, twenty years ago, some who are now heads of state, ministers, and we maintain close relationships. And really we created this spectacular Solidarity with Chile movement, one of the greatest solidarity campaigns known, unimaginable.

. . . My first world was quite ghettoized at first, the Chilean ghetto, then it became Chile-Democrático, and I did a good deal of traveling. . . . The first six years were really a ghetto, then when we realized it wasn't worth it to live with our bags packed. . . . Do you know the PCCH wrote a paper around 1977 saying the dictatorship was about to fall, and we believed it then, but gradually we realized that the PCCH really had no idea what was going on in Chile.

We began to acculturate more, to learn from our Italian friends about the nature and prolongation of fascism, and we gradually unpacked our bags. We realized we would not be authorized to return to Chile. So we began to focus on our personal lives a bit more, so after six, seven, eight years our ghetto began to expand, and we began to establish links with the society in which we lived. I finished my studies in Italy, finished my sociology degree, received a master's in international politics, then a doctorate in philosophy.

I began to work in the universities, in the think tanks, and I earned my living writing, I became an expert in surviving as an academic. I wrote things I was asked to write, like something on the politics and economy of Argentina, or the oil problems of Venezuela, Ecuador, a series of themes that weren't mine, but were in the interests of the Europeans. So I could do this at night at home, in the library, and I dedicated myself to politics during the day.

I think from Europe we perceived the durability of the dictatorship far better than the clandestine party leadership in Chile. Those in Chile were living in a micro-world, while we could reflect, study what fascism, dictatorship could really be, reading Poulantzas and others, one realized that dictatorships weren't easy to remove. And we all received our party analyses, but we often met with people like José Antonio Viera-Gallo [of the MAPU-OC], Enrique Correa [of the MAPU], et cetera, and we commented ironically on our party documents, examining Chile with different lenses.

I think we are all extremely marked by our exile experiences and by the countries in which we were in exile. My political changes, my understandings of politics would have been impossible to explain if it hadn't been for my contact with the PCI. Or they would have been much more gradual changes, in my reflections on 1968, for example, on the ideologized period then.

For Leal, Italian exile was in a sense a return to a moderate version of his experiences in Paris of 1968. Already attuned to European intellectual debates surrounding the May movements, analyses that were ongoing upon his arrival in Italy, Leal, after some time to adjust to the idea that return to Chile would not be an option, immersed himself in the Eurocommunist debates. Chilean exiles in Italy described their integration into what they termed an Italian "catholocommunist" culture much like their own. Chileans were absorbed into the debates of the 1970s within the European left and within the international communist movement, and the Italian left political class was at the vanguard of such debates. For the European left, the Allende experience became an important focus of intellectual discussion. Only two months after the coup, PCI leader Enrico Berlinguer published the party's interpretation of the fall of the Popular Unity government and its significance for the Italian communists. According to Berlinguer, the primary lesson of Chile was that in order to avert reactionary violence and a return to authoritarian rule, progressives must ally with antifascists in a new historic compromise.[19]

While the cultural and ideological connections between the Chilean left and the Italian left proved strong, Chileans were also impressed by the political power that the PCI possessed at the local, and—increasingly for a time, it seemed—at the national levels of government. From 1973 to 1976, Chilean exiles witnessed a period in which the PCI gained in strength against the Italian Christian Democratic Party in important local elections, and the Italian communists captured 34 percent of the national vote in the June 1976 general elections. By the early 1980s, the PCI controlled half of Italy's municipalities.[20] Thus, the Chilean left and the Italian left engaged in rich interaction in an institutional setting that was by no means at the margins of Italian politics.

For Chilean communists in particular, coming to terms with the realities of the socialist bloc provoked some of the most contentious debates:

> Between my contact with the PCI and my link with the PCCH youth, which had its headquarters in Budapest, it meant that already by the late 1970s the majority of us on the Central Committee, at least the Executive Committee of the Jota, understood that the world had changed radically, that the socialist bloc had serious defects, that there

couldn't be democracy without human rights. I was a part of a group that in 1979 participated in a historic plenary in Budapest where we took on three questions: First, the defects of the socialist bloc—not that we homogenized all of them, not all were so black, like in Romania, with the degree of control, others like Hungary, where the political dialectics were quite vast, politically, culturally, I perceived them as party dictatorships, as paternalistic, led by a handful of leaders, the *nomenclatura*, tremendous bureaucracies. Many of these leaders were loved, the Hungarian leader would walk down the street with his wife and be embraced, he was like some kind of uncle . . . There had been social conquests, not political ones. . . . The paternalistic presence of the state was profound, but not as a repressive phenomenon. Let's not confuse it with the police phenomenon, it was an *ideological* repression, a quasi-hegemonic question.

So in 1979 we critiqued this question. Second, we formulated critiques of the Chilean economy; and third, we formulated critiques of the PCCH leadership, which was already on its way to the armed rebellion strategy. We were the generation of young Communists, 99 percent of whom have left the party by now, we were talented, intellectuals of the working class, student, and youth movements, the best the PCCH ever had.

In addition to his contacts with the PCI and the young Communist leadership in Budapest, Leal attributes his ideological transformation to the influence of Antonio Gramsci's thought:

And I would say that a lot of [my challenge to the PCCH leadership] came from Gramsci. I really began to study Gramsci in 1977, and I began to publish articles about Gramsci in 1978. I remember a great feeling of revelation when I took *Prison Notebooks* with me to a conference in Poland and read it over fifteen days, and I returned to Italy transformed. I realized there was an alternative Marxism to the Stalinist one. Gramsci had created political categories that transcended the Marxist-Leninist ones, the concept of hegemony so appropriate for socialists today.

And from there I began to read Togliatti, Berlinguer, scholars of the Frankfurt School, Lukacs, I begin to read Western Marxists, and I begin to realize that I am in a distinct world from the Chilean communists. I continued to stay in the PCCH, painfully, being accused of reformism, everything, but out of solidarity I felt a need to stay out of commitment to that world I grew up in—to La Victoria, La Bandera (shantytowns of Santiago), the mineworkers, that working-class, popular-class culture so rooted in our people.

I hoped to create a counterculture within the PCCH. I drew a great deal upon Gramsci, pushing his work on people, together with Guastavino, and the politics of the PCI. So, yes, yes, the Italian experience weighs heavily on my understandings, my analysis, just as the experience of East Germany for others, the dogmatism, in spite of the fact that many wanted to leave there, it continues to weigh upon them, the dogmatism.

Leal linked his intellectual and professional pursuits in exile to providing political direction to the party:

I envisioned my intellectual learning as part of my political activity. My work on Gramsci has been primarily to allow me to put forward an alternative culture, an alternative political culture using, in a sense, the tools that a Gramscian analysis provides. . . . It was an attempt to instill in the PCCH a kind of thinking that was also going on in the PSCH, in the PCI, in Western socialist and communist thought—to permit a kind of linking or bridge.

Unlike Luis Maira and his fellow party leaders, who supported the need to rethink party structure and, ultimately, to collapse the Christian Left into the Socialist Party, Leal faced a recalcitrant Communist Party whose internal structure would be unsympathetic to or incapable of the kinds of transformations that he advanced.[21] In 1989, after several years of bitter internal struggles over party direction, Leal was expelled from the party. In 1990, he and fellow former PCCH leader and friend in exile Luis Guastavino founded the Party of the Democratic Left, modeled and financed by the renovated Italian Communist Party. In 1994, Leal and Guastavino disbanded their small party, and Leal joined the PPD. Recognized for his intellectual strengths and his work on reconceptualizing a left program, Leal was quickly absorbed into the political commission of the PPD, and in 1997, for the first time in his life, he put himself forward as a congressional candidate.

I've always been a "political worker," becoming a militant at fourteen, I've always felt very political, and I had always been more involved in party direction than in public representative positions, exactly because I had always been more interested in playing a political-intellectual role. My specialization is political science, political philosophy, and I had always rejected the possibility of being in a public representative role in order to dedicate myself to the intellectual side of politics. Nevertheless, we are in a process of trying to reach greater social equality after having achieved democracy and we have to be able to talk about and with people. So I asked to run in a district where the left had lost, after our return to democracy, a very poor, mining district, far from Santiago. I chose a real challenge, on the one hand electorally, and I did get the first majority in the elections, and, on the other hand, to translate and interpret, as a person who is really an academic, a series of themes that have not been addressed within my constituency until now, to insert the themes of modernity, postmodernity, globalization into a reality, the reality of the copper mining community, an area where there is a lot of wealth in terms of investment, but where there is a lot of poverty at the same time. So it was a pretty fascinating challenge, the possibility of conducting what might be thought of as a great political laboratory experiment.

Within the Chilean Chamber of Deputies, Leal has attempted to insert himself into broader debates on the role of the parliament as a political institution. Under an extremely presidentialist constitution, the Chilean parliament is a very weak legislator. Leal is dedicating himself to elevating the parliament as institution.

It is necessary from the parliament to begin to launch an intellectual agenda that will modify the current Chilean political scenario, and we're working to create a new convergence within the parliament, a new agreement to modify certain policies, and my role in parliament, more than being involved in other aspects, has been at a more macro, institutional level, how to modify the institution as such. Last week, for example, I spoke in parliament about the theme of plebiscites, the referendum. I've just sent *La Epoca* newspaper an opinion editorial that represents a critique about what we have accomplished and what we haven't over the past several years from within governing political institutions as such. So my concern, certainly I'll also have to be concerned about the concrete concerns of the people, that is, the cost of water, the concerns of the small copper miner, the realities of my district, but at the same time I am working to figure out from within the parliament how to empower the parliament itself.

We have a political system where the parliament has very little power, it has little legislative authority, there is a lack of prestige, negative ratings of elected representatives and of politics. How, then, do we generate more sense of a collective, overcome the past, in this post-Pinochet period, how do we create a vision of politics more linked to the future than to the Pinochet dictatorship, how do we contribute to a debate within the parliament about the renovation of politics. . . .

I believe the only way to renovate politics is to relegitimize the institution and the only way to do that is for politicians to become far more humble and to listen more to the people, that people feel more of a priority in the parliamentary agenda and in the governmental agenda. I feel we're in a real political crisis today, and every day it grows worse, in terms of the political party system. Today all the political parties have a quota of power that is far bigger than society has actually granted them in terms of true social and political representation. In the last elections, more than a million Chileans abstained, a million and a half young people did not register, demonstrating a big disenchantment with the political system. I feel the parties don't really perceive the degree of disapproval, or they don't get it. . . . And that we must begin to develop a public critique of where we are as we approach the end of the century, for there is a great deal of bad feeling, a great deal, not simply because of the lack of means, but it is also an existentialist bad feeling.

Today Leal finds political inspiration from an interesting source:

And I feel we have to produce a kind of politics similar to what Tony Blair has pulled off in England. The only thing is he did it from the opposition, which is easier. This great idea that England can be more, is what we need, Chile can be more, overcoming the great canons of neoliberalism, which Blair is doing, and which we must do from the government, for we're in the government. At the same time, think about Chile in 2000, what is the Latin American continent going to look like, globalization themes, labor mobility, human mobility.

When asked about the evolution of his understanding of socialism, Leal described his profound ideological transformation:

My concept of socialism has changed radically, radically. I didn't know the realities of the socialist bloc. I have realized that one cannot buy equality at the price of freedom. The vision of socialism, with freedom, with respect for human rights is an absolute necessity. I have come to believe that the socialist bloc ideologies were unviable. Not only concretely have they collapsed, but entire national identities have collapsed. Dead for me is the orthodox notion of Marxist-Leninism as something that is really viable. It was expressed in the concentration of power in the hands of one party. The idea of the dictatorship of the proletariat transformed into the dictatorship of the party.

I have also changed radically concerning the notion of the centralization of property. . . .

The third question for me is the question of citizenship. Democracy, freedom, human rights, aren't empty words.

When asked about the most powerful influences on his political thinking and action, Leal responded from his desk in the Congress with a range of left and not-so-left political figures:

Gramsci, Gorbachev, Brandt, Blair, and in some ways, Clinton. It's a mix of the left that wanted to change the world, where I come from, and the newness of Blair, Clinton, how to formulate a politics with social content in the context of the market—it is an enormous challenge—one can either deny the market and try to create another society or accept that the market is a planetary phenomenon but that it can't do everything, and for that reason it is necessary to create a market society that is more egalitarian, that has a strong citizenship dimension, to reinvent the social. . . . Otherwise the market becomes the provider of everything, even in value terms, and increasingly this is occurring. . . . The market offers you sex, love, status, values, everything. . . . And we are facing an enormous challenge of absorbing what the great technological advances mean for our societies. For example, thirty years ago in my district, an investment of three million dollars would have meant thousands of jobs. Today it means two hundred jobs. This is a huge transformation.

Gramsci because he provided a new interpretation in an old sea of eliminating certain aspects of Leninism, Gorbachev because he had the courage to shake up the world although he did not have the possibility to construct another one, Brandt because he was a great innovator of social democracy, Blair the newest, who has taken on many of the challenges necessary to govern England in a democratic context, and I admire Clinton as well. . . .

I have in many ways become a reformist. Nevertheless, I continue to believe that capitalism is incapable of resolving basic human rights, questions of social justice and dignity. Today in Latin America the people are poorer than they were in the 1960s. Neoliberalism has deepened the phenomenon of extreme poverty in the world, not lessened it. So if we are unable to generate an alternative to capitalism—over the long term—not inspired by the idea of change, of a more just society, then we are betraying our citizens. I continue to be inspired as a Marxist, but not as a partisan one. . . .

Our new ideological vision must be based in a multiplural, multidimensional cultural project, recognizing the diversity of our global civilization. Our new program has to be conceptualized globally, but in all the globe's diversity. . . . It cannot deny modernity, technology, the great leaps we are experiencing. . . . We face rights today—in contrast to the 1920s with the birth of the international communist movement—rights that in a sense are more existential yet vitally important. We need to understand how to open socialism to a plurality of needs or issues. . . .

Much of Leal's discourse echoes that of strong currents within the European left, particularly his emphasis on new categories of rights, on the notion of a multidimensional cultural project based in global diversity, and his emphasis on citizenship and identity. In contrast to Luis Maira's response to the question of visions of socialism, gone is even a mention of the role of the state. Its absence in Leal's lengthy response is noteworthy. Leal's is a deliberate focus on his radically changed conceptualization of civil society.

FERNANDO CONTRERAS

Manuel Fernando Contreras has undergone dramatic ideological transformations in the course of his political life.[22] As a political thinker of the Chilean Communist Party through the late 1970s, Contreras was a committed Stalinist. In exile in East Germany, influenced largely by the marginalization of the Salvadoran and Nicaraguan Communist Parties in their local struggles, Contreras turned toward Che Guevara and an armed insurrectional stance against the Chilean dictatorship. Upon his return to Chile, he ultimately abandoned Guevarism and the Chilean Communist Party altogether. He now searches for a new ideological framework and a new political vehicle (a party or movement) that he feels will promote the interests of Chile's popular sectors.

Fernando Contreras was born in 1945. His mother came from a family of poor dressmakers from what was then the rural zone of Maipu. His father, Contreras said, belonged to the "comfortable middle class, with strong aristocratic pretensions." Fernando was a twin in his family of five brothers and sisters.

In 1963, at the age of eighteen, Contreras joined the Communist Party. It was during the heated campaign of Eduardo Frei.

> When I reflect on why I entered the PCCH, it is for very personal factors, I think. My family was very united, yet we had a very authoritarian, castigating father. Among my siblings we were very united. My father was very dismayed by our showing of self-identity [in our joining the PCCH]. . . . In our house we were inundated with culture, music was so important to my father, reading the papers each day, yet it was all conducted in a very authoritarian way. . . .
>
> I entered the university thinking I would study biochemistry, this was really my vocation. Yet it was the 1960s, Allende, the left on the rise, the Cuban revolution—I ended up in sociology and politics became my life. My siblings were members of the PCCH out of conscience. I made it a vocation.

Contreras's interview with me makes a fascinating study because the text places an almost obsessive emphasis on the psychoanalytic aspects of the relationship between militants and their parties to the exclusion of almost all other issues. Contreras stresses the relationship between what he terms the "personal biographies" of individual militants and their decisions to join parties that serve particular emotional interests, that fill specific emotional gaps. For Contreras, "external" explanations for joining a party, such as the political or historical moment, are secondary.

Contreras quickly rose to the Central Committee of the Jota while serving as a student leader at the University of Chile. When the coup came, he was ordered by the party into exile. He would spend fifteen years in exile in East Germany.

> Exile isn't like anything else. It tended to symbolize memories. It inspired national unity among us. We *lived in memory*. Exile united us [in the PCCH] in spite of the divisions. Workers and the middle class militated in exile as Chilean nationalists, moralists, we created a *family*.

This notion of living in memory pervades the texts of several former exiles interviewed for this study. As Chilean psychologist Ana Vásquez and Uruguayan sociologist Ana María Araujo (themselves former exiles) have found, there is a common initial stage among exiles marked by the trauma of the departure itself: the pain of profound loss, of separation, of an unrelenting nostalgia. In this stage, political exiles develop defense mechanisms, which may include rejection of the country of refuge and its symbols, as well as rejection of communities other than exile communities. There is a tendency to idealize both the "there" and the "before."[23] Political militants attempt both to displace their pain and to uphold their political convictions by dedicating themselves to the resistance, and, particularly, to their political parties, which become, as Contreras said, the second families, the stepfamilies, "the family."[24]

Contreras's feelings about the exile "family" in East Germany illustrate a linkage between the public/private component of individuals' cognitive structures and the types of political cultures they faced in their places of exile. Despite the distinct language and social barriers that Chilean exiles confronted in Italy, as we have seen, exiles tended to be more open to acculturation there. In Italy, the phenomenon of ghettoization seemed far less acute over time than in East Germany or even in Mexico. In Italy, the range of sources for economic survival was much wider than in East Germany, from governmental and nongovernmental organizations, including church-sponsored agencies and research institutes, to state and university academic grants, and, in some cases, partial salaries from their parties.

In East Germany, access to resources of the government, to travel visas, and to other bureaucratic procedures was tightly controlled by the Chilean political party delegate. While the links between the party and family—the party as a virtual stepfamily—was a theme that ran throughout the accounts of former exiles in regions across the globe, it seemed to be at an extreme in East Germany. In addition, Contreras's allusion to the "moralism" of the PCCH in exile is a theme echoed by several former Chilean Communists who resided during their exiles in the former Soviet Union and Eastern Europe. The Communist Party as family carried strong connotations of party leaders as moral judges of private behavior, particularly regarding marital relations and how militants chose to spend their incomes. Nevertheless, several working-class Chilean exiles who resided in East Germany stated categorically that they had never lived better materially in their lives. They had access to free education through the graduate level, they received generous government stipends, and they and their families lived securely.

Contreras played a leading intellectual role in what has become known as the Leipzig Group, a group of young Chilean Communist Party thinkers in exile in East Germany.[25] Yet in our interview Contreras was virtually silent about the Leipzig Group. Much of the description and analysis of the group is my interpretation based on interviews with other group members, former PCCH members, and written analyses.[26]

The Leipzig Group is generally recognized as being responsible for the theoretical foundations of both the PCCH's change in interpretation of the downfall of the Popular Unity government and its strategy against the dictatorship. Until 1979, the PCCH advanced an analysis of the Popular Unity defeat that was analogous to that of the Italian Communist Party previously described. The Leipzig Group, on the other hand, held that the lack of a comprehensive military strategy, including a strategy for arming the popular sectors, had undermined any defense of the UP government. The group also swayed the PCCH leadership into moving its oppositional strategy to the military regime from one of building a multiparty, "antifascist" alliance against the regime, toward one of defeat of the dictatorship by any means necessary, including armed rebellion.

The Leipzig Group's armed rebellion strategy was based on a Guevarist concept of revolutionary man, described as a "disciplined, sacrificing, moral" militant prepared to confront his oppressors in a virtually religious sense.[27] The group was heavily influenced by its analysis of the Salvadoran and Nicaraguan guerrilla struggles, and it argued that the objective conditions existed in Chile to launch assaults that would be supported by the Chilean citizenry. Contreras and his fellow Leipzig Group members also saw the popular rebellion strategy as a way to renovate the PCCH internal party structure, to infuse new life into a party that had taken the antifascist, multiparty, multiclass alliance position toward socialist transformation for several decades.[28]

In retrospect, certainly, one can draw interesting parallels between the young thinkers of Leipzig and Michael Walzer's account of the Marian exiles, sixteenth-century expatriates of England. In Walzer's description, isolation for the Marian exiles led to increasingly radical positions regarding action but also regarding the capacity of revolutionary man:

> The saint was a new political man . . . a revolutionary; a private man
> in the old order and according to the old conventions, who laid claim to
> public status upon the basis of a new law. . . .

In the old political order, the saint was a stranger. It was appropriate, then, that he be the creation of an intellectual in exile. The cleric, disillusioned with the old world, alienated from a conventional and routine obedience, turned upon England with his "spiritual hatred"—a hatred deepened and given intellectual form by Calvinist theology. Physically exiled, he had moved outside the world of political limitation and into the new world of self-control.[29]

The Leipzig Group's conceptualization of revolutionary man was fueled by its distance from both the day-to-day realities of Chile's popular sectors under the dictatorship and from a range of theoretical analysis regarding the "refoundational" successes of the regime. Drawing inspiration from a somewhat romanticized view of the guerrilla struggles of Central America (rather than, for example, the Eurocommunist debates of Western Europe), the Leipzig Group, indeed, appeared to be "outside the world of political limitation."

In general, however, Contreras avoided discussing the Leipzig Group period. He spoke of his exile in only the most general terms, preferring to describe his sense of the Chilean Communist exile communities in general. What we know from his written work, however, is that he advocated the armed rebellion strategy through the mid-1980s. It was only with his return to Chile in 1988 that he began to rethink the viability of such a strategy.[30]

Because of Contreras's silences regarding his leadership in the Leipzig Group, it is difficult to say with certainty what led him to abandon this ideological current. One can only assume that once back in Chile, Contreras judged that the conditions for popular rebellion were not sufficient and that visions of a cadre of "disciplined, sacrificing, moral" militants risked sacrificing the lives of dozens of young people underground.

Contreras's current analysis of the failures of the PCCH centers on its lack of an ideological vision of the popular sector as the vehicle for socialist transformation, of the PCCH's failure to advance an ideological program that grasped the importance of power and the potential of harnessing the popular sectors as a force for change. Reminiscent of Antonio Leal, Contreras emphasizes the cultural underpinnings of the historic Chilean Communist Party as rooted in *lo popular*. Yet in contrast to Leal, who continues to draw from conceptualizations of *lo popular* but has moved to a new ideological discourse centered on "the citizen," Contreras continues to turn toward the popular sectors as the subjects of social change:

The emergence of *lo popular* challenged the Chilean left in a way it had never known. It conducted itself, and it was a phenomenon full of symbols, lifestyles, it was political-ideological, and it was something we didn't understand. It was an almost mystical thing, and despite the fact that in many ways the PCCH embodied *lo popular*, the party didn't overcome its narrow working class–based theoretical focus. It was a value-filled question. Among our cultural figures, our militants such as Violeta Parra, Victor Jara, Inti Illimani, Patricio Manns, and, of course, Pablo Neruda, there was greater understanding. It should have been something we could grasp theoretically and politically as well as culturally, in our construction of a real socialist force.

Theoretically the PCCH was incapable of conceptualizing this force. The popular sector voted for the symbols generated by our cultural producers, yet the party failed to link theoretically *lo popular* with *la nacion*, as populist, nationalist movements had achieved elsewhere, such as Peronism or the Mexican PRI. We were never a corporatist society, assuming class as a legitimate interest.

Contreras's text then reverts to his arguments concerning the intimate relationship between what he terms militants' "personal biographies" and their attachment to particular political parties:

What existed and continues to exist is a personal morphology of each party, distinct political party cultures and visions, which penetrate even as far as the kind of family ties to particular parties, the distinct cultural symbols of each party. *Militants and leaders link their personal biographies to the party.* The Christian Democratic Party is a perfect example of this, associated with particular notions of family, morality, the Catholic middle class. The Socialist Party is the secular expression of this same phenomenon. For the MIR, these young militants, their obsession with Cuba and Vietnam was like the "absent father" in their lives, it is the comfortable middle class. The hippie tendency, alive even today, is the ignored mother. . . . As for the Communists, they are like the Italian Mafia. . . . I am convinced, for example, that we Communists, the Chilean Communists in particular, have been the greatest believers [in God].

Incorporating the dominant language of the market into his current discourse, Contreras's text continues with the notion that the political parties offer a "moral supply" to meet the demands of individual militants:

And it cannot be reducible to class-party, although certainly there is a strong correlation. Political party options have to do fundamentally with the structure of one's personality. A psychology of parties, if you will, which allows individuals to fulfill their personal needs. It is the only way I feel I can explain certain militancies and certain kinds of political behavior, including my own.

CONTRASTS AND CONTINUITIES AMONG THE THINKERS

Common to the thinkers considered in this study is a pattern of early political activism in high school and in the university, exposure to the leading left political institutions of the country, and the consistent intellectual questioning of those institutions in terms of their capacity to conduct a revolutionary transformation of society. Luis Maira, who had a promising career in the Christian Democratic Party, left the PDC to cofound a Christian left vision of a socialist society. Maira's Christian Left party was to be a testimonial, mass-based movement representing the vast Christian popular sectors of Chile.

Antonio Leal and Fernando Contreras, embedded in the Chilean Communist Party, did not question the party until later. For Leal, it was triggered by his exposure to the May 1968 European movements, even though that did not lead to his abandonment of the PCCH. Contreras did not present an intellectual challenge to the party until his period of exile.

Exile was an important influence on these thinkers' ideological transformations, for some more dramatically than for others. For Maira, in Latin America, the influence of exile was subtle, as he came to appreciate the importance of the managerial capacity of the state and of the role of broad-based nationalist, moderate political parties.

Exile played an even greater role in the ideological transformations of Fernando Contreras and Antonio Leal. In 1990, Contreras, disillusioned with both the PCCH and the merits of the strategies he had advanced from exile, resigned from the Communist Party. Since then, he has focused his energies on a small group of intellectuals and activists, many of whom are former members of the Communist Party, to push the Chilean left toward a "popular sector agenda." Leal, with the backing of the Italian Communists, formed a "citizen-based" party styled after debates within the former Eurocommunist parties, then joined the PPD to promote rights-based issues within a reformist framework.

With the exception of the period of clandestinity and persecution following the coup, the three thinkers have consistently operated at the level of ideas in their involvement in their parties during their early activism, in the universities and think tanks during their exile, and in their current roles as officials and strategists of the government and their parties. In 1991 the Socialist Party appointed Maira, together with sociologist Manuel Antonio Garretón and current ambassador to Austria Osvaldo Puccio, as co-drafters of a new PSCH program, which had not been recast since 1957. Antonio Leal was a key drafter of "The People Speak," a recent document from within the Concertación attempting to reframe the Concertación agenda for the December 1999 presidential elections. It is a platform critical of the "elitist" politics of the governing coalition, and it calls for citizen participation and citizen diversity. (This document will be discussed in the concluding chapter.) Fernando Contreras, who now works as a planner in Santiago's metro system, devotes a great deal of his time to intellectual study and debate.

As is true of the political entrepreneurs treated in the next chapter, the thinkers of this study are engaged in a fairly dynamic relationship with their political parties. While Chilean political parties are highly institutionalized, individuals' embeddedness in parties has changed in important ways. From the years of repression, when entire directorates were physically eliminated, to the contemporary period, new Chilean left party networks have created much more fluid, if somewhat uncertain, forms of individual embeddedness. The thinkers of this study are attempting to influence the parties to which they now belong to open them to a range of conceptions of socialism and of party structure.

Whether their influence has been significant is as yet unclear. In a recent Socialist Party ideological congress, for example, Maira, Garretón, and Puccio attempted to advance their new program for the party to replace the 1957 program. In what was essentially an internal political battle having little to do with their proposal, their program was rejected. The three have abandoned their initiative.

While exile allowed the thinkers of this study to think, the postauthoritarian period has thus far favored those political leaders who are capable strategists, who can draw organizational networks together to advance what might be termed the lowest common denominator in the realm of projects and ideas. Chapter 6 examines the political entrepreneurs, those who consistently match ideas with organization.

ABOVE: President Salvador Allende.

BELOW: Personal loyalist Hernán Del Canto (right) with President Allende.

ABOVE: Relatives of the disappeared with placards asking, *Where Are They?*

BELOW: Chilean modernization: Santiago's barrio El Golf.

ABOVE: Pinochet to Aylwin: The passing of the presidential sash.

BELOW: Protesting congressmen on the day of Pinochet's formal entry into the Congress as a senator-for-life (*senador vitalicio*).

LEFT: Chilean Communist Party leader and party loyalist Jorge Insunza.

BELOW: Congresswoman Isabel Allende addressing a commemoration for the dead and disappeared.

Memoria

ADOLFO ARIEL MANCILLA RAMIREZ			
RODOLFO MARCHANT VILLASECA	D.D.	14 / 03 / 75	LUIS HERNAN NUÑEZ ROJAS
AGUSTIN ALAMIRO MARTINEZ MEZA	D.D.	02 / 01 / 75	JUAN FERNANDO ORTIZ LETELIER
RAMON HUGO MARTINEZ GONZALEZ	D.D.	01 / 01 / 75	JAIME IGNACIO OSSA GALDAMES
GUILLERMO ALBINO MARTINEZ QUIJON	EJECUTADO	06 / 01 / 75	MIGUEL HERNAN OVALLE NARVAE
MARIO OSVALDO MAUREIRA VASO		21 / 01 / 76	MONICA DEL CARMEN PACHECO S
RODRIGO ALEJANDRO MEDINA H		08 / 08 / 76	GREGORIO PALMA DONOSO
NALVIA ROSA MENA ALVARADO		27 / 05 / 76	DANIEL PALMA ROBLEDO
HUMBERTO JUAN CARLOS MENANTEA		29 / 04 / 76	VICENTE SEGUNDO PALOMINO BE
ULISES JORGE MERINO VARA			LUIS JAIME PALOMINOS ROJAS
DARIO FRANCISCO MIRANDA GO		02	ERNESTO ENRIQUE PAREDES PE
EDUARDO FRANCISCO MIRA		08 / 10	REINALDA DEL CARMEN PEREIRA
JUAN RENE MOLINA MOG		07 / 10 / 7	JUAN CARLOS PERELMAN IDE
EUGENIO IVAN MONTTI		9 / 01 / 7	MIREYA DE LOURDES PEREZ VA
JUAN HECTOR MORAG		3 / 02 / 5	MICHELLE MARGUERITE PEÑA H
EDGARDO AGUSTIN MO		2 / 07 / 6	MARIO FERNANDO PEÑA SOLAR
VICTOR HUGO MORALES		06 / 09 / 74	EDRAS DE LAS MERCEDES PINT
		09 / 08 / 7	WALDO ULISES PIZARRO MOLI

ABOVE: First vice president of
the House of Representatives
Adriana Muñoz.

BELOW: Chilean ambassador
to Colombia, the Allendista
Aníbal Palma.

ABOVE: Ambassador Luis Maira with his wife, acclaimed Chilean novelist Marcela Serrano.

LEFT: Congressman and political thinker Antonio Leal.

LEFT: Enrique Correa.

BELOW: Chilean foreign relations minister José Miguel Insulza.

ABOVE: Chilean senator José Antonio Viera-Gallo addressing the Congress.

BELOW: Patricio Rivas (second from right).

CHAPTER 6

THE RETURN:
POLITICAL ENTREPRENEURS AND
THE CHILEAN TRANSITION

■ All of the individuals of this study have been at the forefront of Chilean left politics. In that context, those termed *political entrepreneurs* consistently occupy vanguard positions. Political entrepreneurs were the leading young actors in university-based left politics thirty years ago, and they are among the protagonists of a pragmatic, ideologically moderate center-left alliance today.

The individuals considered in this chapter have proved most adept at altering their own ideologies in response to what they perceive to be their society's changing political climate. Yet, like the other cognitive ideal-types presented, the entrepreneurs' basic approaches to politics have remained constant. While the ideological discourses of the entrepreneurs have changed from the past, their fundamental approaches to politics have not.

For political entrepreneurs, politics is about strategies that produce winning coalitions and popular leadership. Entrepreneurs possess the gift of meshing political ideas with multinetwork organizational vehicles to advance those ideas. The entrepreneurs are effective alliance builders, spanning shades of the political spectrum. In the transition from military to democratic rule, the entrepreneurs of this study have played central roles in forging an unprecedented alliance with the centrist Christian Democratic Party. The entrepreneurs are also effective alliance severers. The alliance with the Christian Democrats came largely at the expense of the Socialist Party's historic alliance with the Chilean Communist Party.

Moreover, in contrast to political party loyalists and personal loyalists, political entrepreneurs regard loyalty to their parties or to particular leaders as less important than being a part of an effective political equation. While the entrepreneurs recognize the continuing need to operate politically within political parties, they have also tended to break ranks with their parties to forge new ground. The exception to this very strong pattern is those political entrepreneurs who as young people were members of the

Chilean Communist Party, for whom breaking ranks proved a longer, more painful process. Such is the case of Raúl Oliva, below. Nevertheless, unlike political party loyalists, political entrepreneurs' embeddedness in their parties is far more fluid.

Political entrepreneurs rise to leadership positions by drawing on their ties to networks outside as well as inside their own parties. Such networks may include other parties, former classmates, professional contacts, the Catholic Church, and their own families. Entrepreneurs thus take advantage of their embeddedness in various networks to position themselves politically and strategically. The political entrepreneurs discussed here come from the Chilean middle class, and university training and leadership during a period of major university reform distinguish their early political careers.[1]

Of the four types presented in this study, political entrepreneurs are most apt to shift political directions in response to traumatic political experiences. Traumatic experiences, ranging from the political polarization of the late 1960s to the military coup and the repression that followed, are the catalysts for the entrepreneurs' new ideological directions and altered relationships to their political parties. While traumatic political experiences tended to lead to ideological freezing among the personal and party loyalists of this study, the political entrepreneurs responded to such experiences by turning away from past ideologies.

Among the political entrepreneurs are those who focus on gaining visibility and votes and those who dedicate themselves to behind-the-scenes strategizing, policy making, and policy implementation. There are those who seek elected office, and others who serve as political appointees and consultants—technocrats of the political order.

This chapter will examine the lives and texts of five political entrepreneurs: Raúl Oliva, a former Communist Party leader and current Socialist Party organizer; José Miguel Insulza, Chile's minister of foreign relations; Clarisa Hardy, director of research in the Ministry of Planning; Enrique Correa, minister of government from 1990 to 1994 and currently director of the Facultad Latinoamericana de Ciencias Sociales–Chile (FLACSO–Chile); and José Antonio Viera-Gallo, speaker of the House of Representatives from 1990 to 1994 and now a senator.

RAÚL OLIVA

Raúl Oliva portrays himself as a self-made man and independent thinker, free today from the missionary role he played for many years as a leader in the Chilean Communist Party.[2] His political journey began as a young man when he left a provincial home in the far reaches of Chile for political activism in the capital. Oliva's politics later led to his exile in Europe, which he says made him aware of the political and cultural provincialism of Chile itself. Today Oliva is an organizer in the Chilean Socialist Party, the party that he believes possesses the power and leadership capable of governing Chile. Oliva views the Communist Party as a political dinosaur, no longer the beacon for the Chilean left that he felt it was thirty years ago. Throughout his life, Oliva has proved himself an able organizer and strategist.

Raúl Oliva was born in 1945 in Osorno, a small city in southern Chile. Oliva described Osorno as "estranged from the world," while Santiago "was civilization for us." The only means of mass communication was by radio. Politics in Osorno took place only at election time. Osorno was a very traditional, hardworking community, where "daily life was mediocre."

Oliva's father was a hatmaker who taught him the trade. His mother, a devoted Catholic, worked in a hospital. From his community and family, Oliva inherited a strong work ethic. He was also an exceptional organizer. In his teens he organized a basketball club, a young people's radio program, a rock-and-roll band, a philosophy club, a French club, and a chess club.

While Oliva remembers his hometown as completely cut off from the world, 1960s events and movements were clearly felt in Osorno. Oliva and his senior high school classmates organized an "Independent Left" group in 1964. He attributed his "feeling of belonging to the left" to the influence of his teachers, who he later learned were Communists. Oliva's desire to continue in politics and to "rise in the world" compelled him to leave Osorno for Santiago:

> When I finished my high school exams, I had achieved excellent
> scores, and my father decided, something which for him was a big leap
> regarding the question of education, that I should do three more years
> of study in administration. His idea for me was that I would work in a
> bank, continue playing basketball, get married. He never liked politics,
> and to this day he's critical. I suffered a minor crisis. I didn't want to
> stay in Osorno. I had no money. My professors said it was absurd for
> me to stay in Osorno, that I should study law. I left for Santiago against
> my father's will. I was nineteen years old. I had a girlfriend who
> worked and who lent me money to go and register. I arrived with a

letter from my French professor to work in a private high school. They gave me food, lodging, and a little money in exchange for my teaching. I didn't know anyone. I spent the weekends hungry because the high school was closed.

The above excerpt marks the first passage in Oliva's text where his expression shifts from first person plural (e.g., "we in Osorno believed," "we students") to first person singular. This shift marks Oliva's coming into his own as a self-sufficient young man ready to engage in Chilean political life. Oliva also knew that to become involved politically, he had to choose a party:

All this was in 1965. I began to come in contact with students from different parties. Being an independent was viewed as a weird thing. I began to feel the need to define myself. I saw the people on the right as people with money. I had a friend who was a committed Communist militant. He began to lend me books, to take the time to listen to my great concerns. I had supported Allende in 1964, but I was only a passive Allendista. I began to read. There were two dailies on the left: *El Siglo* of the Communist Party and *La Ultima Hora* of the Socialist Party. *El Siglo* was a great paper, with articles on culture, portraits of the workers' movement. . . .

In the summer of that year [1965] I went to work in the countryside [where I'm from]. My parents separated. I began to read *El Siglo* every afternoon and to identify with everything the PCCH represented. I returned [to Santiago], I began to work as a teacher, I had my own place, and I bought *El Siglo* every day. Then I remember that a *compañero* at the university, a very good friend, had seen me often with *El Siglo* and he approached me and asked me if I was a communist and I said to him, "Yes," [Oliva laughs] and he invited me to a meeting. I left that meeting having found my reason for being and I began to work.

Immediately I was a class candidate in the student elections. The PCCH was a great organization, massive, it was, perhaps, the Communist Youth was the most influential youth group in Chile in the 1960s. From '65, '66 until '73. . . .

My vision [of Communist Party culture] rested somewhere between reality and the idyllic. I thought that everything we did was important, decisive, full of humanity. . . . A party militant was a missionary day and night, didn't know Saturdays or Sundays, everything had a political

character. We were youth with a great mystique. We were carriers of
an idea of change, of the revolution, which was the solution, which
permitted us to resolve all the problems of this country. And we had
great admiration for the party, a mythical admiration. . . . It was a blind
vision, closed, we had tremendous leaders who were cultured, wise,
and they had in their hands the possibility of bringing their vision to
fruition. . . . We studied to learn, to be faithful.

Oliva recounts that there was no separation among party, ideology, and praxis. Through the PCCH leadership and meetings, the party provided ideology
and program. Through *El Siglo*, the PCCH provided an interpretation of day-
to-day events. For Oliva, it was a period when individual political identity became inseparable from Communist Party activism. It was his "reason for
being." To achieve party recognition, Oliva performed as a "missionary," and
it earned him a leadership position in the Young Communists.

Throughout Oliva's text, the narrative moves from first person singular
to first person plural whenever he discusses the party. This parallels his
first narrative transition from first person plural to first person singular
when he moves from Osorno to Santiago. It is as though in the PCCH Oliva
had rediscovered a sense of place for his organizing and leadership skills,
a place he held on to from 1965 until his exile, when he began to question
the PCCH's strategy and direction.

Oliva remembers himself as a proselytizer, guided by the party, a student of faith. The PCCH also provided the most important relationship of
Oliva's life:

> It was during that period that I met Alicia. She was a PCCH high school
> student leader and I was a university student leader. In the middle of this
> great revolutionary atmosphere, we found love. We married in 1969.

Oliva and his wife were swept up with the Allende period, organizing in
the student movement. On the day after the coup, Oliva and other student
resisters were taken prisoner and held, along with several hundred Chilean citizens, in the national soccer stadium. In the process of being
moved to the National Stadium two weeks later, Oliva escaped. He went
underground, while his wife worked for the party at the Finnish Embassy.

Life underground was traumatic. It was a period in which communists
were systematically persecuted and dozens of PCCH organizers were arrested, were murdered, and disappeared. It was also a period when Chilean

leftists were forced to question what had gone wrong during the Allende period and what their own roles had been in that going wrong. For Raúl Oliva, it was also a period when Communists doubted one another. As militant after militant fell into the hands of Chile's security forces, and as the military discovered and murdered the majority of the internal PCCH leadership in 1976, PCCH organizers began to suspect one another's complicity with the military. Oliva felt that his comrades viewed him with suspicion, primarily because he had not yet been captured. "Either you were an informant or you were a *desaparecido!*" he remembered. Such sentiments of suspected betrayals did irreparable damage to Oliva's relationships with fellow Communists. By 1977, Oliva and his wife, wanted by the military, were sent by the PCCH to Sweden as political refugees. It was not until Oliva received asylum in Sweden, he claimed, that the PCCH realized he could not have been an informant.

From 1977 to 1980, Oliva was a reporter for the Soviet-funded World Youth Organization based in Budapest. There he came into contact with communists and other left militants from around the globe. The debate he remembered being most engaged in centered on the questions of ethics and betrayal:

> The most troubling problem for us [Chilean Communists] was the betrayal. What kind of people were we? What kind of ethics could have existed to deliver the lives of other people to save your own life? Why had we been defeated? What were we pretending to be, we who were so-called pacifists, who didn't want to kill anyone, who accepted private property? Two explanations emerged: [one was that being] communist militants required even greater political will, ready to engage in armed struggle if necessary; the other, that we had been too narrow-minded in our process, our approach to change.

Here Oliva presents a fascinating linking of ethics with strategy or means. In one sector of the Communist Party (namely the Leipzig Group, described in chapter 5), party members were expected to take the moral high ground, to answer defeat and oppression with moral and political will and a commitment to give their lives in a battle against the dictatorship. In another sector, which included Oliva, the party had to recognize that the Allende government should have had a more inclusive program that systematically strove to incorporate the political center and the middle class. Oliva portrayed the Leipzig Group as exercising a kind of ethical "overkill" and he, himself, as having to separate ethics from the reality of politics in order to advance a politically viable program:

> These distinct visions of reality provoked tremendous internal conflict for me. If being a communist meant such a Manichaean vision of things, then I'm different. If I'm different, with whom do I identify? The only communist party I related to was the Italian Communist Party. So I became one Italian communist more living in Sweden. I read the daily *Renascita*, I read Italian literature, Gramsci, et cetera. But there was one problem. It was the Communist Party, but it was a European one. It was *very* European.
>
> I continued as a militant in the PCCH, but as a militant with a dissident status. A person not to be trusted. It was almost like being a *"sympathizer."* People began to watch themselves with me because I could be a very negative influence.

Oliva temporarily retreated from exile politics to study in Sweden and Spain, and he earned a master's in law. In 1983 and 1984, as signs of a political opening began to emerge in Chile, Raúl and Alicia Oliva concentrated on building capital for their return. Oliva began to draw on educational and professional networks to redefine his identity.

For Oliva, exile represented what former Brazilian exile and historian Valentina da Rocha Lima termed a "confrontation with individuality," an "individual search for identity."[3] Oliva was shocked by the control that Chilean Communist delegates exercised over their militants in Eastern Europe, possessing the authority, for example, to grant or deny their members travel privileges. "Personal freedoms, one's right to make personal decisions," Oliva recounted, "frankly were limited by the party." In exile, Oliva's complete self-deliverance to the PCCH as its "missionary" gave way. He felt increasingly "stifled" by the PCCH, uncomfortable with the fact that he was forced to remain with the Chilean Communist Youth when he was well over thirty, dismayed by the insularity of the PCCH leadership. "Communist parties are like two bulldogs fighting under a rug," Oliva said. "You see the rug moving, but you don't even hear a sound! It is a deaf and inaccessible struggle."

Through his connections to networks outside the Communist Party, Oliva developed professional contacts and secured funding from a United Nations agency to support independent research upon his return to Chile. The Olivas were granted permission to return in 1984, and after his arrival

Oliva began to work as a human rights lawyer. He remained in the PCCH but did not assume an official party role. His new networks gave him a sense of independence that he felt he had not enjoyed since his pre- PCCH days. He joined a small group of Communist intellectuals who formed a think tank to pressure the PCCH to abandon its armed rebellion strategy. There Oliva oversaw survey studies that convinced him that Chilean citizens had overcome their fear of the dictatorship but were against violence as a means to the regime's end. It also became clear to him that the PCCH itself had lost its historic popular foothold within the left. By 1988, surveys that Oliva and his colleagues conducted indicated that the PCCH would receive no more than 5 or 6 percent of the vote in national elections.

In his description of the Chilean transition from authoritarianism during the mid- to late 1980s, Oliva presents himself as virtually alone with respect to several strategic political issues. When the PCCH and others on the left claimed 1986 to be "the decisive year" to defeat the dictatorship through mass mobilizations and general strikes, Oliva claimed that he knew such a call was premature and ill-conceived. He favored negotiations with the regime. In 1987 he attempted to convince the PCCH to abandon its armed rebellion stance and push for free elections, for universal inscription in the election rosters. In 1988, Oliva, along with a small group of fellow Communists, pressed the PCCH to reverse its policy calling for abstention from the plebiscite, urging that the party join those sectors of the opposition calling upon Chilean citizens to vote "No." Oliva also pushed the PCCH, which was an illegal party according to the 1980 constitution, to consider joining the Party for Democracy, an instrumentalist party created by the Socialists. The PCCH rejected this proposal. Finally, Oliva claimed that at one point in early 1989 there was a window of opportunity for the party to join the center-left Concertación alliance, and, he alleged, he unsuccessfully pressed the PCCH to do so.

Following the 1989 elections, in which the Chilean Communist Party failed to win a single national seat, Raúl Oliva and a group of former fellow PCCH leaders held a press conference:

> We had to go public. To be a communist was like being a person of the past. You felt this kind of moral shame that you belonged to that world. People identified you as a leader of that world. . . . The alternatives were to participate in the refounding of the party, or to found our own movement with other groups.

Oliva's group condemned the PCCH's alienation of party dissidents and announced their resignation from the PCCH to form ARCO, an alternative group composed of a hundred former PCCH members. Shortly thereafter, Oliva led the entry of ARCO as a bloc into the Chilean Socialist Party:

> I believe there isn't space for another party in Chile. In politics one has to make cold choices, and you have to have access to power. This is what politics is about. It is why I opted for the Socialist Party.
>
> I think we have to produce a new identity of a progressive left in this country. And that identity doesn't exist. Who can do it? The Socialist Party, the Party for Democracy. . . . Parties have to be the representative vehicle. They also have to change. And I'm not clear yet in what sense they have to change, but they have to change. . . . None of the parties today function like parties. Historically parties organized immense sectors of the population. They represented very diverse worlds. Today they appear very weak [in terms of their organic connection to civil society]. Parties aren't attractive in a world where individuality has become so pronounced. Parties will have to engage in a practical renovation of relating on an individual-by-individual basis.

Oliva's conception of socialism today differs from his past conceptions in several ways. First, it is no longer statist. Second, it allows for economic inequality. Third, it is not an end but a process:

> I frankly think we must break with our past conception of socialism. I would say that socialism is not a final society, not a type of society, but rather a form of human conduct, a type of politics, a conception that is in the first place ethical, that refers to political and social development. I don't associate public property today with socialism. Socialists have to understand how our economy really works. They have to understand how the market functions. I believe in the necessity of [state] planning to some degree. The most developed countries in the world continue to plan—France, Spain, Italy, Germany. . . . Socialist ideals continue to be important, for example, overcoming the exploitation of man by his fellow man. . . . Yet profit will always exist. Always. Exploitation seen from an ethical point of view means establishing a limit that guarantees basic human dignity, a reasonable daily wage, recreation, education, equality of opportunity according to capacity.

Socialists have to understand that it is impossible for the country to move forward without the businessmen of this country. This country operates with eight hundred thousand businessmen. If these eight hundred thousand hear the news that the government is going to raise taxes or something like that, these eight hundred thousand go to work depressed. The investments they had planned become paralyzed. They are human beings with characteristics that are sometimes conservative, sometimes revolutionary, audacious. We need to change the basic culture of our society.

Oliva's current ideological discourse is a far cry from his discourse of thirty years ago. Yet he continues to organize and strategize, now within the Socialist Party, working with former Communists to create and sustain a power bloc that might gain him a seat on the PSCH's Political Commission. Oliva has a successful law practice. He is hopeful about the left's chances of producing a successful presidential candidate, namely, Ricardo Lagos, to usher Chile into the second millennium.

CLARISA HARDY

Clarisa Hardy is an astute political analyst and strategist.[4] From her early twenties, when she worked in the Allende government, to today as a key assistant to government minister Jorge Arrate, Hardy has used her intellect and her skills to seek credibility as a policy maker and implementer. Like Raúl Oliva, Hardy portrays herself as an independent, self-made person, adept at using her political and professional networks to advance her work and beliefs.

Hardy comes from a liberal Jewish family. She was born in Buenos Aires in 1945. In the early 1950s, when she was a very young girl, Clarisa's father rejected Perón's request that he work for him as a filmmaker; instead he moved the family from Argentina to Chile. They moved into a middle-class neighborhood in Santiago, where Clarisa and her two siblings enrolled in a private Italian school in the neighborhood. There the Hardy children came face-to-face with anti-Semitism:

I ended up in a private Italian school, purely by accident because it was in our neighborhood, but this was in 1952, and you had many Italian fascist immigrants here, so the social composition of the people there was absolutely adversarial. . . . My father was firmly nonreligious, so we three brothers and sisters did not participate in religious classes, and that marked me in school, as you can imagine. It was quite uncomfortable. Sometimes I would sit in on the religious classes and discover that the Jews had killed. . . [pause] . . . it was a terrible situation for me.

Hardy was very influenced by her father and family, and she grew up in a household where "everyone voiced their opinions at the table," a family that was "extraordinarily permissive." The family encouraged independent, liberal-minded children. She denies that her family was political, although she describes their annual trips to Argentina to visit an extremely political side of the family, including an aunt and an uncle who were "*bolche, bolche, bolche* [Bolsheviks]."

What can be gathered from Hardy's anecdotes about her home life and her first years of education is her notion of a virtual separation of politics and the political from the moral, social, or ethical foundations of her upbringing:

My father was a Mason and ever since I was a girl I heard discussions about social justice, the persecution of minorities, et cetera. They were recurrent themes, which contributed to a kind of language of values, not political options, but in value terms—the themes of equality, justice, love.

Hardy's first involvement in politics came in the university. She portrays her period there as one of solidifying certain friendships and a social life, as much as a time to search for political direction. By her third year in college, Hardy had joined the Socialist Party, a decision apparently made by virtue of her immediate circle of friends and influences. She was an excellent student and an articulate young militant. She was chief organizer of a socialist university brigade to work in the Chilean countryside, and she demonstrated a talent for strategizing and dealmaking in concessions that she won from the government for student-peasant initiatives in the rural areas.

In reflecting on her university years, Hardy has come to believe that the Socialist Party sought her out as a leader because she was both a woman and a good student and thereby made a "good token." For Hardy, political party politics was about power and influence, exercised by males. Hardy's storytelling features a strong gendered dimension. She consistently offered portraits of the physical, even sensual, attributes of political friends and militants and her relationships to them. Like all the middle-class Chilean intellectuals interviewed, Hardy begins her narrative in the first person rather than in the collective "we" voice. Yet, unlike those of her male colleagues, Hardy's voice shifts to the "we," referring to "my husband and I," throughout much of her adult life. When Hardy is not using "we," her spouse as a referent is assumed as an underlying presence. Among the male interviewees, with the exception of political party loyalist Patricio Rivas, this was not a storytelling pattern.

From 1967 to 1970 Hardy lived in England with her husband, where she earned a postgraduate degree in anthropology. When they returned to Chile, both she and her husband took government posts in the Allende administration, where Hardy continued to exercise her negotiating abilities in struggles over property rights. She claims that throughout the Allende period, she was "more a '*gobernista*' [a "government loyalist"] than a PSCH militant." Hardy attributed this in part to her frustrations with intraparty struggle and in part to her husband's influence as a member of the Chilean Communist Party. She sought to bridge and sustain effective party alliances within the Popular Unity administration, particularly within her own ministry. In Hardy's description of this period is the recurrent theme of an implicit assumption that the Socialist Party was a thorn in the side of the government.

> I was very much convinced of the need to defend the government
> more than the intraparty struggles of that period. I would say that I
> was an exemplary government militant, much more than an exemplary
> socialist militant, so much so that I had trouble in my neighborhood,
> La Reina. I was seen as very "*gobernista*," and very allied with the
> Communist Party.

Hardy had little desire to discuss the immediate aftermath of the coup. Apparently she had lent her name to protect someone else, a situation that caused a great deal of difficulty and drama in her personal life. She left for Argentina in December 1973, where she and her husband remained for a two-month period. Her husband was given a post in Geneva with the United Nations, but Hardy went to Mexico City, where many of her friends had gone into exile. Once in Mexico, Hardy decided she would stay with the children there.

> I decided I wasn't leaving Mexico, because in Geneva I would have had
> to dedicate myself to raising the children, learning a language, I wouldn't

find work. So Alejandro had to resign from his UN job, and we spent nine years in Mexico City.

Hardy presents this period as the beginning of her own kind of liberation, primarily as she developed herself professionally in Mexico.

Unlike other interviewees who had been in exile in Mexico, Hardy portrayed herself as a person who became quite engrossed in Mexican politics and culture, for whom Mexico offered her first opportunity to study "on the ground."

> Before my work in Mexico I was a book academic. Here I learned how to do fieldwork, because I worked in a research center on rural issues. I traveled all around Mexico. I spent fifteen days a month working in peasant communities.

Hardy claimed that on the personal as well as the professional side, she would have been quite capable, even happy, to live the rest of her days in Mexico if need be. Her children were in Mexican schools, her work was with Mexicans, and she became involved intellectually with the Mexican left. Nevertheless, as the image of her large circle of personal friendships emerged during the interview, it was clear that the core of that circle remained Chilean friends. In exile Hardy became quite close to political party loyalist Isabel Allende, to painter José Roca, to Aylwin's minister of energy, Jaime Tohá, and to a number of other Chilean political thinkers and activists. She hosted solidarity meetings in her home, organized benefits for Chile, and participated in other events against the dictatorship.

Yet Hardy did not consider herself an active socialist militant, and she neither worked for the party nor attended PSCH meetings. She claimed that she was increasingly dismayed by the perspectives and behavior exhibited by many of her compatriots toward Mexico, by a view of Mexicans as *"indios,"* by the "little respect some Chileans showed toward Mexican society." Moreover, she found it strange, "in some ways a little sick, this disassociation between the personal and the political, of an 'outside militancy' very weirdly connected to either country, to Chile or to Mexico." While this contradicts her own disassociation of the personal from the political rooted in her childhood, Hardy herself virtually gave up on the Socialist Party and concentrated on her professional development and alternative networks in Mexico. Unlike party loyalists, who continued to be embroiled in their parties in exile, Hardy maintained a looser relationship with her party, involving herself in other professional and intellectual networks.

Presented with opportunities for work and professional development, Hardy and her family elected to integrate more fully into Mexican life. She taught at a Mexican university, worked at a Mexican research institute, and engaged in debates with Mexicans about Mexican politics and culture.

Hardy described how Mexico had influenced the ways in which she had come to view questions ranging from the meaning of socialism to state-society relations and gender issues:

> For me, curiously, the great leap [toward a renovated socialist position] wasn't due to theoretical political discussion nor to great international moments, no, nor to the conditions leading to the downfall of the Berlin wall. . . . I think it was really a product of my professional work in Mexico and my contact with an extraordinarily more heterogeneous society than I had ever experienced, where it was not merely a question of class differences, but of something else. . . . Where only today in Chile this is appearing and has a marked political and ethnic mix, in Mexico it was basically a cultural struggle, eh, the awakening of the whole feminist theme coincided with my time in Mexico, a society extraordinarily restrictive with women. . . .
>
> My contact with the Mexican university was a contrast to the Chilean university. In Mexico the university had an enormous student body and very little of "class heritage" claims. You gave classes to kids who were asleep in their seats, and when you asked why, it was because they were hungry, not because they were tired, and I discovered how Chile was a brutally stratified society. From the day you are born [in Chile] you move in an extraordinarily homogeneous world, that from birth you live in a neighborhood of a specific type, you attend schools of a specific type. So for me Mexico was the discovery of an enormous diversity irreducible to class struggle. . . .
>
> I realized I was part of the guilty Chilean middle class that one tries not to claim or confront as part of one's identity but tries instead to assume another. For me Mexico was *extremely* important, the impact of modernity and poverty I lived there more strongly than the people who live it here in Chile.

Mexico represented to Hardy not only an opportunity for professional growth and accomplishment but a window on a dramatically distinct politics and culture as well. This led her to discoveries about her own society and culture of which she had previously been unaware. She perceived that she and her fellow left intellectuals had attempted to "assume another identity," as champions of the workers, transcending class boundaries. Hardy now saw Chilean society as profoundly stratified, so much so that she felt many of her colleagues and fellow militants were blind to their own class isolation. On the other hand, she had come to believe that socialism could not be envisioned solely in class terms, that ethnicity and gender issues had to be fully incorporated in a socialist project.

It was her professional achievements and contacts in Mexico that allowed Hardy to return to Chile in 1983 as an externally financed academic researcher, an arrangement that enabled her to establish herself with a leading private research institute in Chile long enough to demonstrate her abilities and to be offered a salaried position with the institute when her financing from Mexico ran out.

The timing of Hardy's return proved fortuitous on the personal and political fronts as well. The year 1983 was a pivotal year in Chilean politics, marking what many experts term the beginning of the Chilean transition from authoritarian rule. "It was a euphoric time, with the first protests," Hardy recounted. In retrospect it is clear that Chilean exiles who were returning were at some advantage if they were able to return this "early" in the transition, to integrate themselves into the large antidictatorial movements of that period, before the waning of mass mobilizations and the onset of an elite-negotiated transition process. During this period, Chilean political returnees could more readily establish their political party identities in Chile, as parties and party factions redefined their goals and strategies. In addition, there was an apparent psychological advantage for those returning early. Based on interviews and on written accounts, it is clear that the "euphoric moment" of political opening made the psychological adjustment to return less difficult for them than for those, say, who returned in 1986 and 1987 to a comparatively diminished and uncertain opposition movement.

Hardy immersed herself in her new fieldwork in Chile, which took her to organizations representing the urban and rural poor. She also became active again in party politics, although in the interview her focus regarding this period was on her contribution to organizing a federation of socialist women, a "thorn in the side" of the Socialist Party. At the time, Hardy felt, such "semiautonomous" movements as the feminist movement could practice an alternative form of power politics to challenge traditional political practices. She has since given up on that strategy.

Under the 1990–1994 Aylwin administration, Hardy became research head of Fondo de Solidaridad a Inversión Social (FOSIS), a government agency whose primary function is to make small grants and loans to micro enterprise projects. After a failed attempt in 1989, Hardy was elected in 1993 to the Central Committee of the Socialist Party.

When asked about her vision of the role of the Socialist Party in Chilean society, Hardy responded somewhat contradictorily. On the one hand, she emphasized the themes of civil society autonomy from the party, of a new understanding of the public/private divide, of a new and problematic "modern" society. On the other, she urged a restructuring of the party that would breathe new life into local-level concerns, in which the party would penetrate civil society's preoccupation with day-to-day issues and projects. On the one hand, Hardy saw a virtual divorce between the Socialist Party of the Allende period and the Socialist Party of today. On the other, she felt that the Socialist Party leadership and a significant portion of the militancy held fast to a thirty-year history, that their identities were intimately tied to the historic Socialist Party, and that a new party had to discover a way to incorporate this identity. The great challenge, as Hardy expressed it, is to develop a socialist project that reflects what can be learned from PSCH history with a complex process of modernization taking place in Chilean society and culture. Hardy suggested that the Party for Democracy might be the logical venue for such a process:

> The great challenge is how to construct a brilliant socialist proposal for this country and for the people of this country and for the history of the last twenty years that this country has lived. I think perhaps the PPD has an attraction because . . . it's a party that expressed, at a particular moment, the necessity of a democratic coming together, it didn't have any real proposal, no real project, and today it has demonstrated that it created an image using the signs that people want to see—modern, successful, accomplishments, new, different things that don't really have anything to do with the PPD in practice as just another party machine. It also benefits from not having the vast claims made upon it by a historic, organic membership. . . . The PPD's success comes from its image as something people want.

Hardy claimed that within the Chilean socialist sphere today it is possible to recognize two tendencies: one that no longer holds firm to a belief in socialism as an end and a second that still places value on socialism as a goal for society. Her descriptions and her hopes for the PSCH echoed those of many members, belying a sense of frustration with the incapacity of the party to define a clear and cohesive project, while at the same time voicing an appreciation of the internal debate over what that project should be. Hardy predicted that change within the PSCH would depend more on internal balances of power than on ideas:

> But, look, it's all a process, it's a process that will break the old internal structures, the small leadership pockets, the ways of doing politics that, ultimately, [have] substantially to do with the exercise of power. You have the pressure for change given what Chile lived through, as well as the real limitations placed by the defensiveness of those very leaders, many of whom are the most resistant to big change because it threatens their own party position. . . . There is constant pressure among the parties for change, yet the only thing that moves them is the logic of power.

In reflecting about her own balancing between the public and the private, Hardy appeared nostalgic about the life she left in Mexico, about a simplicity in her life there when she was not playing "hardball" politics. On the other hand, she admits she enjoys playing hardball politics. Today, Hardy is part of a small group of socialist women who are challenging the men from within the party to cede a degree of control. Her political identity represents a relatively new and rare type for Chilean politics, for it combines roles and value structures uncommon to the Chilean political class: first and foremost, Hardy is a woman and a respected thinker. She has written extensively and does a great deal of public speaking on poverty and social welfare policies in Chile. While women are not entirely new to the Chilean political party elite, women intellectuals are. On the other hand, while women intellectuals are numerous in Chile, for the most part they have steered clear of postauthoritarian party politics, "out of disgust," as several have expressed it. Hardy today plays a key role in Chile 21, the think tank of Socialist Party leader and presidential hopeful Ricardo Lagos. Should Lagos be elected in 1999, Hardy is likely to earn a high-level cabinet position.

When asked to name the two or three most important events in her life, Hardy laughed, and responded with little hesitation. "The coup, of course," she said. "And then, you may think this is strange or funny—motherhood."

ENRIQUE CORREA

Enrique Correa has consistently exhibited an entrepreneurial approach to politics, from his involvement as a cofounder of MAPU in 1969 to his role as the country's first minister of government in the postdictatorial period.[5] Correa is considered one of the top four strategists of the negotiated transition from authoritarian rule of the late 1980s, credited with convincing the left that Christian Democrat Patricio Aylwin was the best candidate to lead Chile's transition. As minister of the agency that serves as the "communicator from the president to the people" from 1990 to 1994, Correa was perhaps second only to President Aylwin as the government's most visible representative. Within the Chilean political class, Correa has tended to win more praise from the right than the left. As one right-wing congressman said of him, "Aylwin should erect a monument to Correa, because he has been an indispensable man for the government."[6]

Enrique Correa grew up in the mining province of Ovalle, north of Santiago. His mother came from a working-class Catholic family and considered herself a devoted communist, and his father was a Mason from a middle-class Santiago family. In addition to the influence of growing up in a mining region representing Chile's oldest left stronghold, Correa attributed his early political leanings to progressive, activist currents within the Catholic Church:

> I was a Christian. Why? Because at the time [of my youth], the most developed, most new, most exciting and vibrant community was the Christian community. It was an explosive force, particularly when combined with the student movement at the end of the 1950s, beginning of 1960s. . . .
>
> I really think that for all of us the most important referent was the church. Today I'm a pretty "Lutheran" Catholic. I really don't accept any of the moral directives from the church. I'm quite a liberal. Really my sense of belonging to the Catholic Church is a social, a *cultural* thing. It provides me with family roots. A sense of belonging. And I strongly believe that it's impossible to understand our history, Chile, without understanding this sense of belonging to the church that we all feel.

Correa's explanation of his attraction to the church suggests that he was as drawn by the power and leadership potential as by the message of the church. He does not identify with the church's moral teachings. Correa views the church as a site for social and political identity and activism.

Nevertheless, when Correa was a young person, his attraction to the Catholic Church represented more than just a "sense of belonging." At the age of twelve he had joined the Young Christian Democrats. In his early teens, Correa cofounded a Catholic Student Youth chapter in Ovalle. At sixteen, he entered the seminary. After a year, he returned home to help support his family and ailing father. A year later, instead of returning to the seminary full-time, Correa entered the philosophy department of Catholic University in Santiago. Throughout his adolescence, Correa felt "torn between his vocation for politics and his vocation for the priesthood."

At Catholic University, Correa was strongly influenced by several of his religious professors, all of whom were politically active, including Brazilian exile and philosophy professor Paulo Freire; Father Gonzalo Arroyo, a leader of the Christians for Socialism Movement; and Jesuit priest Hernan Larraín, who was also director of the leading Catholic journal *Revista Mensaje*. At the university and through his political work, Correa also became close friends with an array of young Christian political activists, including fellow political entrepreneur José Antonio Viera-Gallo, María Antonieta Saa (socialist mayor of Conchalí from 1990 to 1994, now a congresswoman), and Jaime Ravinet (Christian Democratic mayor of Santiago). Correa described his Catholic University period as an "agitated one," a period of struggle over university reform and of heated debate over new directions inspired by Vatican II (1963–1965).

At twenty-two, Correa was elected president of the Young Christian Democrats. Yet, like many of his colleagues, he found that his initial support for Frei turned to dismay over the "reformism" of the administration. "The Frei government," Correa stated in a 1968 press conference, "has exhausted its reformist efforts. Only a revolutionary alternative remains."[7] In 1969, the Christian Democratic Party brought Correa before its Disciplinary Tribunal for public statements urging the PDC to join forces with the revolutionary left:

> What the Young Christian Democrats want is that in 1970 the electoral battle be between two sides, between two opposing and exclusionary blocs: on one side, the right and imperialism, and on the other, all those forces which advocate the substitution of capitalism. Because today the dilemma is clear: socialist revolution or right-wing regression.[8]

After publicly condemning President Frei for ordering troops to remove a group of squatters, an action that resulted in six deaths, Correa was removed from his post as president of the Young Christian Democrats. In May 1969, after an ideologically charged PDC Congress in which President Eduardo Frei Sr. advocated and won the PDC's continued adherence to "forging its own path," rather than allying with the left or right, the majority of the young PDC leadership left the party to form the MAPU, which became a formally recognized Marxist-Leninist party and a staunch supporter of the Allende candidacy for president.

Correa describes the MAPU's shift from Catholicism and Saint Thomas to Marxism-Leninism and Althusser as a logical process of replacing one all-encompassing framework and vision for another:

> I really think we of the MAPU were the most successful at being a revolutionary vanguard party. We had Catholicism on the one hand, and Marxism on the other. Althusser was a guru of ours. I even had the chance to meet him—a very strange meeting. It was in Berlin, and a friend took me to meet him, and I remember Althusser was sitting in the dark, all the lights out, and I introduced myself and mentioned some people he knew. . . . And he said, "Ah, you were one of the founders of the MAPU." And I said, "Yes, professor." And he asked, "And do you think that was a good idea?" And I said, "No, professor." [Correa laughed.]

This anecdote is telling in that the memory of Correa's historic meeting with a political "guru" focuses on what they both recognize as a failed strategic decision to form the MAPU.

Together with fellow entrepreneur José Miguel Insulza (discussed below), Correa worked during the Popular Unity period in the Ministry of Foreign Relations under the leadership of Clodomiro Almeyda. In 1972, when the MAPU split between the faction that favored Allende and the PCCH's more moderate approach to transformation and the ultra left's call for a less compromising, rapid transformation of society, Correa chose the former. Together with José Antonio Viera-Gallo, José Miguel Insulza, and a handful of others fresh from the same university networks, Correa cofounded the MAPU–Worker Peasant Party (MAPU-OC).

At the time of the coup, Correa fled into exile:

> I lived in Moscow, in East Berlin, I came to know well the principal communist leaders in Europe. We were never very friendly with the Cubans. Sure, Oscar Guillermo Garretón[9] [a former MAPU leader who

headed Chile's metro system for the transportation ministry under President Aylwin] lived there, he was more to the left, we all were in a sense. We were pretty Leninist. Yet by 1975 we were changing.

I'm a bad case to discuss about daily life in exile, because while I was proscribed from entering Chile for ten years, I have to say that about 60 percent of that time I lived in Chile and 40 percent abroad. In any case, there were two phases to my exile. The first in 1973 and 1974 in Moscow, and the second, say between 1977 and 1981 between Berlin and Rome.

Correa described the dynamic debates among the Chilean left and the European and Soviet left over the Popular Unity experience. More important to him than the theoretical battles over socialism, however, were the battles over means and strategy. Being a Leninist, for example, was not so much at issue as was the interpretation of Lenin regarding the question of necessary class and organizational alliances. For Correa, the exile experience "taught" the Chilean political class how to compromise. It transformed what he termed the "absolutism" and "integralism" of the Chilean left into more "rational," "civilized" political players:

> I really believe that the Chilean exiled political class gained a great deal of political sophistication abroad. I think that the *política de los acuerdos* ["politics of agreements"] today has two roots: one, of course, was to bring a close to the dictatorship, [and] it was absolutely necessary; the other was that we have a more developed, more *civilized* way of doing politics today. We learned how to do politics. Before we didn't do it and today we do. We have learned to distinguish between politics and war. Before 1973 we were not distinguishing between them. Today we do. I would suggest this is a *synthesis* of what was going on, what changed after 1973. War is war and politics is politics.

After returning to Chile clandestinely under several guises, Correa returned as himself in 1983 and threw himself into opposition politics, first at the side of the Chilean labor leaders who organized the first mass mobilizations against the dictatorship. By 1986 he had judged that the social and political landscape would not support a dramatic, "rupturist" approach to ending the dictatorship. He was among the first on the left to advocate a strategy of alliance with the Christian Democrats behind the transition path outlined in the 1980 constitution.

Correa became the "number two man" behind chief Christian Democratic strategist Genaro Arriagada in the Comando Por el No, the opposition's 1988 plebiscite campaign. On the heels of the opposition's victory in the plebiscite, Correa became executive secretary of the Concertación alliance, the seventeen-party center-left coalition that would bring Patricio Aylwin to the presidency. Aylwin, who more than two decades earlier had led the charge for Correa's expulsion from the Christian Democratic Party, would now consider Correa his closest ally on the left.[10]

Today Correa is regarded as an ultra-pragmatist, a political realist whose hopes for social transformation are tempered by the balance of power in Chile. Correa's political behavior, his gift as a dealmaker, is consistent with his past. Correa also recognizes that his fellow members of the left political class have little taste for political conflict:

> For example, Boeninger, Foxley, Cortázar, and I,[11] the four of us are really the nucleus of the modernizing organ of the [Aylwin] government, and it has been amazing to us to see the kinds of errors committed out of fear of conflict, errors either of bad organization or the rapid resort to exercise the "*mano duro*" [meaning, "to send in the police or troops"] to resolve conflict or protests.

Correa's discussion of fear of conflict in Chilean society today (to which we will return in the final chapter) raises the issue of the difference between "rational" and "irrational" conflict, particularly in light of his previous discussion of the difference between "war" and "politics." He does not resolve this issue.

With regard to the direction of political parties, Correa favors moving away from party adoption of all-encompassing programs. He is uncomfortable with the old style of party militancy, which he views as alienating and out of touch with a modernizing Chile. He depicts a Socialist Party leadership divorced from its internal base:

> I believe that the concept of a partisan-based militancy, understood as adherence to a line, to a thesis that applies to the national, regional, and local levels, is going to be in real crisis as the country civilizes more. I think that politics will become more "single-issue," based around certain themes rather than doctrines, not even around global issues. I think that the regionalization process was successful, and I

think that ten years from now we'll see other kinds of alliances, other forms of understanding. Which I see as quite positive. I have the impression that people will continue to belong to parties based on certain general visions, certain loyalties, certain men who want to be president, but they'll do so expecting very little. Parties will become less important to problems in the communities, the problems of a region, the party will no longer be the dominating force. I think the concept of militancy in a party will be extremely reduced to party bureaucrats, for those who aspire to state positions.

Take me, for example. In two years from now, I'm going to be in a far more relaxed position politically than I am today. And I don't want to go around campaigning for the socialists. Of course I'll be involved in the presidential campaign, but I don't want to go around carrying keys for the socialists. The PPD is an interesting phenomenon, because its members are more relaxed. It's still a little too light for me, floppy.

When I say I'm a socialist today, it means I'm interested in forwarding a long-term vision for the left of this country. Secular. I think as Chile becomes more developed, the central questions will be the struggles for particular civil freedoms—now the question of divorce, for example, freedom for young people, reform of the police, and there will be less timid approaches to these issues. The PPD is better equipped than the PS for this, because the core of the PS is filled with extremely traditional members.

Let's take a look at the first ten or twelve public figures recognized as important leaders of the country and look at who the socialists are: Lagos, who is fourth after Aylwin, Frei, and Foxley, then I come in somewhere after that, then Viera-Gallo. If you take Lagos, Viera-Gallo, and myself, we represent half or more of the Central Committee, but we are far from representative of this internal order of militants, these young guys who live extremely insulated in their world, and I think the logic of being a militant leads them to this.

Enrique Correa recently headed the Chilean branch of the Latin American Social Sciences Faculty (FLACSO-Chile), whose senior members chose Correa for his visibility and his potential for raising substantial financial support, particularly from the Chilean government.[12] Today he is a successful private sector entrepreneur. In our interview Correa said he planned to make an eventual run for the Senate.

JOSÉ ANTONIO VIERA-GALLO

Like his close friend and political party colleague Enrique Correa, Chilean senator José Antonio Viera-Gallo[13] has been a key strategist in the Chilean left's consensus politics. Correa and Viera-Gallo share the controversial distinction of being the two leaders of the left to sit down at the table on more than one occasion with General Augusto Pinochet. Viera-Gallo was Chile's speaker of the House in the 1990–1994 Aylwin administration, and Enrique Correa considers Viera-Gallo an ideal future president.[14]

Viera-Gallo's text emphasizes pragmatism. Yet he is a conflicted thinker and admits to the contradictions within his discourse, claiming to be both a liberal and a social Christian, an individualist and a collectivist. In contrast to Enrique Correa's air of comfort with his political beliefs, Viera-Gallo projects discomfort with what he perceives as a failure to replace his "totalizing" past visions with an alternative framework. Moreover, Viera-Gallo assumes an ironic tone in his narrative, as he portrays his past self as somewhat divorced from his present self. He exaggerates his past identity as a revolutionary in light of his current image as a reformist politician. The tension between past and present identity pervades Viera-Gallo's narrative.

Use of irony is a common narrative approach, as oral historian Alessandro Portelli describes with reference to the narrative mode of *The Autobiography of Malcolm X*:

> Narrators are capable of reconstructing their past attitudes even when they no longer coincide with present ones. . . . In one of the most important oral testimonies of our time, *The Autobiography of Malcolm X*, the narrator describes very vividly how his mind worked before he reached his present awareness, and then judges his own past self by the standards of his present political and religious consciousness. . . . *Irony* is the major narrative mode: two different ethical (or political, or religious) and narrative standards interfere and overlap, and their tension shapes the telling of the story.[15]

Viera-Gallo was the only child of a diplomat, and the family lived in countries throughout the world, "under several forms of authoritarianism—Argentina under Perón, Peru of Odría, Portugal of Oliveira Salazar, and the Dominican Republic under Trujillo." Viera-Gallo's father was a staunch conservative, and Viera-Gallo's first political affiliation (which lasted less than a year) was with a conservative youth group at sixteen.

Viera-Gallo was considered a prodigy, educated within the Chilean Catholic establishment and highly influenced by progressive Catholic intellectuals. At the age of twenty-one, he graduated from the Catholic University Law School. He began teaching law and working with the Instituto Latinoamericano de Doctrina y Estudios Sociales (ILADES), a Jesuit intellectual center, where Viera-Gallo came into contact with leading liberation theologians. He became increasingly active in politics, joining the "rebel" wing of the Young Christian Democrats, the wing that would form the MAPU. At twenty-five, Viera-Gallo was named an undersecretary in the Ministry of Justice of the Allende government.

As undersecretary, Viera-Gallo most remembers the trauma surrounding two issues of utmost importance to the Popular Unity government: first, his work on constitutional reform regarding property rights and state ownership; and second, his struggles to improve Allende's relationship with the Catholic Church and with the Christian Democratic Party. Viera-Gallo was a key figure in orchestrating what proved to be unsuccessful meetings between the president and the cardinal and between the president and then president of the Christian Democratic Party Patricio Aylwin. The failure of these leaders to reach an accord regarding the government's program and direction foreshadowed the Christian Democratic Party's support for a military overthrow of the government. The impasse during these meetings made a lasting impression on Viera-Gallo.

With the aid of his wife's family immediately following the coup, Viera-Gallo was granted political asylum by the Vatican. He secured work with the ecumenical research institute Partito Comuniste di Italia (IDOC) and served as a United Nations consultant on questions of development and disarmament. In Rome, he was soon swept into the debates between Chilean exiled intellectuals and politicians and the thinkers and politicians of the Italian Communist Party.

Viera-Gallo traced what he perceived to be the common traditions in the countries' political cultures, particularly the peculiar blends of Communist and Catholic culture and ideology within the Italian Communist Party:

> I took the significance of Italy to be that a group of Catholics who were in the armed resistance against Mussolini joined the resistance with Communists and, in the end, became Communists themselves yet continued being Catholics. The overall mentality of the Communist state is that mentality which believes there is a global vision of the world, that there is a kind of integralist vision that undergirds a scientific politics,

in this case Marxist, but also religious. . . . Well, we Chileans and Italians alike knew perfectly well then that the world was headed toward communism. [He laughed.]

Nevertheless, set back by several events domestically, internationally, and internally, the PCI failed to maintain electoral momentum at the national level. Viera-Gallo alluded to the many struggles of the PCI, and, tangentially, of the exiled Chileans, throughout the 1970s and early 1980s:

> We lived through all the phases, the historic compromise, Communist dissidence with Carillo [head of the Spanish Communist Party], with Marchais [of the French Communist Party], all the Italian polemics with the Soviets, with the Chinese, the discussions of Prague. . . .
> We experienced the crisis of Italian communism before Gorbachev. I witnessed all my friends who had been so committed, who had been through the bombing in Vietnam, who had been in Cuba, who had been to fight in Angola, or to help, in short, all those people began to feel uncomfortable with the [Italian Communist] Party . . . and they began to publish in the papers, they began to be in crisis, and we were struck with a good deal of confusion throughout this period, because for us the Italian Socialists were really on the back burner . . .

With support from the Europeans, Viera-Gallo founded *Chile-América*, the leading Chilean left polemical journal during the dictatorial period. *Chile-América* became a forum for left debate regarding such questions as responsibility for the fall of the Popular Unity government, necessary alliances to defeat the dictatorship, and the form and program for a transitional government. The journal was also the site for Chilean intellectuals' early explanations of socialist renovation and the reformulation of the meaning of democracy. Viera-Gallo discussed the origins of the socialist renovation process:

> The most profound motive [for the socialist renovation process] was the 1973 crisis, because it was a total defeat. Then there is the influence of exile, of international events, and of the urgency to define a left position before the country that is viable, for a country that has changed dramatically, that is another country.
> All this took us in two directions. The first was the recuperation of democratic values, for which we were struggling against Pinochet. It was absurd for us in our struggle against Pinochet, invoking the ban-

ner of human rights, democracy, and freedom if what we wanted was
the dictatorship of the proletariat. That is a contradiction, a contradiction that all the parties, including the PCCH, were facing. It was such a
strong contradiction that we couldn't avoid it. So we came to champion
democracy in all its luster because this is what we were struggling for.

The other renovation, which was much more difficult, which required
much more work, was the question of the logic of the market, because if
you want democracy, well, the only way to organize the economy collectively that we are aware of until now is through dictatorship, so it became
a very difficult question, one that still requires much more thought.

In 1983 the Pinochet regime granted Viera-Gallo permission to return
to Chile. Like his fellow MAPU-OC leaders, Viera-Gallo threw himself into
strategizing for an alliance between the Christian Democrats and the left
in Chile. Viera-Gallo played a key role in securing improved relations between sectors of the left and the Catholic Church, a role reminiscent of his
role during the Popular Unity years. For his effective work as a negotiator,
Viera-Gallo garnered the support of the Concertación to run for Congress
in the 1989 elections. In 1990 Viera-Gallo became Chile's speaker of the
House, a role that he felt demanded his greatest efforts to date as a con-
sensus-seeker.

Today as a national senator, Viera-Gallo wrestles with establishing a coherent political vision, though he finds little time to devote to the question.
He urges the left to explore systematically the relationship between democracy and the market:

In this last period, there has been a great recuperation of liberalism . . .
particularly the exaltation of the market, economic freedom, and a kind
of ignoring of the question of political freedom, leaving to one side the
whole critique of social inequality made by some liberals, some thinkers, from which socialism really emanates. I think that socialism must
recover in some sense the liberal tradition as socialists reflect on the
totality of the socialist experience.

In an interview with journalist Faride Zerán, Viera-Gallo discussed the
political and philosophical contradictions with which he lives:

It's very possible, in the course of one's life, and under distinct circumstances, to think black one day and white the next, concerning the

same issue, because that material has different meaning in different contexts. And in that sense, one has the right to be contradictory. . . .

I live the contradiction [of being a liberal and a Christian]. I am like Harlequin. Harlequin was made up of pieces. I'm a little communist, a little liberal, a little bourgeois, a little Catholic. . . . We're all made up of pieces of things, not of one great, coherent, total truth.[16]

In an important sense, José Antonio Viera-Gallo reflects the top leaders of the Chilean left today: leaders of a political class who have proved themselves able to return to national political leadership, focused on political process rather than on a comprehensive alternative vision for the country.

I like my parliamentary political role. My work has concentrated on reforming the judicial system. I hope the Concertación remains united, and I am doing everything possible to see to that. I think the best and most probable candidate for the future is Ricardo Lagos.

I feel people do what they can given the conditions in which they live, the circumstances in which they're able to participate, in other words, there is a big part of our lives not dependent upon ourselves. It depends on others. You just have to deliver yourself over to life's chances, history. I can't say I have a particular project. I hope I am contributing to making a better Chile, given the experiences we have lived. . . .

I love these expressions of Gramsci, like: "To be a pessimist reflects intelligence, optimism reflects real will." I think it's important to be pessimistic in terms of not shielding yourself from certain realities, but to be optimistic regarding the future and the possibilities. There are clearly many things that worry me a great deal, within the Concertación—those, for example, who aren't supporting Lagos, this worries me, it has to do with a bit of an idiotic vision of society. What worries me the most is that I do not exclude the possibility [that] the right will win in the next elections. And this worries me not only because I do not share many of their ideas, but because I think politically, historically, it will be very bad for the country. It would be like a return to some kind of renovated Pinochetism.

JOSÉ MIGUEL INSULZA

In a December 1998 national survey concerning the Pinochet arrest and the Chilean government's handling of the situation, Chileans from left to right gave Foreign Minister José Miguel Insulza[17] the highest approval rating of all those politicians involved in the crisis.[18] Insulza is recognized as one of Chile's foremost political strategists in the arena of international relations. Over the past five years, Insulza has been involved in the country's chief bilateral and multilateral negotiations regarding such issues as free trade, multinational investment in Chile, and the Chilean debt. Insulza's performances on these issues earned him his current cabinet post as minister of foreign relations. Insulza also has a gift for behind-the-scenes dealing, a gift he has employed since his early days in Christian left politics.

Insulza was born in a middle-class Santiago family in 1943. Like Correa's parents, Insulza's mother was a Catholic and his father a Mason. Politics was not a particular concern in Insulza's family. Rather, his father admired individual achievement. Insulza did well in school. In his systematic way, he entered the University of Chile in April and joined the Young Christian Democrats in May because, he said, he saw the Christian Democratic Party as the great new force with a number of capable leaders. Insulza would become a major Christian Democratic Party student leader and the head of the Federation of Students his last year in law school.

Insulza's narrative is frank, matter-of-fact, and a bit sarcastic. He portrays himself as personally distant from his fellow party members:

> In terms of my friends—my best friends were not my political friends. Of course I became closer with people with whom I worked closely, but my personal friends were not my political friends—not even my girl-friend was in the PDC.

Unlike the other individuals in this study, Insulza claimed to have no guiding political figures in the course of his political career and thought:

> I have to tell you that I wasn't one of those great admirers of leaders. I can't think of anyone who was a really important figure for me. I suppose Frei was [he said, in the context of our discussion of the Frei administration].

When asked about his participation in student political projects, Insulza downplayed any enthusiasm for work on behalf of the common good:

> My generation was a generation that did a great deal on behalf of the poor, worked in the urban shantytowns, in the countryside. Not me.

> I lived with my parents until the day I married at twenty-seven, and I
> liked it that way. I never liked to participate in these great projects in
> the countryside.

After graduating from law school, Insulza worked in the Ministry of
Education. In 1967 he returned to study, first at the left intellectual center and degree-awarding institute, the Latin American Social Science Faculty (FLACSO-Chile), where he studied political science, then at both the University of Chile and Catholic University, also in the field of political science.

After a good deal of internal deliberation, Insulza left the Christian
Democrats in 1969 to join the MAPU. He did not leave the PDC at the same
time as his fellow PDC-turned-MAPU members. He questioned the strategic
sensibility of forming a new party, a strategy that he worried would only
contribute to increased ideological and political tension in the country.
Like Luis Maira, Insulza was being groomed by the PDC to be a future national leader. Nevertheless, he left the PDC after what he felt were the Frei
administration's dangerous capitulations to the military following retired
army general Viaux's failed coup attempt. He became a cofounder of the
MAPU-OC, the more moderate of the New Left intellectual parties, whose
tendency was to stand behind Allende against the more radical Socialist
Party leadership.

In 1970 Insulza was awarded a scholarship to continue his political science studies at the University of Michigan. He attended the university that
year and for part of 1971, until political events at home lured him back to
Chile, where he was immediately appointed an adviser to Allende's foreign
relations minister, Clodomiro Almeyda.

Despite Insulza's interest and immersion in international relations, he
did not believe that international movements or events had had an important impact on his thinking or on the course of events in Chile in the 1960s
and early 1970s:

> In terms of international influences on my thinking then, of course
> there were things going on, Cuba, et cetera. But looking back on it all,
> I'd say that our conflicts, the way things went, were extremely national
> in focus. Chileans have always been an internally focused people.

On September 11, 1973, the day of the coup, Insulza was in Paris at-
tending a conference of the non-aligned countries. On September 12, he
flew to Buenos Aires and began to organize his family's exodus from Chile.

He sought exile in Italy, because it represented the heart of MAPU-OC's political organizing, and "they were party orders." Insulza was based in Rome from January 1974 until 1981, when he received financing to teach and do investigative work at CIDE in Mexico.

> Throughout my exile, I was the MAPU-OC's chief organizer and fundraiser. I survived personally with small academic projects. We had militants all over the world, and we were constantly organizing, strategizing to reunite and renovate what had been the Popular Unity coalition. We participated heavily in the debates between the two wings of the Popular Unity coalition. When the Socialist Party split in 1979, things were quite shaky. It affected us a good deal. We had good relations with the rest of the left. We really only fought heavily with the MAPU. I was head of the MAPU-Exterior.

Insulza sketched a detailed map of Chile's exile network, complete with political party headquarters, factions, and leaders spread across the globe. He described the arduous process of organizing the negotiations that took place in the 1980s among the many sectors of the left leadership—the meetings in East Berlin, Rome, Mexico City, Paris, and Caracas, the splits and realignments, and the rise and fall of left coalitions, including the Popular Unity coalition, the Convergence, the Democratic Alliance, the Popular Democratic Movement, and the socialist bloc. Insulza led the reuniting of the MAPU and the MAPU-OC, and as a member of MAPU's Political Commission, he was a crucial strategist in both the 1989 Concertación campaign and MAPU's joining the Chilean Socialist Party.

During this period, Insulza was also a prolific writer, best known for his work on the globalization of production and the question of United States hegemony. His writing has consistently been with an eye toward the ramifications of international trends for Chile:

> The paradox today is that while the advanced capitalist world has begun to speak of a recomposition, of a new institutional organization of production, in our countries we are still experiencing the profound crisis phase that those countries experienced much earlier.
>
> Because the great problem for us is that while the world advances toward greater regionalization, we continue looking to the horizons of the North and continue fragmented internally, realizing that we have nothing to do with our neighbors and with those at our level.[19]

While Insulza has been a strong promoter of Latin American multilateral accords, his focus over the past five years and in his present position as minister of foreign relations were on "the horizons of the North," namely, on a NAFTA accord for Chile. When questioned about his political transformations over the years, Insulza responded uncomfortably and somewhat defensively:

> I find it problematic to try to look back on what my thinking was then and compare it to what it is now. I was not among the most rebellious of that period, yet certainly I and my political group have moderated . . .
>
> That's the reality of the times, and it clearly has been appropriate for us to adapt to the political moment.

While Insulza's politics have become more moderate, he still professes a profound concern for social transformation and social equality:

> We have gotten rid of a lot of the dogma, and I view that as positive. Today we are in far better shape to confront the challenges we are all aware of, particularly the challenge of democracy, but also the challenge of justice. . . . If history has been the history of injustice, of confrontation, of class struggle, of international inequality, our history has yet to be entirely written.

In a 1995 informal editorial comment in its "gossip" section, the daily *El Mercurio* criticized Insulza for his performance at the funeral of Socialist Party leader and former senator Aniceto Rodríguez. At the funeral, Insulza joined his fellow socialists in the singing of the party anthem, "The Marseilles," which *El Mercurio* stated had not been "renovated" for the times. Specifically, *El Mercurio* disapproved of the foreign relations minister's singing of a line alluding to the "imperialist creature" when he was in the midst of "negotiations with the 'imperialist creature' regarding the incorporation of Chile into NAFTA."[20] While *El Mercurio*'s jab was in jest, the image of Insulza singing the anthem reflects the old, seemingly sentimental attachments long overshadowed by "modern," pragmatic, moderated perspectives that leaders like Insulza harbor.

POLITICAL ENTREPRENEURS COMPARED

Samuel Huntington claimed that he who organizes his country's politics holds the key to his country's future.[21] Of the four cognitive orientations presented in this study, the political entrepreneurs as a group have consistently been the top "players" in their generation's left Chilean politics. They are keen judges and interpreters of the political moment. They possess a talent for negotiating and strategizing and for forging and severing alliances.

It is no coincidence that three of the five political entrepreneurs came from the MAPU, an extremely small yet ideologically and strategically significant New Left party. In 1969, the MAPU represented the political entrepreneurs' perfect achievement. The party's top membership was composed of elements of the most important political and educational elite networks in the country, including some of the left elite of the Catholic University Law School and the young left elite of the Christian Democratic Party. Together, these networks housed a revolutionary political ideology within a Leninist vanguard party structure. It was an explosive formula that, as Enrique Correa alluded in his interview, its founders would later regret. Nevertheless, the political entrepreneurs from this grouping would be primary architects in the transition from military rule and the postauthoritarian government.

Today the ideas housed within the Socialist Party–Party for Democracy bloc are not totalizing, proactive projects. Rather, they tend to take the form of defensive postures within a neoliberal economic framework and a political scenario highly sensitive to the demands of the civilian right and the military—thus the language of "defense" of the poor and disenfranchised, "protection" of the old, "defense" of human rights.[22]

Chilean political analyst Antonio Cortés characterized the tenor of the Concertación government as "entrepreneurial." "It would be aprioristic and arbitrary to speak of the rightward shift of the government," Cortés wrote. "It is really an 'entrepreneurialization,' due to the logics of its development strategy."[23] Such a characterization certainly favors the leadership embodied by this study's political entrepreneurs.

POLITICAL IDENTITY, POSTAUTHORITARIANISM IN THE 1990S, AND THE POLITICS OF THE POSSIBLE

■ The contrasts between the Chile of the 1960s and the Chile of today are apparent. Gone are the mass mobilizations in the streets and the calls for revolutionary change. Polling, focus groups, "spins," and sound bites have overtaken grandstanding, hand-pumping, and rallying militants as valued political party talents and resources.[1] While the Chilean Communist Party has by no means disappeared, it is no longer a major force in national politics. The military continues to be a significant factor, and for the past nine years, the Christian Democratic Party, the Chilean Socialist Party, and the Party for Democracy have been the leading partners in a governing alliance for democratization and peace. The Chilean executive branch and the legislature have engaged in consensus-based politics, the "politics of gentlemen."[2]

In contrast to the 1960s, brazen insularity has characterized 1990s Chilean politics. This insularity is marked by what has often been termed the "cupola politics" of the Chilean political parties and by what political thinker Luis Maira first termed an "encapsulation" of political decision making within the executive branch. Sociologist Tomás Moulián asserts that "an exaggerated political elitism" best describes contemporary Chilean politics.[3] Certainly this is not atypical of regime transitions.[4] And in Chile, where political and ideological divides ran deep and the repression of politics was so prolonged, it should not be surprising that throughout the 1990s, the *process* of consensus-building within the political elite appears to have dominated politics as much as program itself.

Underlying this elite insularity and consensus are complex and instructive realities. First, in addition to the institutional parameters of the 1980 constitution, a crucial source of the encapsulation and consensus of the past decade has been latent fear. This fear has been based on memories of the political chaos and traumas of the past, memories that have limited the political imagination and that may not prove a sound long-term basis for consensus. As the 1990s draw to a close and the December 1999 presidential elections loom large, renewed sectarianism is publicly resurfacing, playing upon the very fears that served as the basis for transitional government unity. For those political leaders vested in sustaining the Concertación alliance, it has become a worrisome political moment.

Second, in spite of (or even as a result of) memories of political trauma, there are those political elites who remain committed to totalizing ideologies that are virtually frozen in a past, as well as those who place tremendous value on mass mobilization and on militant party recruitment. Since the December 1997 congressional elections, such leaders are reemerging as prominent figures.

Finally, in light of the results of the 1997 elections and the upcoming presidential elections, innovative political thinking is taking place with regard to a progressive agenda. Though inspired by past visions and memories, this thinking is cognizant of dramatic political changes and a new political moment. Much of it centers on "repoliticizing the political," that is, empowering citizens to feel vested in Chile's future through their participation in local political discussion and debate.

This book centers on how individual elite political identities are formed and internalized, as well as how such identities both respond to and are privileged by particular political moments. The study advances a model to address these questions, to explore how individual elites have conceptualized their political visions, practices, and the meanings they derive from their participation in this political process. Intensive exploration of the leaders presented here reveals a broad panorama of identities on the Chilean left. Within that context, this study has arrived at a model of cognitive ideal-types, types whose members vary in their preoccupation with ideas and organizational forms and in their responses to traumatic political experiences. While individual human beings are clearly quite complex and multidimensional, I argue here that individuals possess core political identities, which form early in life and which continue to shape their political behaviors and approaches.

This concluding chapter will take a final look at contemporary Chilean politics and debates through the lens of the individual cognitive types. It will focus on political understandings and roles among different cognitive types today, including individual perspectives on the relationships among democracy, socialism, and modernization. I suggest here that the study of individual political identity is a useful approach for uncovering the political culture of a society itself, the patterns of doing politics that are cast and recast, at play with the historical moment.

For those who have been designated political party loyalists, the party as organization is paramount to conceptualizations of their visions and roles in politics. Party loyalists sustain ideologies and images from the past, working to assure their parties' popular bases and solid cadres. Based on my examination of the lives and texts of the party loyalists of this study, as well as other research, I suggest that party loyalists in general enjoyed positions of greatest prominence in the 1960s mobilizations and the victory of Salvador Allende, where their priorities and skills were most valued and where largely working class–based sectors experienced comparative visibility and power. Party loyalists also worked to sustain their parties organizationally during the trauma of the dictatorship's early years, when many were repressed or withdrew from politics altogether.

The images and representations of the 1960s and the Popular Unity period continue to be the dominant referents in the ideological and activist formulations of party loyalists today. In moments of traumatic political crisis, such as the 1973 coup d'état, party loyalists fight for their parties' survival. Their memories of such trauma bind them to their parties, even as those parties ebb in prominence and/or viability.

Current Communist Party leader Jorge Insunza, who best fits the party loyalist ideal-type, has evidenced no visible ideological transformation from his identity of the 1960s to his identity of today. He remains frozen in Leninist conceptualizations of internal party structure and the role of the political party in society. Memories of traumatic political experiences have served to affirm his ideological convictions and political actions. Despite his defensiveness regarding the PCCH's relationship to liberal democracy in Chile, Insunza continues to view socialism as an end signifying society's redistribution of wealth and some form of public ownership of the means of production. He continues to believe in the need for a vanguard party representing the popular sectors, albeit not limited to the working class.

Today Insunza struggles to reassert the PCCH as a voice for the popular sectors. As a "preacher," he acts as a "moral conscience" for today's left. He and the Communist Party protest Chile's neoliberal economic policies, pointing to the greatest disparities between rich and poor that the country has ever known and to the lack of popular participation in everyday political practice. While there has been a tendency to dismiss the PCCH as inconsequential, the party garnered a surprising 4.98 percent of the national vote in the December 1993 elections and 7.5 percent of the vote in the December 1997 elections, making it an important ally or foe in any potential reconfiguration of a left coalition. Inspired by his early ideological convictions, Insunza continues to concentrate on organizing the Communist Party as a vehicle for the disenfranchised and disillusioned.

The Allendistas—the personal loyalists of this study—represent a different kind of moral conscience. Personal loyalists Aníbal Palma, Hernán Del Canto, and Eduardo Reyes invoke the memory of Allende as a political and ideological symbol of socialist commitment to a progressive, nationalist agenda and to formal democratic institutions. Like party loyalists, personal loyalists are party organizers. In moments of political crisis, they cling to their leaders, seeking political identity in the public attributes for which their leaders are recognized or remembered.

It is no coincidence that personal and political party loyalists are embedded largely within the Chilean working class and the lower middle class. Their structure of opportunities, or access to important alternative professional and political networks, such as educational elite networks, is limited. Historical working-class networks, such as the trade union movement, have been considerably weakened and now no longer represent the political force they once were in Chilean politics. Personal and political party loyalists have a strong tendency to elevate the 1960s period, in which working-class movements enjoyed perceptibly greater social and political power and could be greater sources of mobility than they are today. This would suggest that class embeddedness powerfully shapes political identity.

Personal and political party loyalists represent continuity within contemporary Chilean political culture. Compared with the Popular Unity period, the immediate aftermath of the coup, and even the 1983–1986 mobilizations against Pinochet, the personal and political party loyalists were seemingly invisible in postauthoritarian transition politics. This reflected a larger contemporary Chilean phenomenon: a civil society that was politically silent during the 1990s. Personal and party loyalists, though effective organizers, still lack the professional and political networks and the political imagination that might spark renewed interest in political participation. Resources and imagination are particularly important in a society deeply wounded by ideological polarization and repressive authoritarian rule.[5]

Nevertheless, one party loyalist who also possesses political imagination is Patricio Rivas, whose cognitive framework tends to approach that of a political thinker. Rivas seeks to rebuild a collective inspired by his subjective image of his former party, the Revolutionary Left Movement, the MIR. For

Rivas, the MIR was a serious, ethical, idealistic, youthful party, impervious to the institutional parameters of traditional Chilean political society. Chided for his insistence that the Brazilian Workers Party (PT) was a useful model for the Chilean left, Rivas actively denied the conventional wisdom that such a collective no longer exists. Rivas does admit that a democratic socialist project linking civil and political society has yet to be formulated:

> What I've come to conclude is that the construction of a revolutionary leadership, in the strictest sense of being anticapitalist, is of such complexity that we don't really understand it well. To construct a leadership of men and women who are capable of launching an anticapitalist program, of having a concrete national strategy to meet each challenge . . . we don't know how to do that yet. . . .
>
> The Chilean social structure has clearly changed dramatically, and it has significant meaning for what has been the historic class base for Chilean left parties. I don't believe that the working class has gone away, as many have suggested. In fact, the working class has increased. But, yes, it is far more disaggregated. It is no longer a working class with its great centers, "locatable," you know what I mean? Second, this whole capitalist consciousness, oriented around competition, individualism, is the product of the destruction of cultural links that had existed for decades prior to the dictatorship. And third, in psychosocial terms, this capitalist consciousness, a product of both the dictatorship and the defeat of the left, means that people today require success and they require new things. It can't be like the sixties, where you evoke images of the great utopias, although certainly the utopian aspect remains a part of your reflections politically. . . .
>
> I think we must distance ourselves, in a solidaristic way, from the "real socialist" models, proposing a project that is democratic, socialist, anticapitalist. We have to recuperate our sense of adventure and launch, rather than a revolutionary socialist project of armed struggle of the sixties, a democratic socialist project today. . . .
>
> I really think that what is happening in the world, I really believe this, is that the conditions are being created to create a society that is enormously just. They already exist. What was once a highly utopian discourse, today is much more possible to achieve. I think it is possible to design a project that draws from the classic republican discourse on the citizen, who has the right to decide and to be involved, together with a new socialism, emerging from civil society.

In contrast to the political party loyalists, the political thinkers of this study are idea-focused rather than organization-focused. While personal and political party loyalists have been agents of survival and continuity, Chilean political thinkers have been agents of change. Political thinkers played crucial roles in their parties during the late 1970s, a period of political reflection and reassessment that produced radically new visions regarding the role of the political party and social transformation. The best fit within this ideal-type is former Communist Party leader Fernando Contreras, who, unlike Patricio Rivas, feels little loyalty for his past affiliation. Contreras's architectural role in conceiving the PCCH's armed rebellion strategy during the dictatorship reflected an individual completely uninhibited by his country's objective conditions and his party's organizational limits. The Leipzig Group's promotion of arming and training young militants to combat the Pinochet regime was inspired by Guevarist notions of the revolutionary socialist man, whose combative energies were matched by his ethics and sense of sacrifice for the common good. Such a strategy proved suicidal and, in fact, sacrificed a significant number of young people. Contreras now ponders the psychosocial dimensions of political action, uncertain of his organizational fit. He, I would argue, is representative of a larger group of former revolutionary intellectuals and activists who have been alienated from the entrepreneurial politics characteristic of the better part of the 1990s.[6]

Political entrepreneurs represent those who tightly link ideas with the organizational expressions necessary to carry them out. As consummate strategists, political entrepreneurs attempt to realize their visions by drawing together strands of key networks. Major political experiences sharply influence political entrepreneurs, and they are skillful at adapting to changed political conditions, reworking ideas and organizational forms. Political entrepreneurs have the capacity to draw from and organize resources and political imagination. Based on my study of those whom I term entrepreneurs, I would argue that while entrepreneurs have always played prominent roles in Chilean politics, the 1990s have favored their hierarchy of values and skills unlike any other type.

In Chile today, it is the political entrepreneurs who have championed a political discourse of "modernization." For former Communist Party youth leader Raúl Oliva, modernization requires that the left understand "a world where individuality has become so pronounced," and where the "eight hundred thousand businessmen" of the country are confident regarding Chile's economic direction. For Clarisa Hardy, the Chilean Socialist Party must at least project a "modern image" in whatever way it can if it is to sustain popular support. Precisely what modernization means or looks like for these political entrepreneurs remains vague, however.

José Antonio Viera-Gallo argues that the Chilean modernization process is making politics less central for important sectors of society's citizenry:

> Chilean citizens are more modern today. Politics have become relativized, and while still influential, politics has little probability of touching the world of the economy. Here businessmen couldn't care less about politics. They go on with their businesses, they export, et cetera, it's not an issue, and many people, whether they're professionals or well-paid workers, why should they care? Now the problem is that there are many in Chilean society who are poor, who can only emerge and have their demands felt through politics, so parties are somewhat the expression of that part of society, the more backward part of society, not the modern part, because the modern part doesn't need parties.

Viera-Gallo makes a provocative distinction between those in society whom he terms "modern," and the "more backward party of society," Chile's poor. His comments allude to contemporary intellectual debates on the meaning of modernity for Latin America, in which Latin Americans see a hybridization of the modernization process in their societies.[7] "Modern" lifestyles, practices, and technologies are juxtaposed against "backward" living conditions of abject poverty and the lack of basic amenities. Viera-Gallo suggests that modern man can be free of politics, while the poor require representation to have their needs expressed. He downplays the importance of political participation or ethics in the course of modernization.

Political entrepreneur Enrique Correa has elevated the discourse of modernization to new heights. In a 1995 opinion editorial, Correa argued that the Chilean modernization process required not only primary and secondary school educational reform but also the development of Chile's capacity to "export intelligence, creativity, [and] knowledge" as one of its potential comparative advantages in the world market.[8] "The struggle to be competitive on the world market is not only nor principally a question of material production, but rather an intelligence contest in which knowledge and information are a key factor."[9] Correa views modernization as a process of acquiring knowledge.

What appears to be absent from the entrepreneurs' adoption of modernization into contemporary political discourse is any questioning or critique of modernization itself. It is as if modernization has become the new ideology for a future Chile. The discourse of modernization is widely accepted and is also employed by the political right. There is something self-assured and safe about the images that modernity conveys—access to material desires, market freedoms, educational excellence, freedom from the state, and so forth. For political entrepreneurs, ideas of modernization can be ably expressed in their political party caucuses and coalitions without provoking protest or backlash.

I would argue that underneath the entrepreneurs' use of a consensus-based language of modernization has been an exaggerated fear of political conflict, stemming from a political legacy that continues to haunt protagonists of the Chilean left. Enrique Correa recognized that his fellow members of the left political class have little taste for political conflict today:

> There was indeed a loss of control before 1973. I think none of us really had experienced the degree of political conflict like that under Allende. We are extremely uncomfortable with conflict. The president of the country was always considered like a kind of father figure, authoritative, his hand conferred the blessing or not. . . . It is really too much fear of conflict, and too much fear of freedom, to put it another way. . . .
>
> I think there is also a great deal of fear in this country regarding institutional conflicts. If you look, for example, at the recent moves concerning constitutional reform and at the supreme control that the executive has been able to exercise over the nature of the reform, that there was fear over the creation of a mixed committee of congressmen and senators, something perfectly democratic, that the socialists would constitute one front, the right the other, et cetera, it was clear that the memories of legislative battles over the constitution under Allende were still fresh and still scare us.

There is no question that memories of the political conflicts and traumas of the past have deeply influenced all of Chile's political protagonists. Throughout the texts of my interviewees is the message that their own sense of failure has led to their determination not to fail again. Nevertheless, how "not to fail" holds different meanings for distinct cognitive types. Party loyalists concentrate their efforts on stronger, more disciplined, and better organized political parties. Allendistas promote the man they feel embodied love for Chile and its democratic institutions.

Political entrepreneurs have championed a "politics of consensus" political style at the expense of bolder political projects. Translated into the politics of transition from authoritarianism, this has meant a gradual, careful promotion of social, political, and electoral policy reforms within an extremely presidentialist constitutional framework and virtual autonomy for Chile's armed forces. Political entrepreneurs have shrunk from the challenge of a comprehensive political vision for Chile's future, or even a more nuanced adaptation of the ideology of modernization.

Political thinkers have tended to be more critical of consensus politics and the new ideology of modernization, though their critiques have not been accompanied by proposals for alternative policy directions. Drawing from modernization and dependency debates of the 1960s, many (though not all) thinkers question the notion that a society in which politics becomes irrelevant and individuals are viewed primarily as producers and consumers is a meaningful or even viable basis for the common good.[10]

Socialist Party leader and current ambassador to Austria Osvaldo Puccio, who argued that the very concept of modernization came from the world's left, challenged fellow socialists to "repoliticize" their politics by moving away from consensus politics and adopting an explicit democratic socialist program for the Socialist Party. Unlike Viera-Gallo's version, Puccio's conceptualization of modernization emphasizes an "ethical, utopian content." Modernization would be led by "secular man," striving for a socially just society of citizens. Puccio continues to be inspired by 1960s globalizing visions, though he recognizes a global left teleological crisis.[11] In ways analogous to the views of political thinker and Chilean ambassador to Mexico Luis Maira, Puccio observes Chilean politics largely from abroad, engrossed in Austrian civil society movements and intellectual currents.

Like Patricio Rivas and Osvaldo Puccio, former Communist Party youth leader and political thinker Antonio Leal also links a future socialist agenda to the discourse of citizenship, couched in the language of modernization. Unlike Rivas, however, Leal does not believe it necessary that a radical democratic project be anticapitalist. In a 1994 opinion editorial on ideological debates taking place within the Socialist Party, Leal challenged the left to abandon both the idea of revolution and the doctrine of Marxism. He urged the left to concentrate on deepening democracy and elaborating a "democratic politics of the market":

> Today we can talk of socialist ideals and action as the way toward a
> broader form of democracy and, as such, the way toward configuring a

new map of social rights, of citizenship rights and of those rights linked to a new planetary structure of the world and to an overcoming of the world's great contradictions. . . .

[We need] a left which grasps the critiques of the present, broadening the practice of democracy to all those who inhabit a pluralist society capable of generating a democratic project for a modern society. This, without the need to insist on the overcoming of the confines of capitalism, in favor of a communitarian and solidaristic society more humane than the present. . . .

This is the alternative: Either a neoconservative individualism in a totally exclusionary society, or a democratic individuality that does not relegate the responsibility of one's fate to the state, but instead demands that the state guarantee the conditions in which all can be free and responsible, without baseline conditions of inferiority.[12]

For Leal, socialism is no longer an end but a process. Socialism is a means to deepen democracy, which he understands as the recognition of a broad range of rights in a diverse, tolerant, pluralistic society. This echoes much of the renovationist thinking that took place in the Chilean left during the late 1970s and early 1980s—a newfound appreciation of civil and political as well as social and economic rights.

The political thinkers are embedded in a dynamic relationship with their political parties and their government, constrained by their institutions yet challenging them to reinvigorate the left programmatically. In June 1998 Leal was a key drafter of "The People Are Right," a document signed by prominent party leaders and policy makers. "The People Are Right" was a response to a document produced the previous month by high government officials, titled "Renovating the Concertación: The Force of Our Ideas." Leal's group found the previous document too self-congratulatory regarding the 1990s Concertación record. Leal himself maintained that "The Force of Our Ideas" was "an institutional interpretation," not "from civil society" but rather from the "debatable premise that Chileans are already integrated into the fruits of modernization without recognizing sufficiently that an essential part of the country is still excluded and lives in a Chile far from it." Leal criticized the previous document as "elitist," as coming from a "technocratic efficiency camp," rather than from a dimension inclusionary of "political values" and "citizen's rights."[13]

José Antonio Viera-Gallo apears to represent the "elitist" sector to whom Leal is referring:

I feel my views are very well represented by the "Renovating the Concertación" document, in terms of very basic things. I feel we're on a
good road as a country, we live the contradictions of a very accelerated
modernization, transformation process, to which there is a demand to
imprint upon it a more humane, more just, more solidaristic sense.
Not to deny we are in a progressive mode already, but there is a
demand for a more human progress. As this document says, however,
perhaps the most complicated challenge of where we are is that there is
a serious part of the political elite which has lost confidence in this
project, because they have a wrong diagnosis, in my view, of where the
country is. . . . There is a confusion of ideas, and of feelings about
what's going on, which we try to take on in this document.

So my feeling is that the most important thing is that we persevere
with our project, recognizing that there are problems we have to take
on, things we must do, for example in terms of health, in terms of the
university system, in terms of unemployment questions.

I feel that the confusion comes when people expect from politics
what politics can't give. So that when someone says, "Look, what's
going on is that people are less happy. People feel more insecure."
Politics is lost here. Politics can't give this. It produces a great deal of
dissatisfaction. The public sector cannot be expected to resolve many
problems that are, on the one hand, individual problems, or, on the
other hand, conditions of the society that are universal ones! We can't
be expected to be this great idyllic Chile that at the same time is growing, exporting, that people live better, but they're not consumerist, or
whatever, I just don't see how we can do that.

Thus, public differences over programmatic emphasis and discourse have
now begun to appear in earnest. How this will translate into programmatic policy, however, is not clear. Election campaigns for the Chilean president who will launch his country into the new millennium have begun in
earnest. The first half of 1999 was marked by a very public struggle between Christian Democratic presidential hopeful Andrés Zaldívar and Party for Democracy–Socialist Party candidate Ricardo Lagos over who would
represent the Concertación alliance on the December 1999 ballot. The
struggle between the two men, interestingly enough, indicates little in the
way of programmatic differences. Rather, it focused on personality differences, party loyalties and affiliations, and, last but certainly not least, allu-
sions to Socialist Party performance in the executive during the Popular

Unity years. In many ways, the Zaldívar-Lagos rivalry has been about proving and disproving claims regarding continuities with the past, including bitter memories of pre-1973 partisan struggles.

Few would deny that this has been the most interesting period in Chilean politics since the return to democratic rule in 1990. The arrest of Pinochet in London colors all current analysis of Chilean politics, society, and culture, particularly as the country has firmly initiated presidential campaign politics for the 1999 elections. Yet important shifts in the political current were evident before Pinochet's October 16 arrest, symbolized best by the December 1997 elections, the increasingly tense political rivalry between Andrés Zaldívar and Ricardo Lagos, and the acts, reflections, and debates surrounding the twenty-fifth anniversary of the 1973 military coup d'état. The *"política de acuerdos,"* the "cupola" politics, the "politics among gentlemen" that have marked the past decade have been shaken, challenged by political discord and by the deep-rooted and inescapable conflicts of the past, which continue to "presence" themselves in uncomfortable ways.

In a paradoxical sense, the Chilean political class is now immersed in a battle it had very much hoped to avoid: all must confront, albeit through a polarized set of interpretive lenses, the political past. Until recently political elites had engaged in a kind of "forgetting," or silence, about the past thirty or more years. For members of the left political class, memories of the past were too painful and guilt-ridden, and left leaders in government felt they had already expressed remorse for past mistakes.

Members of the left political class have often dismissed calls to examine the past by claiming that society is uninterested in such revisiting. They point to surveys that indicate that Chileans are most preoccupied with personal security, a stable and healthy economy, education for their children, and so forth. They point to the low turnouts to commemorations of the past, to dedications attended only by families directly affected by the violence or by Communist Party activists. This is certainly true at one level. Yet there are other indicators that suggest that Chileans are strongly interested in—even obsessed with, though publicly repressing such obsession—the past. Over the past two years, for example, books about the Allende period, the military coup, the years of repression, and the broad question of reconciliation have topped best-seller lists in Chile.[14] Television networks record all-time-high public viewership of special television documentaries or debates on the 1960s, the Popular Unity years, the coup, the Letelier case. Citizens' preoccupations with the past have been expressed over the last decade in much the same ways that political debate itself has taken place in Chile in the 1990s (and for much of the past twenty-five years, for that matter)—behind closed doors, within the family, and in private meetings.

In spite of political class desires to "forget" the past, to move on, to avoid tense and unresolvable disagreements over who was wrong and why "it" happened, political "irruptions" have become closer and closer together, and the unanticipated arrest of Pinochet (who is termed in *all* the major Chilean press as the senator and "former President of the Republic," as opposed to the international press's terming him "the former dictator") has forced political memories, for better or for worse, into full view of Chile and the world.

A recent national survey found that only 41 percent of the Chilean population believes that national reconciliation about the past is possible.[15] Divides run very deep. The politically charged generations that lived through the late 1960s, the Popular Unity government, the dictatorship and redemocratization can readily recall traumatic political memories, and perspectives regarding the roots of such trauma are well formulated and unchanging.

Close attention to individual leaders of the left reveals a broad ideological mosaic that includes major transformations as well as continuities in left thinking concerning means and visions of the common good. Nevertheless, despite traumatic political events and historic changes, individuals' basic approaches to politics—that is, individual cognitive frameworks—do not change, from their early activism in politics to the present. Political identity represents the often fitful product of individual cognitive frameworks that deliberate and act amid such trauma and change.

NOTES

Introduction

1. The concept of cognitive frameworks developed in this book draws to some degree from the work of Erik Erikson and from Kristen Renwick Monroe, Michael C. Barton, and Ute Klingemann, "Altruism and the Theory of Rational Action: An Analysis of Rescuers of Jews in Nazi Europe," in Kristen Renwick Monroe, ed., *The Economic Approach to Politics: A Critical Reassessment of the Theory of Rational Action* (New York: HarperCollins, 1991), pp. 325–330. As Erikson has emphasized, identity is intimately tied to the perceptions of one's self in relation to others. See "The Problem of Ego Identity," in *Identity and the Life Cycle* (New York: Norton, 1980), p. 109.

2. The term *embeddedness* is used predominantly by sociologists to counter a dominant tendency in the social sciences that views individual behavior as somehow autonomous or as analytically separate from the social relations of which individuals form a part. As Mark Granovetter argues, embeddedness emphasizes the notion that individual behavior and individual social institutions "are so constrained by ongoing social relations that to construe them as independent is a grievous misunderstanding." See Granovetter, "Economic Action and Social Structure: The Problem of Embeddedness," *American Journal of Sociology* 91, no. 3 (November 1985): 482.

3. Karl Mannheim, *Ideology and Utopia: An Introduction to the Sociology of Knowledge* (San Diego: Harcourt, Brace, Jovanovich, 1985), p. 36.

4. While Erikson's classic studies *Young Man Luther* (New York: Norton, 1958) and *Ghandi's Truth* (New York: Norton, 1969) are the most recognized of his studies on identity, see also "The Problem of Ego Identity," in *Identity and the Life Cycle*, pp. 109–174.

5. Clifford Geertz's essays from the 1960s were gathered in what has now become a classic for those studying the broad questions of meaning and identity: *The Interpretation of Cultures* (New York: Basic Books, 1973). A rational actor–oriented challenge to Geertz's assertion is Abner Cohen, *Two-Dimensional Man: An Essay on the Anthropology of Power and Symbolism in Complex Society* (Berkeley: University of California Press, 1974). Political scientist David Laitin provides a useful synopsis of these distinct approaches in his influential *Hegemony and Culture: Politics and Reli-*

gious Change Among the Yoruba (Chicago: University of Chicago Press, 1986). Anthropologist Kay Warren's *The Symbolism of Subordination: Indian Identity in a Guatemalan Town* (Austin: University of Texas Press, 1978) is largely inspired by Geertz and has become an important reference. Virginia Domínguez's *People as Subject, People as Object: Selfhood and Peoplehood in Contemporary Israel* (Madison: University of Wisconsin Press, 1989), brings the dimension of power firmly into identity debates. James Scott's *The Moral Economy of the Peasant* (New Haven: Yale University Press, 1976) and *Weapons of the Weak: Everyday Forms of Peasant Resistance* (New Haven: Yale University Press, 1985) are also essential political science references on identity construction.

6. See, for example, David Laitin, *Hegemony and Culture*, and Juan Linz and Alfred Stepan, "Political Identities and Electoral Sequences: Spain, the Soviet Union, and Yugoslavia," *Daedalus* 121 (Spring 1992): 123–139, in which the authors signal the importance of state crafting, particularly the choice of all-union versus regional elections, in regime transition. For an altogether distinct model linking individual identity to nation building and national identity, see William Bloom, *Personal Identity, National Identity, and International Relations* (Cambridge: Cambridge University Press, 1990).

7. The groundbreaking work in this vein was Benedict Anderson's *Imagined Communities: Reflections on the Origin and Spread of Nationalism* (London: Verso, 1983). See also Robert Smith, "Los Ausentes Siempre Presentes: The Imagining, Making, and Politics of a Transnational Community Between Ticuani, Puebla, Mexico, and New York City" (Ph.D. diss., Columbia University, 1994). The concept of identity has also formed the basis for leading area-studies programs throughout the United States that have sponsored important scholarship in such areas as Chicano studies, Puerto Rican studies, and Hispanic studies. These and other literatures on identity use interdisciplinary approaches.

8. See, for example, Lewis Coser, *Men of Ideas: A Sociologist's View* (New York: Free Press, 1965); Juan Linz and Alfred Stepan, eds., *The Breakdown of Democratic Regimes* (Baltimore: Johns Hopkins University Press, 1979). For a more recent example arguing the importance of the study (and bitter condemnation) of intellectuals because of their powerful influence on society and culture, see Tony Judt, *Past Imperfect: French Intellectuals, 1944–1956* (Berkeley: University of California Press, 1992).

9. Robert E. Lane, *Political Ideology: Why the American Common Man Believes What He Does* (New York: Free Press, 1967), pp. 1–11.

10. Jennifer Hochschild, *What's Fair? American Beliefs About Distributive Justice* (Cambridge: Harvard University Press, 1981), pp. 1–26.

11. Luisa Passerini, *Fascism in Popular Memory: The Cultural Experience of the Turin Working Class* (Cambridge: Cambridge University Press, 1987), p. 8.

12. Hochschild develops this argument in *What's Fair?*, p. 24, as does Stanley Renshon, "Psychological Perspectives on Theories of Adult Development and the

Political Socialization of Leaders," in Roberta S. Sigel, ed., *Political Learning in Adulthood: A Sourcebook of Theory and Research* (Chicago: University of Chicago Press, 1989), pp. 203–264.

13. Luisa Passerini, "Memory: Resume of the Final Session of the International Conference on Oral History, Aix-en-Provence, September 26, 1982," reprinted in *History Workshop* 15 (Spring 1983): 195–196. See also Alessandro Portelli, *The Death of Luigi Trastulli and Other Stories: Form and Meaning in Oral History* (Albany: SUNY Press, 1991).

1. Interpreting Political Identity

1. Mostafa Rejai and Kay Phillips provide a useful overview of such literature in *Loyalists and Revolutionaries: Political Leaders Compared* (New York: Praeger, 1988), pp. 3–14. See also Maureen Mancuso, "The Ethical Attitudes of British MPs: A Typology," *Parliamentary Affairs* 46 (April 1993): 179–191.

2. In a recent study of Latin American revolutions, Eric Selbin criticizes political leadership studies for their failure to link leadership types and actions to revolutionary ideology, and he develops leadership categories that examine revolutionary vision and its implementation. See Selbin, *Modern Latin American Revolutions* (Boulder: Westview, 1993), pp. 74–92. A number of individual biographies of political leaders do, in fact, discuss the relationship among leaders' personalities, motivations, and political beliefs and ideals; see, for example, such classics as Erik Erikson's *Young Man Luther* (New York: Norton, 1962) and *Ghandi's Truth* (New York: Norton, 1969) and Alexander and Juliet George's *Woodrow Wilson and Colonel House: A Personality Study* (New York: Dover Publications, 1964). These, however, are intensely psychological treatments that miss important contextual elements, such as the links of individuals to class interests, groups, and political institutions. Such contextual elements are crucial to the political identity orientations presented here.

3. Erik Erikson, *Life History and the Historical Moment* (New York: Norton, 1975), p. 173.

4. For a useful discussion of individual altruism and for an inspiring general read, see Kristen Renwick Monroe, *The Heart of Altruism: Perceptions of a Common Humanity* (Princeton, N.J.: Princeton University Press, 1996). In this book Monroe also suggests individual cognitive frameworks for explaining behavior on behalf of the common good, and though our definitions and methods differ, Monroe's earlier work was an important influence on my own.

5. Kristen Renwick Monroe, ed., *The Economic Approach to Politics: A Critical Reassessment of the Theory of Rational Action* (New York: HarperCollins, 1991), p. x.

6. Norman Frohlich, "Self-Interest or Altruism: What Difference?" *Journal of Conflict Resolution* 18, no. 1 (March 1974): 57.

7. Ibid., 58.

8. For a useful overview of the influence of Olson over the past two decades, as

well as of recent challenges to concepts deeply influenced by Olson's work, see Carol McClurg Mueller, "Building Social Movement Theory," in Aldon Morris and Carol McClurg Mueller, eds., *Frontiers in Social Movement Theory* (New Haven: Yale University Press, 1992), pp. 3–25. See also Jean Cohen, "Strategy or Identity: New Theoretical Paradigms and Contemporary Social Movements," *Social Research* 52 (1985): 663–716.

9. See Kristen Renwick Monroe, Michael C. Barton, and Ute Klingemann, "Altruism and the Theory of Rational Action: An Analysis of Rescuers of Jews in Nazi Europe," in Monroe, *The Economic Approach to Politics*, pp. 325–330. For examples of rational actor theorists' approaches to altruism, see Kenneth Arrow, "Gifts and Exchanges," in E. Phelps, ed., *Altruism, Morality, and Economic Theory* (New York: Russell Sage Foundation, 1975)pp. 13–28; Gordon Becker, *The Economic Approach to Human Behavior* (Chicago: University of Chicago Press, 1976); and R. Wintrobe, "It Pays to Do Good. But Not More Good Than It Pays," *Journal of Economic Behavior and Organization* 2, no. 3 (1981): 201–213.

10. Cohen, "Strategy or Identity," p. 688.

11. Ibid., p. 677.

12. Bert Klandermans, "The Social Construction of Protest and Multiorganizational Fields," in Morris and Mueller, *Frontiers*, p. 77.

13. Cited in Morris and Mueller, *Frontiers*, p. 9.

14. William Bloom, *Personal Identity, National Identity, and International Relations* (Cambridge: Cambridge University Press, 1990), p. 47. Bloom provides an extremely useful summary of Habermas's contribution to identity theories.

15. Jürgen Habermas, *Legitimation Crisis* (Boston: Beacon, 1973), p. 69.

16. Bloom, *Personal Identity*, p. 47.

17. Habermas, *Legitimation Crisis*, pp. 3–4.

18. David Laitin, *Hegemony and Culture: Politics and Religious Change Among the Yoruba* (Chicago: University of Chicago Press, 1986).

19. Ibid., pp. 19–20. See also ibid., ch. 7, "Rational Choice and Hegemony," pp. 136–169.

20. Laitin provides a detailed appendix regarding his research methodology in *Hegemony and Culture*, pp. 185–205.

21. Juan Linz and Alfred Stepan, "Political Identities and Electoral Sequences: Spain, the Soviet Union, and Yugoslavia," *Daedalus* 121 (Spring 1992): 123–139.

22. Ibid., p. 124.

23. Ibid.

24. Bloom, *Personal Identity*, p. 22.

25. Ibid., pp. 23, 25–53.

26. Ibid., p. 23.

27. Monroe, Barton, and Klingemann, "Altruism," pp. 326–328.

28. Ibid., p. 318.

29. Jane Mansbridge, "The Rise and Fall of Self-Interest in the Explanation of

Political Life," in Jane Mansbridge, ed., *Beyond Self-Interest* (Chicago: University of Chicago Press, 1990), p. 20.

30. David Johnston, "Human Agency and Rational Action," in Monroe, *The Economic Approach to Politics*, p. 95.

31. Erikson's two general theoretical works on identity are *Identity and the Life Cycle* (New York: Norton, 1980) and *Identity, Youth, and Crisis* (New York, Norton, 1968). His two classic case studies of ego identity are *Young Man Luther* and *Ghandi's Truth*. For a fairly succinct explanation of identity, see Erikson, "The Problem of Ego Identity," in *Identity and the Life Cycle*, pp. 109–174. For a brief and useful analysis of Erikson's work on identity and its potential significance for theories of international relations, see Bloom, *Personal Identity*, pp. 35–40.

32. Erikson, *Identity and the Life Cycle*, cited in Bloom, *Personal Identity*, p. 37.

33. Erik Erikson, *Life History and the Historical Moment* (New York: Norton, 1975), pp. 19–20. For a useful exploration of the self-other identification process within the field of sociology, see Orville Brim Jr. and Stanton Wheeler, *Socialization After Childhood: Two Essays* (New York: Wiley, 1966).

34. See, for example, David Snow, Louis Zurcher Jr., and Sheldon Ekland-Olson, "Social Networks and Social Movements: A Microstructural Approach to Differential Recruitment," *American Sociological Review* 45 (1980): 787–801. See also Debra Friedman and Doug McAdam, "Collective Identity and Activism: Networks, Choices, and the Life of a Social Movement," in Morris and Mueller, *Frontiers*, pp. 156–173. For a useful overview of network theory approaches, see Barry Wellman and S. D. Berkowitz, eds., *Social Structures: A Network Approach* (New York: Cambridge University Press, 1988), ch. 1. For an extremely useful social network theory application to the study of intellectuals, see Robert J. Brym, *Intellectuals and Politics* (London: Allen and Unwin), 1980.

35. Carole Pateman, "The Civic Culture: A Philosophic Critique," in Gabriel Almond and Sidney Verba, eds., *The Civic Culture Revisited* (New York: Sage, 1989), pp. 57–102. See also Wayne Cornelius and Ann Craig, "Political Culture in Mexico: Continuities and Revisionist Interpretations," in ibid., pp. 335–337.

36. Pateman, "The Civic Culture," p. 60. Works on the relationship between class status and political views are far too numerous to cite. Perhaps the best-known political socialization texts in this regard are Seymour Lipset, *Political Man* (New York: Doubleday, 1960), and Sidney Verba and N. H. Nie, *Participation in America* (New York: Harper and Row, 1974).

37. Markos J. Mamalakis, *The Growth and Structure of the Chilean Economy: From Independence to Allende* (New Haven: Yale University Press, 1976), p. 215. See also Helio Varela Carmona, "Estratificación Social de la Población Trabajadora en Chile y Su Participación en el Ingreso Nacional, 1940–1954," in *Memoria en ciencias económicas* (Santiago: Universidad de Chile, Escuela de Economía, 1958); Ricardo Lagos Escobar, *La concentración del poder económico* (Santiago: Editorial del Pacífico, 1961); ECLA, *Economic Survey of Latin America, 1964* (New York: United Nations,

ECLA, 1965), p. 32; and Sergio Molina, *El proceso de cambio en Chile* (Santiago, 1972), p. 85.

38. Mamalakis, *Growth and Structure*, p. 217.

39. Indeed, it is no small coincidence that in the December 1993 presidential elections, the leading contestants were Eduardo Frei Jr. and Arturo Alessandri, the son and nephew, respectively, of former Chilean presidents.

40. For a useful historical and analytical lens on the politicization of the university, see Iván Jaksic, *Academic Rebels in Chile: The Role of Philosophy in Higher Education and Politics* (Albany: SUNY Press, 1989). See also Patricia Weiss Fagen, *Chilean Universities: Problems of Autonomy and Dependence* (Beverly Hills: Sage, 1973). For accounts of this relationship during the late 1960s and 1970s, see Manuel Antonio Garretón, "Universidad y política en los procesos de transformación y reversión en Chile, 1967–1977," *Estudios Sociales* 26, no. 4 (1980): 83–109.

41. For a classic conceptualization of a generational analysis to understanding history and social change, see Karl Mannheim, "The Problem of Generations" (1928), in Philip Altbach and Robert Laufer, eds., *The New Pilgrims: Youth Protest in Transition* (New York: McKay, 1972), pp. 101–138. This anthology includes several analyses of the sixties generation as a unique twentieth-century cohort. For an overview of the generational debate, see Michael Delli Carpini, "Age and History: Generations and Sociopolitical Change," in Roberta S. Sigel, ed., *Political Learning in Adulthood: A Sourcebook of Theory and Research* (Chicago: University of Chicago Press, 1989), pp. 11–55. See also Vern Bengston, Michael Furlong, and Robert Laufer, "Time, Aging, and the Continuity of Social Structure: Themes and Issues in Generational Analysis," *Journal of Social Issues* 30, no. 2 (1974): 1–30.

42. Examples of the former include Ronald Inglehart, *The Silent Revolution* (Princeton, N.J.: Princeton University Press, 1977), and M. Kent Jennings and Richard Niemi, *The Political Character of Adolescence: The Influence of Families and Schools* (Princeton, N.J.: Princeton University Press, 1974). Examples of the latter are Karl Mannheim's classic "The Problem of Generations," and Richard Braungart and Margaret Braungart, "Political Career Patterns of Radical Activists in the 1960s and 1970s: Some Historical Comparisons," *Sociological Focus* 13 (1980): 237–254.

43. José Antonio Viera-Gallo, *Chile: Un nuevo camino* (Santiago: CESOC, 1989), p. 21.

44. Ibid., pp. 29–30.

45. On Vietnam veterans, see Robert Laufer, "The Aftermath of War: Adult Socialization and Political Development," in Sigel, *Political Learning*, pp. 415–457. On Holocaust victims, see Irving Louis Horowitz, "The Texture of Terrorism: Socialization, Routinization, and Integration," in Sigel, *Political Learning*, pp. 386–414. Sigel's edited volume provides a series of excellent critiques of the limits to standard political socialization arguments, whose conventional wisdom holds that individuals' political worldviews tend to be formed and fixed by adolescence. The authors assume that "political attitudes, preferences, interest and involvement in

politics" depend less "on a person's cognitive maturity than on his or her life expe-riences—education, occupation, reference group, and the times in which the per-son lives. Here is where we can anticipate considerable change with chronological age and change in life circumstances" (Sigel, *Political Learning,* p. 1).

46. One of the chief initiators of these inquiries was Salvadoran social psychol-ogist and former academic vice rector of the José Simeón Canas University Ignacio Martín Baró, who was one of several Jesuit priests murdered in their residency in 1989. His most influential works included *Guerra y salúd mental* (San Salvador: UCA, 1984) and *Acción e ideología* (San Salvador: UCA, 1985). Chilean pioneers in this field include social psychologists Elizabeth Lira, María Isabel Castillo, David Becker, Valentina Arcos, Julia Cienfuegos, and Cristina Monelli. Important compi-lations of their work can be found in David Becker and Elizabeth Lira, eds., *Dere-chos humanos: Todo es según el dolor con que se mira* (Santiago, ILAS: 1990); Eliza-beth Lira and María Isabel Castillo, *Psicología de la amenaza política y del miedo* (Santiago: ILAS, 1991); and the Fundación de Ayuda Social de las Iglesias Cris-tianas, *Escritos sobre exilio y retorno (1978–1984)* (Santiago: FASIC, 1984).

47. An important note of clarification is in order here. While I have termed a se-lect group of individuals in this study the "thinkers," this is in no way meant to imply that those in other categories of my typology do not think. Indeed, all of the participants of this study are extremely intelligent and reflective individuals.

48. The term *irruption* has been coined by political scientist Alexander Wilde. See his "Irruptions of Memory: Expressive Politics in Chile's Transition to Democ-racy" (paper presented to the Authoritarian Legacies Working Group of the Insti-tute of Latin American and Iberian Studies, Columbia University, Buenos Aires, Argentina, August 27–29, 1998).

49. Karl Mannheim, *Ideology and Utopia: An Introduction to the Sociology of Knowledge* (San Diego: Harcourt, Brace, Jovanovich, 1985), p. 236.

2. Chile's Revolutionary Generation

1. For an excellent account and analysis of the post-1973 trajectories of the two dominant parties of the Popular Unity coalition, the Chilean Socialist and Com-munist parties, see Kenneth Roberts, "In Search of a New Identity: Dictatorship, Democracy, and the Evolution of the Left in Chile and Peru" (Ph.D. diss., Stanford University, 1992).

2. For a description of the process of "renovation" of important sectors of the Chilean Socialist Party from 1973 to the mid-1980s, see Ignacio Walker, *Socialis-mo y democracia: Chile y Europa en perspectiva comparada* (Santiago: CIEPLAN-HACHETTE, 1990). There are also several published memoirs, as well as per-sonal interview and essay collections, that recount this process and their roles in it, including Jorge Arrate, *El retorno verdadero: Textos políticos, 1987–1991* (Santi-ago: Ediciones Ornitorrinco, 1991); Alexis Guardia, *Chile, país centauro: Perfil del socialismo renovado* (Santiago: Ediciones BAT, 1990); Ricardo Lagos, *Democracia*

para Chile: Proposiciones de un Socialista (Santiago: Puhuén Editores, 1985); José Antonio Viera-Gallo, *Chile: Un nuevo camino* (Santiago: CESOC, 1990); and Hernán Vodanovic, *Un socialismo renovado para Chile* (Santiago: Editorial Andante, 1988).

3. Among the most path-breaking works in this vein are Norbert Lechner, *Los patios interiores de la democracia: Subjetividad y política* (Santiago: FLACSO, 1988); José Joaquín Brunner, *La cultura autoritaria en Chile* (Santiago: FLACSO, 1981); Pilar Vergara, "Las transformaciones del estado chileno bajo el régimen militar," in FLACSO, eds., *Chile: 1973–198?* (Santiago: FLACSO, 1983), pp. 65–104; Brunner, "La cultura política del autoritarianismo," in *Chile: 1973–198?*, pp. 211–228; and Eugenio Tironi, *Autoritarismo, modernización, y marginalidad* (Santiago: Ediciones SUR, 1990).

In addition, several Chilean social psychiatrists have been among the pioneers in work on the effects of political repression on Latin American culture and society. See, among others, Elizabeth Lira, "Consecuencias psicosociales de la represion en Chile," *Revista de psicología de El Salvador* 7, no. 28 (1988): 143–159; Elizabeth Lira, David Becker, Juana Kovalskys, Elena Gómez, and María Isabel Castillo, "Daño social y memoria colectiva: Perspectivas de reparación," in David Becker and Elizabeth Lira, eds., *Derechos humanos: Tódo es según el dolor con que se mira* (Santiago: ILAS, 1989), pp. 195–213; and Elizabeth Lira and María Isabel Castillo, *Psicología de la amenaza política y del miedo* (Santiago: ILAS-CESOC, 1991).

4. I am grateful to Tomás Moulián for his clarification of this point with me in an interview in November 1993.

5. Until quite recently, it was difficult not to note the irony in much of the left's uncritical use of the term *modernization* in light of the resounding debates around the question of modernization in the late 1960s and 1970s. Chilean sociologist Manuel Antonio Garretón raised this point in an opinion editorial, "Actores sociales y gobierno: La cara oculta del problema," *Apsi* 492 (March 1995): 23. Nevertheless, over the past year, debates regarding the relationships among modernization, quality-of-life issues, and politics have begun to emerge; they will be discussed in the concluding chapter.

6. Brian Loveman, *Chile: The Legacy of Hispanic Capitalism* (New York: Oxford University Press, 1988), p. 20. For an understanding of Chile's historic dependence upon copper and its relation to the international economy, see Theodore Moran, *Multinational Corporations and the Politics of Dependence* (Princeton: Princeton University Press, 1974).

7. On the state-led industrialization process in Chile, see Marcelo Cavarozzi, "The Government and the Industrial Bourgeoisie in Chile, 1938–1964" (Ph.D. diss., University of California at Berkeley, 1975).

8. The Jorge Alessandri government (1958–1964) proclaimed a "technocratic revolution" to free the economy of state control. Eduardo Frei pronounced his administration (1964–1970) a "Revolution in Liberty." One of the popular slogans of

the Allende government was the *"vía chilena"* toward revolutionary socialism. The Augusto Pinochet regime was responsible for the *"revolución silenciosa."* See Eugenio Tironi, *Los silencios de la revolución: Chile—La otra cara de la modernización* (Santiago: Editorial La Puerta Abierta, 1988), p. 11.

9. The classic study of the Chilean political party system in the pre-1970 period is Federico Gil, *The Political System of Chile* (Boston: Cambridge University Press, 1966). For analyses of the Chilean political party system of the pre-1973 period, see Arturo Valenzuela, *The Breakdown of Democratic Regimes: Chile* (Baltimore: Johns Hopkins University Press, 1979); Adolfo Aldunate, Angel Flisfisch, and Tomás Moulián, *Estudios sobre sistemas de partidos en Chile* (Santiago: FLACSO, 1985); and Manuel Antonio Garretón, *El proceso político chileno* (Santiago: FLACSO, 1983).

10. Loveman, *Chile*, p. 265.

11. Excellent accounts of this history can be found in Charles Bergquist, *Labor in Latin America* (Stanford: Stanford University Press, 1986); Peter DeShazo, *Urban Workers and Labor Unions in Chile, 1902–1927* (Madison: University of Wisconsin Press, 1983); and Alan Angell, *Politics and the Labor Movement in Chile* (London: Oxford, 1972).

12. Bergquist, *Labor in Latin America*, pp. 47–48. For a forceful analysis of the critical juncture marking this shift in Chilean labor-capital-state relations, see Ruth Berins Collier and David Collier, *Shaping the Political Arena: Critical Junctures, the Labor Movement, and Regime Dynamics in Latin America* (Princeton: Princeton University Press, 1991).

13. Regis Debray in NACLA, eds., *New Chile* (New York: Waller Press, 1972), p. 9.

14. For a synthetic history of the PCCh, see Carmelo Furci, *The Chilean Communist Party and the Road to Socialism* (London: ZED Books, 1984). For the official account of the early years of the PCCh, see Hernán Ramírez-Necochea, *Orígen y formación del Partido Comunista de Chile* (Santiago: Editorial Austral, 1965). On Recabarren's thought, see Augusto Varas, "Ideal socialista y teoría Marxista en Chile: Recabarren y el Komintern," in Augusto Varas, ed., *El Partido Comunista en Chile* (Santiago: CESOC-FLACSO, 1988), pp. 17–63.

15. For a detailed account of the transition from the Frente Unico position of a worker-peasant alliance leading to revolutionary struggle to the Popular Front position of broader alliances and the necessity of a bourgeois democratic phase, see María Soledad Gómez, "Factores nacionales e internacionales de la política interna del Partido Comunista de Chile (1922–1952)," in Varas, *El Partido Comunista en Chile*, pp. 66–73. See also Kenneth Roberts, "In Search of a New Identity," pp. 196–207; and Tomás Moulián, *Democracia y socialismo en Chile* (Santiago: FLACSO, 1983), pp. 75–84.

16. This is a conservative estimate based on interviews with PCCh leaders and former leaders, as well as with Socialist Party leaders. Several referred to the Young Communists (la Jota) as the fourth-largest political party of the times, behind the Christian Democrats, the Socialists, and the Communists.

17. For a detailed account of the 1932 Socialist Republic and the birth of Chilean socialism, see Paul Drake, *Socialism and Populism in Chile, 1932–1952* (Urbana: University of Illinois, 1978), pp. 71–98. For a discussion of the influences of this period based on in-depth oral interviews with socialist leaders and activists, see Peter Winn, *Weavers of Revolution: The Yarur Workers and Chile's Road to Socialism* (New York: Oxford University Press, 1986), pp. 55–57.

18. Roberts, "In Search of a New Identity," pp. 125–126. For an official history and analysis of the pre-1970 Chilean Socialist Party, see Julio Cesar Jobet, *Historia del Partido Socialista de Chile*, 2nd ed. (Santiago: Ediciones Documentas, 1987). For an excellent analysis of the PSCh until 1952, see Drake, *Socialism and Populism in Chile*. For an additional study of the PSCh, see Benny Pollack and Hernán Rosenkranz, *Revolutionary Social Democracy: The Chilean Socialist Party* (London: Pinter, 1986).

19. On the appeal of such figures in Chile, see Drake, *Socialism and Populism in Chile*.

20. Interestingly enough, this period in the PSCh's history was drawn upon as an important source of strength for the reunifying efforts under a far less radical program in the mid- to late 1980s. See Jorge Arrate, *El socialismo chileno: Rescate y renovación* (Barcelona and Rotterdam: Instituto Para el Nuevo Chile, 1983); and Jorge Arrate and Paulo Hidalgo, *Pasión y razón del socialismo chileno* (Santiago: Ediciones Ornitorrinco, 1989).

21. Jobet, *Historia del Partido Socialista de Chile*, pp. 292–293.

22. Second resolution of XXII Congreso General, reprinted in ibid., p. 313.

23. See ibid., pp. 386–398.

24. For a synopsis of this process, see Roberts, "In Search of a New Identity," pp. 129–133.

25. See Jobet, *Historia del Partido Socialista de Chile*, pp. 288–289.

26. Loveman argues, for example, that the breakdown of democracy in Chile can be attributed largely to attempts to bring an end to landowner hegemony in the Chilean countryside. See his *Chile*, particularly pp. 265–288.

27. Discussion of the ideological meaning of "*lo popular*," "the popular sector," will be developed in chapter 5.

28. Tomás Moulián, "Evolución histórica de la izquierda chilena: La influencia del Marxismo," in *Democracia y socialismo en Chile*, p. 73.

29. Ibid., p. 74.

30. Tomás Moulián, *La forja de ilusiones: El sistema de partidos, 1932–1973* (Santiago: ARCIS/FLACSO, 1993), pp. 238–240.

31. Ibid., p. 252.

32. This point has been made most forcefully by Arturo Valenzuela in *The Breakdown of Democratic Regimes*.

33. Moulián, *La forja de ilusiones*, p. 268.

34. For a clear outline and critique of the objectives of the Popular Unity pro-

gram, see Sergo Bitar, *Transición, socialismo, y democracia* (Mexico City: Siglo Ventiuno Editores, 1979), pp. 53–66. Bitar's work provides a detailed chronology and analysis of the political economy of the UP period. An English translation of the "UP Program of Government" appeared in the *North American Congress on Latin America Newsletter* in March 1971.

35. I am grateful to Peter Winn for his signaling of this point, as well as for his close read and critique of this chapter.

36. From the *NACLA Newsletter*, 1971.

37. Until recently, one of the most widely read accounts of the final days of the Popular Unity government, including a blow-by-blow account of the coup itself, was Ignacio González Camus, *El día en que murió Allende* (Santiago: Editorial CESOC, 1988). Over the past year, however, several firsthand or journalistic accounts have been released, including the very powerful *Interferencia secreta* (September 1998) by journalist Patricia Verdugo. The book comes accompanied with a compact disc of taped orders by the coup leaders, including Pinochet's order to put Allende and his chief advisers on a plane and, later, to "throw them from the plane."

38. There are several journalistic accounts of the escape of the Chilean left leadership. For a fascinating account of the flight of Chilean Socialist Party leader Carlos Altamirano, see Patricia Politzer, *Altamirano* (Buenos Aires: Ediciones Melquíades, 1989). For an account of the experiences of approximately thirty of the top leaders, see Faride Zerán, *O el asilo contra la opresión: 23 historias para recordar* (Santiago: Editores Paradox, 1991). See also Mili Rodríguez, *Nunca me verás como me vieras* (Santiago: Ediciones Ornitorrinco, 1990).

39. See *Summary of the Truth and Reconciliation Commission Report*, published by the National Education Campaign for Truth and Human Rights, Ministry of Foreign Affairs, Santiago, Chile (July 1991), and Human Rights Watch/Americas, "Chile: Unsettled Business: Human Rights in Chile at the Start of the Frei Presidency," *Human Rights Watch* 6, no. 6 (May 1994).

40. Americas Watch, *Chile Since the Coup: Ten Years of Repression* (New York: Americas Watch, 1983), p. 3. The human rights record of the Pinochet regime was carefully documented by the Commission on Truth and Reconciliation. The commission's report focuses on deaths and disappearances under the dictatorship and has been criticized for its failure to release publicly the names of the perpetrators of human rights violations. Nevertheless, the report provides a penetrating analysis of the systematic violation of human rights under Pinochet, and it calls for a series of reparations, which have been heeded by the Aylwin and Frei administrations.

41. Manuel Antonio Garretón, "The Political Evolution of the Chilean Military Regime and Problems in the Transition to Democracy," in Guillermo O'Donnell and Philippe Schmitter, eds., *Transitions from Military Rule: Latin America* (Baltimore: Johns Hopkins University Press, 1986), pp. 95–111. For an elaborated version of this argument, see his *El proceso político chileno*. See also Augusto Varas and Felipe Aguero, *El proyecto político militar* (Santiago: FLACSO, 1984).

42. Garretón, "The Political Evolution," p. 103.

43. See Hector Schamis, "Reconceptualizing Latin American Authoritarianism in the 1970s: From Bureaucratic Authoritarianism to Neoconservatism," *Comparative Politics* 23, no. 2 (January 1991): 201–220.

44. For a useful analysis of the evolution of Chile's neoliberal model, see Eduardo Silva, "The Political Economy of Chile's Regime Transition: From Radical to 'Pragmatic' Neo-Liberal Policies," in Paul Drake and Iván Jaksic, eds., *The Struggle for Democracy in Chile, 1982–1990*, 2nd ed. (Lincoln: University of Nebraska Press, 1995), pp. 98–127. On the weakening of the working class, see Alan Angell, "Unions and Workers in Chile During the 1980s," in Drake and Jaksic, *The Struggle for Democracy*, pp. 188–210.

45. On the effects of Pinochet's neoliberal model on the Chilean financial sector in the early years of the regime, see Fernando Dahse, *El mapa de la extrema riqueza*. See also Eduardo Silva, "Capitalist Coalitions and Economic Policymaking in Authoritarian Chile" (Ph.D. diss., University of California–San Diego, 1991).

46. For an overview of the political institutionalization process of the military regime, see Garretón, *El proceso político chileno*, pp. 151–163. For a study of the 1980 constitution, see Luís Maira, *La constitución de 1980 y la ruptura democrática* (Santiago; Editorial Emisión, 1988).

47. Pilar Vergara, "Las transformaciones del estado," p. 100.

48. Brunner, "La cultura política del autoritarianismo," p. 217.

49. Vergara, "Las transformaciones del estado," pp. 95–100. See also José Joaquín Brunner, "La cultura política del autoritarianismo," pp. 217–221.

50. Vergara, "Las transformaciones del estado," p. 96. It is interesting to note that analyses of Pinochet's project in terms of its long-term influences on redefining Chilean political culture were produced in large part by intellectuals sheltered in small think tanks inside the country. For an overview of this phenomenon, see Jeffrey Puryear, *Thinking Politics: Intellectuals and Democracy in Chile, 1973–1988* (Baltimore: Johns Hopkins University Press, 1994). By the early 1980s, private centers such as the Latin American Social Science Faculty (FLACSO) and CIEPLAN— homes to important Chilean left and moderate thinkers—had perceptibly grasped both the direct and the latent meanings for any transition from authoritarian rule. Those based at FLACSO alone included José Joaquín Brunner, Alicia Frohman, Manuel Antonio Garretón, Norbert Lechner, Tomás Moulián, Teresa Valdés, Augusto Varas, and Pilar Vergara, all of whom produced seminal studies of the political, economic, and social aspects of the dictatorship as well as their implications for the country's future.

51. Roberts, "In Search of a New Identity," pp. 207–208.

52. Partido Comunista de Chile, "Al partido y al pueblo de Chile" (mimeographed; December 1974).

53. Ana Vásquez and Ana María Araujo, *La maldición de Ulises: Repercusiones psicológicas del exilio* (Santiago: Editorial Sudamericana, 1990), p. 11.

54. For an excellent discussion concerning the nature of political exile and political exiles, see Yossi Shain, *The Frontier of Loyalty: Political Exiles in the Age of the Nation-State* (Hanover, N.H.: Wesleyan University Press, 1989). My definition of political exiles comes from his conceptualization.

55. Alan Angell and Susan Carstairs, "The Exile Question in Chilean Politics," *Third World Quarterly* 9, no. 1 (January 1987): 151–152.

56. I base this figure upon interviews with a range of former exiled political leaders and activists who belonged to distinct parties and lived in different regions of the world. During the interviews I asked each of them to estimate the number of key political leaders in exile. Interestingly enough, they all gave about the same figure.

57. These debates are presented and analyzed in detail by Roberts, "In Search of a New Identity."

58. *Documento del Comité Central del Partido Socialista de Chile*, Santiago, March 1974, p. 12. Cited in Roberts, "In Search of a New Identity," p. 137.

59. Ibid.

60. Partido Comunista de Chile, "Patriotas: Sólo unidos derrotaremos el fascismo" (mimeographed; September 1976), p. 4.

61. For a useful analysis of the PCCh that attributes its change to a popular rebellion position to party organizational dynamics, see Roberts, "In Search of a New Identity." See also Tomás Moulián and Isabel Torres, "Continuidad o cambio en la linea política del Partido Comunista de Chile," in Varas, *El Partido Comunista en Chile*, pp. 453–485.

62. Roberts, "In Search of a New Identity," pp. 154–155. For elaborated discussions of renovation from two of its chief protagonists, see Tomás Moulián, *Democracia y socialismo en Chile*, and Jorge Arrate, *El socialismo chileno: Rescate y renovación* (Rotterdam: Instituto para el Nuevo Chile, 1983).

63. Moulián, "Evolución histórica de la izquierda chilena: la influencia del marxismo," in *Democracia y socialismo en Chile*.

64. Moulián, "Democracia, socialismo, y proyecto nacional popular," in *Democracia y socialismo en Chile*.

65. Silva, "The Political Economy of Chile's Regime Transition," p. 110.

66. See Gonzalo de la Maza and Mario Garcés, *La explosión de las mayorías: Protesta nacional, 1983–1984* (Santiago: Educación y Comunicaciones, 1985).

67. Manuel Antonio Garretón, "The Political Opposition and the Party System Under the Military Regime," in Drake and Jaksic, *The Struggle for Democracy*, p. 221.

68. Ibid., p. 222.

69. For an insightful analysis of the Pinochet regime's "carrots and sticks" approach to social unrest, see Carlos Huneeus, "La dinámica de los 'nuevos autoritarismos': Chile en una perspectiva comparada," *Revista de Estudios Políticos* 54 (1986): 105–158.

70. For a detailed and well-written account of the opposition's strategic shifts

from a mass protest to a strategy of accepting the dictatorship's timetable, see Jeffrey Puryear, *Thinking Politics*, 123–159.

71. Brian Loveman, "The Transition to Civilian Government in Chile, 1990–1994," in Drake and Jaksic, *The Struggle for Democracy in Chile*, p. 308.

72. Minister of the Economy Carlos Ominami, cited in the *Latin American Monitor*, February 1990. A member of the MIR until 1973, Ominami today is a Chilean Socialist Party senator.

73. For an analysis of the 1997 election, see Felipe Aguero, "Chile's Lingering Authoritarian Legacy," *Current History* 97, no. 616 (February 1998): 66–70.

74. See "Obispos: Iglesia debe recabar datos sobre paradero de desaparecidos," *La Hora*, September 9, 1998, p. 10.

3. The Binds and Bonds of Party Loyalty

1. In fact, after a long period of dormancy, "generational analyses" reemerged with fervor in the late 1960s as scholars examined 1960s social conflict. Analysts returned to such thinkers as Karl Mannheim and José Ortega y Gasset for explanations of the role of youth in moments of rapid social change. Generational analyses became a major focus of political socialization studies, as both an independent variable and a dependent variable in studies of political and social systems. Such analyses challenged the conventional wisdom of political socialization literature of the period for its emphasis on change rather than continuity. "The biggest distinction between the study of political socialization in general and the particular study of generations," wrote Michael Delli Carpini, "is that the former emphasizes *continuity* in attitudes, opinions, and behaviors between socializer and socialized, while the latter focuses on *discontinuity*." See "Age and History: Generations and Sociopolitical Change," in Roberta Sigel, ed., *Political Learning in Adulthood: A Sourcebook of Theory and Research*, p. 13 (Chicago: University of Chicago Press, 1989).

2. All of my interviews used a primarily open-ended questionnaire to guide but not to control the interview sessions. The interviewees themselves tended to determine how much time was spent on particular issues or periods of their lives.

3. On Socialist Party culture, see Paul Drake, *Socialism and Populism in Chile, 1932–1952* (Urbana: University of Illinois, 1978), and Benny Pollack and Hernán Rosenkranz, *Revolutionary Social Democracy: The Chilean Socialist Party* (London: Pinter, 1986). On the Chilean Communist Party, see Carmelo Furci, *The Chilean Communist Party and the Road to Socialism* (London: ZED, 1984). To my knowledge there are no in-depth studies of the Izquierda Cristiana or the MAPU, parties that were historically short-lived yet whose members were key thinkers in the process of socialist renovation. A history of the formation and evolution of the MAPU would make for an interesting study.

4. I interviewed Jorge Insunza on January 22 and 29, 1992, and June 10, 1998.

5. My interviews with Isabel Allende were conducted on December 3, 1991, January 9, 1992, and June 12, 1998.

6. In a June 8, 1998, meeting with fellow Christian Democratic Party leaders and organizers, presidential hopeful Andrés Zaldívar discussed the 1999 presidential elections and his rival for the presidential nomination, Socialist Party–Party for Democracy leader Ricardo Lagos. Zaldívar was reported to have stated that the Socialist Party might not be capable of governance based on its past. His remarks were covered by the major media, and leaders of the Socialist Party responded with harsh condemnation of Zaldívar.

7. My interviews with Adriana Muñoz took place on December 2, 1991, January 24, 1992, and June 9, 1998.

8. In a press interview, Allende criticized feminists for complaining about the lack of Socialist Party nominees for cabinet positions and for pushing too forcefully regarding the legalization of divorce. Regarding Socialist Party–picked candidates for the 1994 Frei cabinet, she defended the Socialist Party's position that there were not appropriate Socialist women for the jobs. Regarding divorce, she said, "Frankly, it seems to me that there are far more urgent social problems, and in my campaign for congress, it would not have occurred to me to choose divorce as a number one theme. It would have been absurd. When you see people without work, or services or hospitals, frankly divorce is not a priority issue" (*La Epoca*, January 2, 1994, p. 5).

9. Individuals' basic proclivities toward progressive social and political values, such as the defense of the poor and underprivileged, or equality under the law, are rooted in the predominant cultural, religious, and socioeconomic traditions of their families and communities. Class, urban-rural, religious-secular, and politicized-apolitical cleavages in the home and neighborhood combine in complex ways to influence how individuals perceive themselves in relation to others. Such cleavages undergird individuals' basic values, values that provide the foundations for subsequent political militancy and political commitment.

10. In several informal discussions with such Chilean feminists as Teresa Valdés, and others, the author was exposed to a widespread frustration and disappointment with the pervasive machismo of the Chilean political class. There are notably fewer women in public office today than before 1973, an interesting paradox given the high visibility of Chilean women in the struggle against the dictatorship. The visible retreat from politics on the part of Chilean women intellectuals in the post-1990 period would make for a fascinating study.

11. The relationship between the Chilean Socialist Party and the Party for Democracy is a complicated one, as many of the PPD leaders are also closely associated with the PSCh leadership. Since 1989, when the PSCh first created the PPD as an instrumentalist party to accede to the confines of the 1980 Chilean constitution, the PPD has increasingly differentiated itself from the PSCh as a more "modern" left party. The PPD continues to struggle to define itself, though in the area of gender and politics, it has taken the lead over the PSCh in advancing greater participation of women in politics.

12. My interviews with Patricio Rivas took place on November 19 and 21, 1991, and June 12, 1998.

13. Such former Miristas include Carlos Ominami, Aylwin's planning minister, who was recently elected senator; Osvaldo Puccio, currently ambassador to Austria; and Alvaro Díaz, a senior adviser to the Ministry of Planning.

4. Personal Loyalists and the Meaning of Allendismo

1. From interview with Patricio Rivas, June 12, 1998.

2. Alessandro Portelli, *The Death of Luigi Trastulli and Other Stories: Form and Meaning in Oral History* (Albany: SUNY Press, 1991), p. 52.

3. Luisa Passerini, "Memory: Resume of the Final Session of the International Conference on Oral History, Aix-en-Provence, September 26, 1982," reprinted in *History Workshop* 15 (Spring 1983): 195; and Passerini, "Work Ideology and Consensus," in *Fascism in Popular Memory: The Cultural Experience of the Turin Working Class* (Cambridge: Cambridge University Press, 1987), p. 85.

4. Robert N. Bellah, Richard Madsen, William M. Sullivan, Anne Swidler, and Steven M. Tipton, *Habits of the Heart: Individualism and Commitment in American Life* (New York: Harper and Row, 1985), p. 153.

5. For a valuable discussion of the historic roots of populist leadership within the Chilean Socialist Party, see Paul Drake, *Socialism and Populism in Chile, 1932–1952* (Urbana: University of Illinois, 1978).

6. Carlos Huneeus, *Los chilenos y la política: Cambio y continuidad en el autoritarianismo* (Santiago: CERC, 1987), p. 85.

7. See, for example, Arturo Valenzuela, *The Breakdown of Democratic Regimes: Chile* (Baltimore: Johns Hopkins University Press, 1979); Manuel Antonio Garretón and Tomás Moulián, *La Unidad Popular y el conflicto político en Chile* (Santiago: Ediciones Minga, 1983); and Sergio Bitar, *Transición, socialismo, y democracia: La experiencia chilena* (Mexico City: Siglo Ventiuno Editores, 1979).

8. See, for example, Jorge Arrate, *La fuerza demócratica de la idea socialista* (Santiago: Ediciones Ornitorrinco, 1986), pp. 69–77; Gonzalo Martner, "La unidad de la izquierda: Una perspectiva," *Convergencia*, no. 11 (April–June 1987): 39–43; and Aniceto Rodríguez, *Unidad y renovación: Dialéctica para la victoria* (Santiago: CESOC, 1990), pp. 63–66.

9. Cited in "Miedo y amenaza en la propaganda política televisa del plebiscito del 1988," in Elizabeth Lira and María Isabel Castillo, *Psicología de la amenaza política y del miedo*, p. 163.

10. In fact, it is difficult to come across any positive public imagery from those years. For the authoritarian regime's manipulation of societal fear and its quest for stability, see Norbert Lechner, "Hay gente que muere del miedo," in his collection of essays, *Los patios interiores de la democracia: Subjetividad y politica* (Santiago: FLACSO, 1988), pp. 95–109. This article appears in a translated version in a very strong anthology edited by Juan Corradi, Patricia Weiss Fagen, and Manuel Anto-

nio Garretón; see *Fear at the Edge: State Terror and Resistance in Latin America* (Berkeley: University of California Press, 1992).

11. Patricia Politzer, *Altamirano* (Buenos Aires: Ediciones Melquíades, 1989), p. 11.

12. Cited in ibid., pp. 194–195.

13. Ibid., p. 17.

14. Ibid., p. 9.

15. This is also in stark contrast to Altamirano, who, aided by the Chilean Communist Party, managed to flee the country within days after the coup.

16. Martner, "La unidad de la izquierda," p. 39.

17. In 1991 the Allende family established the Fundación Allende, which houses a range of archival material. According to the socialist magazine *Convergencia*, the Centro de Estudios Salvador Allende in Puebla, Mexico, has begun to publish the fifteen-volume *Archivo Salvador Allende*, complete with illustrations, chronologies, and analysis by leading socialist thinkers. Each volume is dedicated to a specific theme: "Latin America, youth, democracy and socialism, the party, the Chilean road to socialism, workers, the international context, man's daily existence." See *Convergencia*, no. 11 (April–June 1987): 45.

18. Remarks by Jorge Arrate in Jorge Arrate, Oscar G. Garretón, Osvaldo Puccio, and Ignacio Walker, "Salvador Allende y la renovación socialista," *Convergencia*, no. 13 (July 1988): 18–19.

19. Remarks by Puccio in ibid., p. 18. Together with Manuel Antonio Garretón and Luis Maira, Puccio was responsible for drafting a new PSCh program, a task that had not been undertaken since 1957.

20. Ibid., p. 21. See also Garretón's opinion editorial, "Qué dignidad, Presidente! Qué dignidad!" *La Hora*, September 8, 1998.

21. Ricardo Nuñez, "La difícil tarea de los socialistas hoy" (speech reprinted in *Convergencia*, no. 18 [May–June 1990], p. 17).

22. See, for example, "El fantasma de Lagos," in the weekly Chilean magazine *Que Pasa*, August 15, 1998, p. 28.

23. My interviews with Hernán Del Canto were conducted on October 31 and November 11, 1991.

24. Javier Martínez and Eugenio Tironi, *Las clases sociales en Chile: Cambio y estratificación, 1970–1980* (Santiago: SUR, 1985); and Jean Blondel, "The Social Backgrounds of Ministers," in *Government Ministers in the Contemporary World* (London: Sage, 1985), pp. 29–54, esp. his table documenting "manual workers, employees, trade union organizers and farmers" holding government ministries since 1945 (table 2–4. p. 43).

25. Public announcements issued by the military junta seeking the whereabouts of high-level officials of the Popular Unity government.

26. Ignacio González Camus, *El día en que murió Allende* (Santiago: Editorial CESOC, 1989), pp. 211–213.

27. Erik Erikson, "On the Nature of Psycho-Historical Evidence," in *Life History and the Historical Moment* (New York: Norton, 1975), pp. 123–124.

28. Portelli, *The Death of Luigi Trastulli*, p. 19.

29. Ibid., p. 50.

30. Ana Vásquez and Ana María Araujo use this term in their study of Southern Cone exiles in France. See *La maldición de Ulises: Repercusiones psicológicas del exilio* (Santiago: Editorial Sudamericana, 1990), p. 6.

31. Portelli, *The Death of Luigi Trastulli*, p. 53.

32. My interviews with Aníbal Palma took place on October 29, November 5, and November 8, 1991.

33. For a description and analysis of the historical role of the Radical Party, see Timothy Scully, *Rethinking the Center: Party Politics in Nineteenth- and Twentieth-Century Chile* (Stanford: Stanford University Press, 1992); and Valenzuela, *The Breakdown of Authoritarian Regimes*.

34. Aníbal Palma, "La verdad sobre la ENU," *Un sólo norte* (Santiago: A.T.G., 1989), p. 131.

35. *Momio* is a derogatory term for members of the right, and it also implied members of the middle to upper classes.

36. My interviews with Eduardo Reyes were conducted on November 5 and 6, 1991, and June 10, 1998.

37. For an excellent source on the politics of voting in the rural areas, see Brian Loveman, *Chile: The Legacy of Hispanic Capitalism* (New York: Oxford University Press, 1988), pp. 229–270.

38. The Tupamaros were a 1960s Uruguayan urban guerrilla movement.

39. Exemplified by Che Guevara's expedition into Bolivia, guerrilla *focos* were small groups of armed militants whose purpose was to live among and recruit the peasantry into support for socialist revolution.

40. The notion of the immediacy of traumatic political moments in national history is developed in Henri Rousso's study of Vichy France. See Rousso, *The Vichy Syndrome: History and Memory in France Since 1944* (Cambridge: Harvard University Press, 1991).

41. This is not the case for all former Allende cabinet ministers. Former minister of mines Sergio Bitar, for example, is now a Chilean senator. Though he was not a participant in this study, I did interview him briefly and am familiar with his thinking and work. Were I to take a guess as to what ideal-type Bitar would be, I would place him as a political entrepreneur, the subject of chapter 6.

5. Exile and the Thinkers

1. Hans Speier, "The Social Conditions of the Intellectual Exile," in Hans Speier, *Social Order and the Risks of War: Papers in Political Sociology* (New York: Stewart, 1952), p. 94.

2. As Bryan Turner has suggested in his preface to Karl Mannheim's *Ideology and*

Utopia, Mannheim's own concepts, most clearly demonstrated in his "free-floating intellectual," are a product of his biographical experience, first as a Hungarian refugee fleeing the White Terror and later as a refugee from fascist Germany. Turner includes among the "floating Jewish intelligentsia" Karl Marx, Georg Simmel, Emile Durkheim, the whole of the Frankfurt School—all of whom, it might be argued, were directly influenced theoretically by their uprootedness. See Turner's preface to Mannheim, *Ideology and Utopia: An Introduction to the Sociology of Knowledge* (San Diego: Harcourt, Brace, Jovanovich, 1985), p. xliii. In Erik Erikson's work on identity and identity crisis, he discusses how the identity crisis of immigrants, including his own experience, opened his eyes to the question of "what world image they were sharing, where they were going, from where they were, and who was going with them." See Erikson, *Life History and the Historical Moment* (New York: Norton, 1975), p. 4. In his reflections in *Exit, Voice, and Loyalty* (Cambridge: Harvard University Press, 1970), Albert Hirschman has also alluded to his refugee experience as influential in his formulation of the concepts of exit and voice.

3. There is a rich literature on the phenomenon of exile, particularly in the fields of history, psychology, sociology, and literary criticism. There are, however, few explicitly theoretical studies of the importance of exiles' thinking and activity upon their countries' politics. What theoretical studies do exist focus upon the impact of political exiles' activities in their *adopted* countries. Classics in this vein include Edward Carr, *The Romantic Exiles: A Nineteenth-Century Portrait Gallery* (Harmonsworth: Penguin, 1949); and Lewis Coser's *Refugee Scholars in America: Their Impact and Their Experiences* (New Haven: Yale University Press, 1984). Others of interest that examine specific national diasporas include R. C. Williams, *Culture in Exile: Russian Emigres in Germany, 1881–1941* (Ithaca: Cornell University Press, 1972). Generally these examine how political exiles, defined as those who flee their country as a result of political persecution, become refugees. They are studies of those who seek new lives abroad and eventually become less and less involved in political activity focused on their home countries, and they do not return. These studies are based largely on the cases of Eastern Europe and the former Soviet Union and have thus treated exile as an implicitly permanent phenomenon. They do not address the theoretical implications for exile repatriation. Important works on the Spanish exiled communities are Louis Stein's *Beyond Death and Exile: The Spanish Republicans in France, 1939–1955* (Cambridge: Harvard University Press, 1979); and Patricia Weiss Fagen, *Exiles and Citizens: Spanish Republicans in Mexico* (Austin: University of Texas Press, 1973). Studies that conceptually include a vast range of diaspora communities are Yossi Shain's *The Frontier of Loyalty: Political Exiles in the Age of the Nation-State* (Hanover, N.H.: Wesleyan University Press, 1989); and Paul Tabori, *The Anatomy of Exile: A Semantic and Historical Study* (London: Habrap, 1972).

4. The centrality of a "sense of place" in the lives of many individuals is suggested by Jerome Bruner in his study of culture and autobiography. It is the dis-

covery that one's home or sense of place, of all the subjective phenomena and sentiments attached with that sense of place, is a constant referent in everyday discourse, as in life. See Bruner, "Life as Narrative," *Social Research* 54, no. 1 (Spring 1987): 24–27.

5. Diane Kay, *Chileans in Exile: Private Struggles, Public Lives* (London: Macmillan, 1987). For an additional study of the public/private dimension in exile and its differential impact on gender, see Valentina da Rocha Lima, "Women in Exile: Becoming Feminist," *International Journal of Oral History* 5, no. 2 (June 1984): 81–99.

6. For an important institutionalist perspective on the realm and flow of ideas across nations, see Peter Hall, *The Political Power of Economic Ideas* (Princeton: Princeton University Press, 1989).

7. Robert Brym, *Intellectuals and Politics* (London: Allen and Unwin, 1980), p. 13.

8. In Yossi Shain's study of political exiles, he distinguishes between two broad segments in the international arena that serve as support institutions for exiles: "1) Governments, including the intergovernmental organizations such as the United Nations, the Organization of American States . . . ; and 2) Civil society, including: a) transnational nongovernmental organizations such as the Socialist International, the World Council of Churches . . . b) national organizations such as political parties, labor unions, student movements, or even exile groups of other nationalities; c) public opinion and the media; and d) private individuals and organizations" (*The Frontier of Loyalty*, p. 111).

9. My interviews with Luis Maira took place on October 22 and November 19, 1991, and November 14, 1993.

10. Cited in Reinhard Friedman, *La política chilena de la A a la Z* (Santiago: Melquíades, 1988), p. 68.

11. Faride Zerán, *O el asilo contra la opresión* (Santiago: Editores Paradox, 1991), p. 91.

12. For a history of the contribution of Spanish Republicans to intellectual and professional life in Mexico, see Fagen, *Exiles and Citizens*.

13. As the secretary-general of Chile's solidarity office for the Americas, Maira traveled extensively to the United States as well as to other countries of Latin America. He visited Washington, D.C., as many as six times per year, focusing a good deal on U.S. foreign policy toward Latin America. In his reflections on intellectuals who had most influenced and challenged his thinking, Maira noted, in addition to prominent Christian and Marxist theorists, social scientist Samuel Huntington, who gave him a dose of "realpolitik": "I want to point out a final current that influenced me from among the social sciences, authors one reads without feeling any great affinity toward them, but who illuminate very concrete questions, nevertheless—who have an important influence on you for their conceptual sharpness, such as Samuel Huntington, whose thoughts are rich and when you must confront them it affects your own thinking, you find yourself accommodating their thinking. So

people from the most varied currents in the field of international relations have had a tremendous influence on my intellectual formulation."

14. In an article he wrote for the socialist magazine *Convergencia*, for example, Maira urged fellow socialists to learn from the Latin American transitions of the 1980s (rather than the Spanish one) as they prepared for the Chilean transition from authoritarian rule. By this he meant more attention to Latin American economic dependency, to fragile political coalitions, and to the primacy of populist leaders. Luis Maira, "La transición chilena: Desafíos y capacidades," *Convergencia* 18 (May–June 1990): 11.

15. Maira, "La Izquierda Cristiana, una mayoría que nace," cited in Friedman, *La política chilena de la A a la Z*, p. 67.

16. My interviews with Antonio Leal were conducted on November 12 and 17, 1991, and June 9, 1998.

17. There is a rich literature on the meaning of *"lo popular"* in Latin America. While today, the "popular sector" tends to be used in purely sociological terms to connote broad sectors of the poor, from those in the working-class sector to the informal sector, in the 1960s and 1970s the term tended to carry a definitively political and ideological content. The popular classes or sectors were agents for protest, for change, for mobilization and demand-making of the state. For a sociological conceptualization that treats the popular sectors as the working and lower middle class, see David Collier, introduction to Collier, ed., *The New Authoritarianism in Latin America* (Princeton: Princeton University Press, 1979), pp. 3–20. For an alternative sociological treatment, which essentially views the popular sector as all those who oppose the elites, see Susan Eckstein, "Power and Popular Protest in Latin America," in Eckstein, ed., *Power and Popular Protest: Latin American Social Movements* (Berkeley: University of California Press, 1988), pp. 1–60. For a politico-ideological conceptualization, see Guillermo O'Donnell, "Tensions in the Bureaucratic-Authoritarian State and the Question of Democracy," in Collier, *The New Authoritarianism in Latin America*, pp. 285–318.

18. *"Yo no soy ni allí,"* means "I couldn't care less," while *"en todo"* means "in everything."

19. Enrico Berlinguer, "Reflections After Events in Chile," *Italian Communists* 5–6 (September–December 1973).

20. For a discussion of the PCI's increased prominence during this period, see Ignacio Walker, *Socialismo y democracia: Chile y Europa en perspectiva comparada* (Santiago: CIEPLAN-HACHETTE, 1990), pp. 106–112.

21. This is reminiscent of Alvin Gouldner's argument regarding contradictions between the vanguard organization and the nature of the intellectual: "The vanguard organization has and develops its own logic, and this comes into contradiction with the grammar of the intelligentsia. . . . In short, the common culture of intellectuals places a central value on talk, particularly self-reflective discourse. But a vanguard structure is an instrument of social combat. Its military exigencies and

dangerous position compel it to insist on disciplined obedience. . . . In bringing the vanguard party into being, the intellectuals also bring the seeds of their own polit-ical disillusionment and displacement." Alvin W. Gouldner, "Prologue to a Theory of Revolutionary Intellectuals," *Telos* 26 (Winter 1975–76), p. 17.

22. My interviews with Fernando Contreras took place on November 26 and 29, 1991, and April 20, 1992.

23. Ana Vásquez and Ana María Araujo, *La maldición de Ulises: Repercusiones psi-cológicas del exilio* (Santiago: Editorial Sudamericana, 1990). See also Juana Koval-skys and Elizabeth Lira, "Exilio y retorno: una aproximación psicosocial," in FASIC, *Exilio: 1978–1986*, pp. 139–145.

24. For a useful discussion of the individual militant-party dynamic in exile, see Eugenia Neves and Ana Vásquez, "La militancia política y los exiliados," *Chile-América* 76–77 (January–March 1982): 53.

25. The Leipzig Group earned its name from a 1979 meeting held among them in Leipzig, although their place of residence was East Berlin.

26. In addition to Contreras, I discussed the Leipzig Group with Alvaro Palacios, another member of the group, as well as with former Communists Raúl Oliva and Antonio Leal. Written analyses include Kenneth Roberts, "In Search of a New Iden-tity: Dictatorship, Democracy, and the Evolution of the Chilean Left in Chile and Peru" (Ph.D. diss., Stanford University, 1992); Boris Yopo, "Las relaciones interna-cionales del Partido Comunista," in Augusto Varas, ed., *El Partido Comunista en Chile* (Santiago: CESOC-FLACSO, 1988), esp. pp. 389–393; Osvaldo Puccio, "La política del Partido Comunista de Chile: Elementos de su evolución y permanencia en el último período," in Varas, *El Partido Comunista Chileno*, pp. 403–437; Luis Corvalán, "Rebelión popular: Política de nuestro partido," in "Rebelión popular: Camino de la victoria" (mimeographed; 1982), pp. 73–80; and a presentation and discussion session led by Contreras and reprinted in ICAL, eds., *Crisis y renovación* (Santiago: Ediciones Medusa/ICAL, 1990), pp. 265–277.

27. This description of revolutionary man was provided by Contreras in our interview.

28. Yopo, "Las relaciones internacionales," pp. 373–388.

29. Michael Walzer, *The Revolution of the Saints: A Study in the Origins of Radical Politics* (Cambridge: Harvard University Press, 1965), p. 110.

30. See, for example, Manuel Fernando Contreras, "Bases para debatir la reno-vación revolucionaria de nuestro partido" (unpublished manuscript, 1990); Contr-eras, "Opiniones en torno a la renovación del Partido Comunista de Chile" (un-published manuscript, 1990); and Contreras, "La renovación del PC de Chile," in ICAL, *Crisis y renovación*, esp. pp. 277–280.

6. The Return: Political Entrepreneurs and the Chilean Transition

1. It would be difficult to underestimate the importance of the national univer-sity reform movement on the political lives of 1960s generation university leaders

and activists. The university reform movement is beyond the scope of this study, but it would make a very strong research contribution to understanding the evolution of the Chilean New Left.

2. My interviews with Raúl Oliva were conducted on October 18, 24, and 31, 1991.

3. Valentina da Rocha Lima, "Women in Exile: Becoming Feminist," *International Journal of Oral History* 5, no. 2 (June 1984): 94.

4. My interviews with Clarisa Hardy took place on February 5 and 7, 1992, and June 12, 1998.

5. My interviews with Enrique Correa took place in New York City on October 27 and November 6, 1993.

6. Interview with UDI congressman Andrés Chadwick, cited in Alicia De la Cruz and Luisa García, "El poder del ministro Correa, para muchos el hombre político de 1990," *La Segunda*, December 21, 1990, p. 16. In this article, National Party senator Sebastián Piñera said, "Correa doesn't have enemies in the opposition. If he has any, they are in the Concertación." Typical also was rightist magazine *Qué Pasa*'s laudatory article on Correa, titled "Eighty-five Kilos of Talent" (June 19, 1993).

7. Cited in María Angélica de Luigi, "Ministro: Cambió Usted o Cambió el País?" *El Mercurio*, May 12, 1991, p. D12.

8. Ibid.

9. Oscar Guillermo Garretón is a former MAPU leader and under President Aylwin headed Chile's metro system for the transportation ministry.

10. A key contributor to the new bond between Aylwin and Correa was a close mutual friend, the Archbishop Carlos González, an early mentor of Correa's and the archbishop of the diocese that encompassed Aylwin's 1960s senatorial district. During the transition, the Catholic Church provided an extremely important facilitating network between the Christian Democratic Party and sectors of the Christian left.

11. Edgardo Boeninger was Aylwin's minister of the presidency and is today a designated senator. Alejandro Foxley was Aylwin's minister of finance and is today an elected senator. Rene Cortázar has been a high-level government official and consultant.

12. Interview with senior fellows of FLACSO. In contrast to FLACSO-Mexico, FLACSO-Argentina, and FLACSO-Quito, FLACSO-Chile is the one branch that does not receive financial support from its government.

13. My interviews with José Antonio Viera-Gallo were conducted on November 18, 1991, January 13, 1992, and June 8, 1998.

14. Interview with the author, October 27, 1993.

15. Alessandro Portelli, *The Death of Luigi Trastulli and Other Stories: Form and Meaning in Oral History* (Albany: SUNY Press, 1991), p. 53.

16. Faride Zerán, "José Antonio Viera-Gallo: 'Soy como el Arlequín,'" *Análisis*, July 8–14, 1991, p. 6.

17. My interviews with José Miguel Insulza took place on November 18 and 29, 1991, and November 13, 1993.

18. January 1999 release of a poll conducted by the reputable CERC (Centro de Estudios de la Realidad Contemporánea), Santiago, Chile.

19. Paper presented at panel on "The Crisis of the Socialist Countries," printed in ICAL, eds., *Crisis y renovación* (Santiago: Ediciones Medusa/ICAL, 1990), p. 20.

20. "El pulpo imperialista," *El Mercurio*, June 11, 1995, p. D36.

21. Samuel Huntington, *Political Order in Changing Societies* (New Haven: Yale University Press, 1968), p. 461.

22. Lucy Dávila, "Lagos, el PPD y el gobierno," *Hoy*, no. 932 (May 29–June 4, 1995): 19; "Socialistas rechazan juicios de Ominami: Defendieron los símbolos socialistas," *El Mercurio*, April 20, 1995, p. B3; "Escalona Afirmó que el socialismo es la mejor alternativa democrática," *El Mercurio*, April 20, 1995, p. B3; "Critican fórmulas de la oposición para solucionar tema de derechos humanos," *El Mercurio*, July 16, 1995, p. C3.

23. Antonio Cortés T., "Hegemonia gubernamental y socialismo," *La Epoca*, October 13, 1994, p. 9.

Conclusion: Political Identity, Postauthoritarianism in the 1990s, and the Politics of the Possible

1. It is interesting to note that the terms *spot, focus group, mass media*, and *spin* have become incorporated in their original English into the Chilean language.

2. Words used by Enrique Correa in an interview with the author in November 1993.

3. Interview with the author, November 1993.

4. For a useful analysis of one such type of consensus-based politics, see Terry Lynn Karl, "Petroleum and Political Pacts: The Transition to Democracy in Venezuela," in Guillermo O'Donnell, Philippe Schmitter, and Laurence Whitehead, eds., *Transitions from Authoritarian Rule: Latin America* (Baltimore: Johns Hopkins University Press, 1986), pp. 196–219.

5. For an important discussion of the need to examine the effects of authoritarian political legacies on the postauthoritarian period, see Frances Hagopian, "After Regime Change: Authoritarian Legacies, Political Representation, and the Democratic Future of South America," *World Politics* 45 (April 1993): 464–500. For a leading Chilean psychiatrist's perspectives on her society's continued fear and fragmentation, see Faride Zerán's interview with Sofía Salamovich, "El alma de Chile," *La Epoca*, July 2, 1995, pp. 14–15.

6. My assertion is based on personal interviews with former revolutionary intellectuals and activists both in Chile and abroad (including those former exiles who did not return to Chile), who are working in a range of capacities, from academic posts to nongovernmental service and development organizations.

7. See John Beverley, José Oviedo, and Michael Aronna, eds., *The Post-Modernism Debate in Latin America* (Durham: Duke University Press, 1995).

8. Enrique Correa, "Exportar inteligencia," *Qué Pasa*, p. 12.

9. Ibid.

10. Manuel Antonio Garretón, "La cara oculta del problema,"*Hoy*, p. 23.

11. I conducted a series of intensive interviews with Osvaldo Puccio on October 15, 23, and 31, 1991.

12. Antonio Leal, "Debate socialista," *La Epoca*, October 8, 1994, p. 10.

13. Remarks taken from June 9, 1998, interview and from opinion editorial, "Ni autocomplacientes ni autoflagelantes," published in *La Epoca*, June 12, 1998, p. 8.

14. "Revista de Libros," *El Mercurio*, September 12, 1998, p. 7. See, for example: Tomás Moulián, *Conversación interrumpida con Allende* (Santiago: LOM Ediciones, 1998); Patricia Verdugo, *Interferencia secreta: 11 de septiembre de 1973* (Santiago: Editorial Sudamericano, 1998); Marco Antonio de la Parra, *Carta abierta a Pinochet* (Santiago: Editorial Planeta, 1998); Armando Uribe, *Carta abierta a Patricio Aylwin* (Santiago: Editorial Planeta, 1998); Tomás Moulián, *El consumo me consume* (Santiago: LOM Ediciones, 1998); Marco Antonio de la Parra, *La mala memoria: Historia personal de Chile contemporáneo* (Santiago: Editorial Planeta, 1997).

15. January 4, 1999, CERC poll, a national survey of twelve hundred Chileans in twenty-nine cities throughout the country.

SELECTED BIBLIOGRAPHY

Abramson, Paul. "Developing Party Identification: A Further Examination of Life Cycle, Generational, and Period Effects." *American Journal of Political Science* 23 (February 1979): 78–96.

Aguero, Felipe. "Chile's Lingering Authoritarian Legacy." *Current History* 97, no. 616 (February 1998): 66–70.

Aldunate, Adolfo, Angel Flisfisch, and Tomás Moulián. *Estudios sobre sistemas de partidos en Chile*. Santiago: FLACSO, 1985.

Almond, Gabriel, and Sidney Verba, eds. *The Civic Culture Revisited*. New York: Sage, 1989.

Americas Watch. *Chile Since the Coup: Ten Years of Repression*. New York: Americas Watch, 1983.

Angell, Alan. *Politics and the Labor Movement in Chile*. London: Oxford University Press, 1972.

——. "Unions and Workers in Chile During the 1980s." In Paul Drake and Iván Jaksic, eds., *The Struggle for Democracy in Chile, 1982–1990*, pp. 188–210. 2nd ed. Lincoln: University of Nebraska Press, 1995.

Angell, Alan, and Susan Carstairs. "The Exile Question in Chilean Politics." *Third World Quarterly* 9, no. 1 (January 1987): 148–167.

Arcos, Valentina, Ana Julia Cienfuegos, and Cristina Monelli. "Represión y daño psicológico: Respuesta subjetiva frente a la ruptura de un proyecto político." *Lecturas de Psicología y Política*. Santiago: Edición Privada, 1982.

Arrate, Jorge. *La fuerza demócratica de la idea socialista*. Santiago: Ediciones Ornitorrinco, 1986.

——. *El retorno verdadero: Textos políticos, 1987–1991*. Santiago: Ediciones Ornitorrinco, 1991.

——. *El socialismo chilena: Rescate y renovación*. Rotterdam: Instituto Para el Nuevo Chile, 1983.

Arrate, Jorge, and Paulo Hidalgo. *Pasión y razón del socialismo chileno*. Santiago: Ediciones Ornitorrinco, 1989.

Arrow, Kenneth. "Gifts and Exchanges." In E. Phelps, ed., *Altruism, Morality, and Economic Theory*. New York: Russell Sage Foundation, 1975.

Baró, Ignacio Martín. *Acción e ideología*. San Salvador: UCA, 1985.
——. *Guerra y salúd mental*. San Salvador: UCA, 1984.
Becker, David, and Elizabeth Lira, eds. *Derechos humanos: Todo es según el dolor con que se mira*. Santiago: ILAS, 1990.
Becker, Gordon. *The Economic Approach to Human Behavior*. Chicago: University of Chicago Press, 1976.
Bellah, Robert N., Richard Madsen, William M. Sullivan, Anne Swidler, and Steven M. Tipton. *Habits of the Heart: Individualism and Commitment in American Life*. New York: Harper and Row, 1985.
Bengston, Vern, Michael Furlong, and Robert Laufer. "Time, Aging, and the Continuity of Social Structure: Themes and Issues in Generational Analysis." *Journal of Social Issues* 30, no. 2 (1974): 1–30.
Bergquist, Charles. *Labor in Latin America*. Stanford: Stanford University Press, 1986.
Berlinguer, Enrico. "Reflections After Events in Chile." *Italian Communists* 5–6 (September–December 1973).
Bermeo, Nancy. "Democracy and the Lessons of Dictatorship." *Comparative Politics* 24 (April 1992): 273–291.
Beverley, John, José Oviedo, and Michael Aronna, eds. *The Post-Modernism Debate in Latin America*. Durham: Duke University Press, 1995.
Bitar, Sergio. *Isla 10*. Santiago: Pehuén Editores, 1987.
——. *Transición, socialismo, y democracia*. Mexico City: Siglo Ventiuno Editores, 1979.
Blondel, Jean. *Government Ministers in the Contemporary World*. London: Sage, 1985.
Bloom, William. *Personal Identity, National Identity, and International Relations*. Cambridge: Cambridge University Press, 1990.
Braungart, Richard, and Margaret Braungart. "Political Career Patterns of Radical Activists in the 1960s and 1970s: Some Historical Comparisons." *Sociological Focus* 13 (1980): 237–254.
Brim Jr., Orville, and Stanton Wheeler. *Socialization After Childhood: Two Essays*. New York: Wiley, 1966.
Brown, Cynthia. *Chile Since the Coup: Ten Years of Repression*. New York: Americas Watch Committee, 1983.
Bruner, Jerome. "Life as Narrative." *Social Research* 54, no. 1 (Spring 1987): 24–27.
Brunner, José Joaquín. *La cultura autoritaria en Chile*. Santiago: FLACSO, 1981.
——. "La cultura política del autoritarianismo." In FLACSO, eds., *Chile: 1973–198?*. Santiago: FLACSO, 1983.
Brunner, José Joaquín, and Angel Flisfisch. *Los intelectuales y las instituciones de la cultura*. Santiago: FLACSO, 1983.
Brym, Robert J. *Intellectuals and Politics*. London: Allen and Unwin, 1980.
Carr, Edward. *The Romantic Exiles: A Nineteenth-Century Portrait Gallery*. Harmonsworth: Penguin, 1949.

Castañeda, Jorge. *Utopia Unarmed: The Latin American Left After the Cold War.* New York: Random House, 1994.

Cavalcanti, Pedro, and Ruben Fernandes. "An Unfinished Conversation: Two Oppressed People Unable to Agree." *Telos* 18 (1973): 136–149.

Cavarozzi, Marcelo. "The Government and the Industrial Bourgeoisie in Chile, 1938–1964." Ph.D. diss., University of California at Berkeley, 1975.

Chalmers, Douglas A. "Dilemmas of Latin American Democratization: Dealing with International Forces." Notes for discussion for the annual meeting of the New England Council of Latin American Studies, Storrs, Connecticut, December 4, 1989.

Chavez, Leo. *Shadowed Lives: Undocumented Immigrants in American Society.* Fort Worth: Harcourt, Brace, Jovanovich, 1992.

Claggett, William. "Partisan Acquisition vs. Partisan Identity: Life Cycle, Generational, and Period Effects." *American Journal of Political Science* 25 (1981): 193–214.

Cohen, Abner. *Two-Dimensional Man: An Essay on the Anthropology of Power and Symbolism in Complex Society.* Berkeley: University of California Press, 1974.

Cohen, Jean. "Strategy or Identity: New Theoretical Paradigms and Contemporary Social Movements." *Social Research* 52 (1985): 663–716.

Collier, David. Introduction to David Collier, ed., *The New Authoritarianism in Latin America.* Princeton: Princeton University Press, 1979.

Collier, Ruth Berins, and David Collier. *Shaping the Political Arena: Critical Junctures, the Labor Movement, and Regime Dynamics in Latin America.* Princeton: Princeton University Press, 1991.

Cornelius, Wayne, and Ann Craig. "Political Culture in Mexico: Continuities and Revisionist Interpretations." In Gabriel Almond and Sidney Verba, eds., *The Civic Culture Revisited*, pp. 335–337. New York: Russell Sage Foundation, 1989.

Corradi, Juan, Patricia Weiss Fagen, and Manuel Antonio Garretón, eds. *Fear at the Edge: State Terror and Resistance in Latin America.* Berkeley: University of California Press, 1992.

Coser, Lewis, *Men of Ideas: A Sociologist's View.* New York: Free Press, 1965.

——. *Refugee Scholars in America: Their Impact and Their Experiences.* New Haven: Yale University Press, 1984.

Crosby, Travis. "Gladstone's Decade of Crisis: Biography and the Life Course Approach." *Journal of Political and Military Sociology* 12 (1984): 9–22.

da Rocha Lima, Valentina. "Women in Exile: Becoming Feminist." *International Journal of Oral History* 5, no. 2 (June 1984): 81–99.

Degregori, Carlos Iván. "How Difficult It Is to Be God: Ideology and Political Violence in Sendero Luminoso." *Critique of Anthropology* 11, no. 3 (1991): 233–250.

de la Maza, Gonzalo, and Mario Garcés. *La explosión de las mayorías: Protesta nacional, 1983–1984.* Santiago: Educación y Comunicaciones, 1985.

de la Parra, Marco Antonio. *Carta abierta a Pinochet.* Santiago: Editorial Planeta, 1998.

Delli Carpini, Michael. "Age and History: Generations and Sociopolitical Change." In Roberta S. Sigel, ed., *Political Learning in Adulthood: A Sourcebook of Theory and Research*, pp. 11–55. Chicago: University of Chicago Press, 1989.

———. *Stability and Change in American Politics: The Coming of Age of the Generation of the Nineteen Sixties*. New York: New York University Press, 1986.

Dennis, Jack. *Socialization to Politics: A Reader*. New York: John Wiley, 1973.

DeShazo, Peter. *Urban Workers and Labor Unions in Chile, 1902–1927*. Madison: University of Wisconsin Press, 1983.

Domínguez, Virginia. *People as Subject, People as Object: Selfhood and Peoplehood in Contemporary Israel*. Madison: University of Wisconsin Press, 1989.

Drake, Paul. *Socialism and Populism in Chile, 1932–1952*. Urbana: University of Illinois, 1978.

Drake, Paul, and Ivan Jaksic, eds. *The Struggle for Democracy in Chile, 1982–1990*. 2nd ed. Lincoln: University of Nebraska Press, 1995.

du Preez, Peter. *The Politics of Identity: Ideology and the Human Image*. Oxford: Basil Blackwell, 1980.

Eckstein, Susan. *Power and Popular Protest: Latin American Social Movements*. Berkeley: University of California Press, 1988.

ECLA. *Economic Survey of Latin America, 1964*. New York: United Nations, ECLA, 1965.

Edinger, Lewis. *German Exile Politics: The Social Democratic Executive Committee in the Nazi Era*. Berkeley: University of California Press, 1956.

Erikson, Erik. *Ghandi's Truth*. New York: Norton, 1969.

———. *Identity and the Life Cycle*. New York: Norton, 1980.

———. *Identity, Youth, and Crisis*. New York: Norton, 1968.

———. *Life History and the Historical Moment*. New York: Norton, 1975.

———. *Young Man Luther*. New York: Norton, 1958.

Escobar, Ricardo Lagos. *La concentración del poder económico*. Santiago: Editorial del Pacífico, 1961.

Fagen, Patricia Weiss. *Chilean Universities: Problems of Autonomy and Dependence*. Beverly Hills: Sage, 1973.

———. *Exiles and Citizens: Spanish Republicans in Mexico*. Austin: University of Texas Press, 1973.

Friedman, Debra, and Doug McAdam. "Collective Identity and Activism: Networks, Choices, and the Life of a Social Movement." In Aldon Morris and Carol McClurg Mueller, eds., *Frontiers in Social Movement Theory*, pp. 156–173. New Haven: Yale University Press, 1992.

Friedman, Reinhard. *La política chilena de la A a la Z*. Santiago: Melquíades, 1988.

Frohlich, Norman. "Self-Interest or Altruism: What Difference?" *Journal of Conflict Resolution* 18, no. 1 (March 1974): 55–73.

Fundación de Ayuda Social de las Iglesias Cristianas. *Escritos sobre exilio y retorno (1978–1984)*. Santiago: FASIC, 1984.

Furci, Carmelo. *The Chilean Communist Party and the Road to Socialism.* London: ZED, 1984.

Garretón, Manuel Antonio. "The Political Evolution of the Chilean Military Regime and Problems in the Transition to Democracy." In Guillermo O'Donnell and Philippe Schmitter, eds., *Transitions from Authoritarian Rule: Latin America*, pp. 95–111. Baltimore: Johns Hopkins University Press, 1986.

——. "The Political Opposition and the Party System Under the Military Regime." In Paul Drake and Ivan Jaksic, eds., *The Struggle for Democracy in Chile, 1982–1990*, pp. 211–250. Lincoln: University of Nebraska Press, 1995.

——. *El proceso político chileno.* Santiago: FLACSO, 1983.

——. "Universidad y política en los procesos de transformación y reversión en Chile, 1967–1977." *Estudios sociales* 26, no. 4 (1980): 83–109.

Garretón, Manuel Antonio, and Tomás Moulián. *La Unidad Popular y el conflicto político en Chile.* Santiago: Ediciones Minga, 1983.

Geertz, Clifford. *The Interpretation of Cultures.* New York: Basic Books, 1973.

George, Alexander L., and Juliet L. George. *Woodrow Wilson and Colonel House: A Personality Study.* New York: Dover Publications, 1964.

Gil, Federico. *The Political System of Chile.* Boston: Cambridge University Press, 1966.

González Camus, Ignacio. *El día en que murió Allende.* Santiago: Editorial CESOC, 1988.

Gouldner, Alvin. "Prologue to a Theory of Revolutionary Intellectuals." *Telos* 26 (Winter 1975–76): 3–28.

Granovetter, Mark. "Economic Action and Social Structure: The Problem of Embeddedness." *American Journal of Sociology* 91, no. 3 (November 1985): 481–510.

Guardia, Alexis. *Chile, país centauro: Perfil del socialismo renovado.* Santiago: Ediciones BAT, 1990.

Guastavino, Luís. *Caen las catedrales.* Santiago: HACHETTE, 1990.

Habermas, Jürgen. *Legitimation Crisis.* Boston: Beacon, 1973.

Hagopian, Frances. "After Regime Change: Authoritarian Legacies, Political Representation, and the Democratic Future of South America." *World Politics* 45 (April 1993): 464–500.

——. "Traditional Power Structures and Democratic Governance in Latin America." In Jorge Domínguez and Abraham Lowenthal, eds., *Constructing Democratic Governance: Latin America and the Caribbean in the 1990s—Themes and Issues*, pp. 64–86. Baltimore: Johns Hopkins University Press, 1996.

Hall, Peter. *The Political Power of Economic Ideas.* Princeton: Princeton University Press, 1989.

Hardy, Clarisa. *La reforma social pendiente.* Santiago: Chile 21, 1997.

Hirschman, Albert O. *Exit, Voice, and Loyalty.* Cambridge: Harvard University Press, 1970.

Hite, Katherine. "Chile: A Rough Road Home." *NACLA Report on the Americas* 24, no. 5 (February 1991): 4–8.

——. "The Formation and Transformation of Political Identity: Leaders of the Chilean Left, 1968–1990." *Journal of Latin American Studies* 28, pt. 2 (May 1996): 299–328.

Hochschild, Jennifer. *What's Fair? American Beliefs About Distributive Justice*. Cambridge: Harvard University Press, 1981.

Horowitz, Irving Louis. "The Texture of Terrorism: Socialization, Routinization, and Integration." In Roberta S. Sigel, ed., *Political Learning in Adulthood: A Sourcebook of Theory and Research*, pp. 386–414. Chicago: University of Chicago Press, 1989.

Human Rights Watch/Americas. "Chile: Unsettled Business: Human Rights at the Start of the Frei Presidency." *Human Rights Watch* 6, no. 6 (May 1994).

Huneeus, Carlos. "La dinámica de los 'nuevos autoritarismos': Chile en una perspectiva comparada." *Revista de estudios políticos* 54 (1986): 105–158.

——. *Los chilenos y la política: Cambio y continuidad en el autoritarianismo*. Santiago: CERC, 1987.

Huntington, Samuel. *Political Order in Changing Societies*. New Haven: Yale University Press, 1968.

Hyman, Herbert. *Political Socialization*. Glencoe: Free Press, 1959.

Inglehart, Ronald. *The Silent Revolution*. Princeton: Princeton University Press, 1977.

Instituto de Ciencias Alejandro Lipschutz (ICAL), eds. *Crisis y renovación*. Santiago: Ediciones Medusa/ICAL, 1990.

Iwanska, Alicia. "Modern Exiles: Spanish, Polish, American." *Polish Review* 23 (1978): 47–61.

Jaksic, Iván. *Academic Rebels in Chile: The Role of Philosophy in Higher Education and Politics*. Albany: SUNY Press, 1989.

Jennings, M. Kent, and Richard Niemi. *The Political Character of Adolescence: The Influence of Families and Schools*. Princeton: Princeton University Press, 1974.

Jobet, Julio Cesar. *Historia del Partido Socialista de Chile*. 2nd ed. Santiago: Ediciones Documentas, 1987.

Johnston, David. "Human Agency and Rational Action." In Kristen Renwick Monroe, ed., *The Economic Approach to Politics: A Critical Reassessment of the Theory of Rational Action*. New York: HarperCollins, 1991.

Judt, Tony. *Past Imperfect: French Intellectuals, 1944–1956*. Berkeley: University of California Press, 1992.

Karl, Terry Lynn. "Petroleum and Political Pacts: The Transition to Democracy in Venezuela." In Guillermo O'Donnell, Philippe Schmitter, and Laurence Whitehead, eds., *Transitions from Authoritarian Rule: Latin America*, pp. 196–219. Baltimore: Johns Hopkins University Press, 1986.

Kay, Diane. *Chileans in Exile: Private Struggles, Public Lives*. London: Macmillan, 1987.

Klandermans, Bert. "The Social Construction of Protest and Multiorganizational Fields." In Aldon Morris and Carol McClurg Mueller, eds., *Frontiers of Social Movement Theory.* New Haven: Yale University Press, 1992.

Kovalskys, Juana, and Elizabeth Lira. "Exilio y retorno: Una aproximación psicosocial." In FASIC, *Exilio: 1978–1986,* pp. 139–145.

Lagos, Ricardo. *Democracia para Chile: Proposiciones de un Socialista.* Santiago: Puhuén Editores, 1985.

Laitin, David. *Hegemony and Culture: Politics and Religious Change Among the Yoruba.* Chicago: University of Chicago Press, 1986.

Lamb, Karl A. *As Orange Goes.* New York: Norton, 1974.

Lane, Robert. *Political Ideology: Why the American Common Man Believes What He Does.* New York: Free Press, 1967.

——. *Political Man.* New York: Free Press, 1972.

Laufer, Robert. "The Aftermath of War: Adult Socialization and Political Development." In Roberta S. Sigel, ed., *Political Learning in Adulthood: A Sourcebook of Theory and Research,* pp. 415–457. Chicago: University of Chicago Press, 1989.

Lechner, Norbert. *Los patios interiores de la democracia: Subjetividad y política.* Santiago: FLACSO, 1988.

Linz, Juan, and Alfred Stepan. *The Breakdown of Democratic Regimes.* Baltimore: Johns Hopkins University Press, 1979.

——. "Political Identities and Electoral Sequences: Spain, the Soviet Union, and Yugoslavia." *Daedalus* 121 (Spring 1992): 123–139.

Lira, Elizabeth. "Consecuencias psicosociales de la represión en Chile." *Revista de psicología de El Salvador* 7, no. 28 (1988): 143–159.

Lira, Elizabeth, David Becker, Juana Kovalskys, Elena Gómez, and María Isabel Castillo. "Daño social y memoria colectiva: Perspectivas de reparación." In David Becker and Elizabeth Lira, eds., *Derechos humanos: Todo es según el dolor con que se mira,* pp. 195–213. Santiago: ILAS, 1989.

Lira, Elizabeth, and María Isabel Castillo. *Psicología de la amenaza política y del miedo.* Santiago: ILAS-CESOC, 1991.

Loveman, Brian. *Chile: The Legacy of Hispanic Capitalism.* New York: Oxford University Press, 1988.

——. "The Transition to Civilian Government in Chile, 1990–1994." In Paul Drake and Ivan Jaksic, eds., *The Struggle for Democracy in Chile, 1982–1990,* pp. 305–337. 2nd ed. Lincoln: University of Nebraska Press, 1995.

Mainwaring, Scott. "Grassroots Popular Movements, Identity, and Democratization in Brazil." Working Paper #84. Kellogg Institute, University of Notre Dame, October 1986.

Maira, Luis. *La constitución de 1980 y la ruptura democrática.* Santiago: Editorial Emisión, 1988.

Mamalakis, Markos J. *The Growth and Structure of the Chilean Economy: From Independence to Allende.* New Haven: Yale University Press, 1976.

Mancuso, Maureen. "The Ethical Attitudes of British MPs: A Typology." *Parliamentary Affairs* 46 (April 1993): 179–191.

Mannheim, Karl. *Ideology and Utopia: An Introduction to the Sociology of Knowledge.* San Diego: Harcourt, Brace, Jovanovich, 1985.

———. "The Problem of Generations." In Philip Altbach and Robert Laufer, eds., *The New Pilgrims: Youth Protest in Transition*, pp. 101–138. 1928; reprint, New York: David McKay, 1972.

Mansbridge, Jane. "The Rise and Fall of Self-Interest in the Explanation of Political Life." In Jane Mansbridge, ed., *Beyond Self-Interest.* Chicago: University of Chicago Press, 1990.

Martínez, Javier, and Eugenio Tironi. *Las clases sociales en Chile: Cambio y estratificación, 1970–1980.* Santiago: SUR, 1985.

Mayhew, Bruce. "Structuralism versus Individualism." *Social Forces* 59 (1980): 335–375.

Molina, Sergio. *El proceso de cambio en Chile.* Santiago, 1972.

Monroe, Kristen Renwick. *The Heart of Altruism: Perceptions of a Common Humanity.* Princeton: Princeton University Press, 1996.

———, ed. *The Economic Approach to Politics: A Critical Reassessment of the Theory of Rational Action.* New York: HarperCollins, 1991.

Monroe, Kristen Renwick, Michael C. Barton, and Ute Klingemann. "Altruism and the Theory of Rational Action: An Analysis of Rescuers of Jews in Nazi Europe." In Kristen Renwick Monroe, ed., *The Economic Approach to Politics.* New York: HarperCollins, 1991.

Moran, Theodore. *Multinational Corporations and the Politics of Dependence.* Princeton: Princeton University Press, 1974.

Moulián, Tomás. *El consumo me consume.* Santiago: LOM Ediciones, 1998.

———. *Conversación interrumpida con Allende.* Santiago: LOM Ediciones, 1998.

———. *Democracia y socialismo en Chile.* Santiago: FLACSO, 1983.

———. *La forja de ilusiones: El sistema de partidos, 1932–1973.* Santiago: ARCIS/FLACSO, 1993.

Mueller, Carol McClurg. "Building Social Movement Theory." In Aldon Morris and Carol McClurg Mueller, eds., *Frontiers in Social Movement Theory.* New Haven: Yale University Press, 1992.

NACLA, eds. *New Chile.* New York: Waller Press, 1972.

National Education Campaign for Truth and Human Rights. Ministry of Foreign Affairs, Chile. *Summary of the Truth and Reconciliation Commission Report.* Santiago: Ministry of Foreign Affairs, July 1991.

O'Donnell, Guillermo, and Philippe Schmitter. *Transitions from Authoritarian Rule: Tentative Conclusions About Uncertain Democracies.* Baltimore: Johns Hopkins University Press, 1986.

Olson, Mancur. *The Logic of Collective Action: Public Goods and the Theory of Groups.* Cambridge, Mass.: Harvard University Press, 1965.

Ortega y Gasset, José. "The Importance of Generationhood." In A. Esler, ed., *The Youth Revolution*. Lexington, Mass.: D. C. Heath, 1974.

———. *The Modern Theme*. New York: Harper and Row, 1961.

Palma, Aníbal. *Un sólo norte*. Santiago, 1989.

Partido Comunista de Chile. "Al partido y al pueblo de Chile." Mimeographed document, December 1974.

———. "Patriotas: Sólo unidos derrotaremos el fascismo." Mimeographed document, September 1976.

Partido Socialista de Chile. "Documento del Comité Central del Partido Socialista de Chile." Mimeographed document, March 1974.

Passerini, Luisa. *Fascism in Popular Memory: The Cultural Experience of the Turin Working Class*. Cambridge: Cambridge University Press, 1987.

———. "Memory: Resumé of the Final Session of the International Conference on Oral History, Aix-en-Provence, September 26, 1982." Reprinted in *History Workshop* 15 (Spring 1983): 195–196.

Pateman, Carole. "The Civic Culture: A Philosophic Critique." In Gabriel Almond and Sidney Verba, eds., *The Civic Culture Revisited*, pp. 57–102. New York: Russell Sage Foundation, 1989.

Phelps, Edmund, ed. *Altruism, Morality, and Economic Theory*. New York: Russell Sage Foundation, 1975.

Politzer, Patricia. *Altamirano*. Buenos Aires: Ediciones Melquíades, 1989.

Pollack, Benny, and Hernán Rosenkranz. *Revolutionary Social Democracy: The Chilean Socialist Party*. London: Pinter, 1986.

Portelli, Alessandro. *The Death of Luigi Trastulli and Other Stories: Form and Meaning in Oral History*. Albany: SUNY Press, 1991.

Post, Jerold. "Dreams of Glory and the Life Cycle: Reflections on the Life Cycle Course of Narcissistic Leaders." *Journal of Political and Military Sociology* 12 (1984): 49–60.

Puryear, Jeffrey. *Thinking Politics: Intellectuals and Democracy in Chile, 1973–1988*. Baltimore: Johns Hopkins Press, 1994.

Ramírez-Necochea, Hernán. *Orígen y formación del Partido Comunista de Chile*. Santiago: Editorial Austral, 1965.

Redfield, Robert. *The Little Community and Peasant Society and Culture*. Chicago: University of Chicago Press, Phoenix Books, 1967.

Rejai, Mostafa, and Kay Phillips. *Loyalists and Revolutionaries: Political Leaders Compared*. New York: Praeger, 1988.

Renshon, Stanley. "Psychological Perspectives on Theories of Adult Development and the Political Socialization of Leaders." In Roberta S. Sigel, ed., *Political Learning in Adulthood: A Sourcebook of Theory and Research*, pp. 203–264. Chicago: University of Chicago Press, 1989.

Renshon, Stanley, ed. *Handbook of Political Socialization*. New York: Free Press, 1977.

Roberts, Kenneth. "In Search of a New Identity: Dictatorship, Democracy, and the Evolution of the Left in Chile and Peru." Ph.D. diss., Stanford University, 1992.

Rodríguez, Aniceto. *Unidad y renovación: Dialéctica para la victoria*. Santiago: CESOC, 1990.

Rodríguez, Mili. *Nunca me verás como me vieras*. Santiago: Editores Ornitorrinco, 1990.

Rousso, Henri. *The Vichy Syndrome: History and Memory in France Since 1944*. Cambridge: Harvard University Press, 1991.

Schamis, Hector. "Reconceptualizing Latin American Authoritarianism in the 1970s: From Bureaucratic Authoritarianism to Neoconservatism." *Comparative Politics* 23, no. 2 (January 1991): 201–220.

Scott, James. *The Moral Economy of the Peasant*. New Haven: Yale University Press, 1976.

——. *Weapons of the Weak: Everyday Forms of Peasant Resistance*. New Haven: Yale University Press, 1985.

Scully, Timothy. *Rethinking the Center: Party Politics in Nineteenth- and Twentieth-Century Chile*. Stanford: Stanford University Press, 1992.

Sears, David O. "Political Socialization." In Fred Greenstein and Nelson W. Posby, eds., *Handbook in Political Science*, 4:93–153. Reading, Mass.: Addison-Wesley, 1975.

Selbin, Eric. *Modern Latin American Revolutions*. Boulder: Westview, 1993.

Shain, Yossi. *The Frontier of Loyalty: Political Exiles in the Age of the Nation-State*. Hanover, N.H.: Wesleyan University Press, 1989.

Sigel, Roberta S., ed. *Political Learning in Adulthood: A Sourcebook of Theory and Research*. Chicago: University of Chicago Press, 1989.

Silva, Eduardo. "Capitalist Coalitions and Economic Policymaking in Authoritarian Chile." Ph.D. diss., University of California–San Diego, 1991.

——. "The Political Economy of Chile's Regime Transition: From Radical to 'Pragmatic' Neo-Liberal Policies." In Paul Drake and Iván Jaksic, eds., *The Struggle for Democracy in Chile, 1982–1990*, pp. 98–127. Lincoln: University of Nebraska Press, 1991.

Smith, Robert. "Los Ausentes Siempre Presentes: The Imagining, Making, and Politics of a Transnational Community Between Ticuani, Puebla, Mexico, and New York City." Ph.D. diss., Columbia University, 1994.

Snow, David, Louis Zurcher Jr., and Sheldon Ekland-Olson. "Social Networks and Social Movements: A Microstructural Approach to Differential Recruitment." *American Sociological Review* 45 (1980): 787–801.

Speier, Hans. *Social Order and the Risks of War: Papers in Political Sociology*. New York: Stewart, 1952.

Stein, Louis. *Beyond Death and Exile: The Spanish Republicans in France. 1939–1955*. Cambridge: Harvard University Press, 1979.

Tabori, Paul. *The Anatomy of Exile: A Semantic and Historical Study.* London: Habrap, 1972.

Tironi, Eugenio. *Autoritarismo, modernización, y marginalidad.* Santiago: SUR Ediciones, 1990.

——. *Los silencios de la revolución: Chile—La otra cara de la modernización.* Santiago: Editorial la Puerta Abierta, 1988.

"UP Program of Government." *North American Congress on Latin America Newsletter.* March 1971.

Uribe, Armando. *Carta abierta a Patricio Aylwin.* Santiago: Editorial Planeta, 1998.

Valenzuela, Arturo. *The Breakdown of Democratic Regimes: Chile.* Baltimore: Johns Hopkins University Press, 1979.

Varas, Augusto, ed. *El Partido Comunista en Chile.* Santiago: CESOC-FLACSO, 1988.

Varas, Augusto, and Felipe Aguero. *El proyecto político militar.* Santiago: FLACSO, 1984.

Varela, Carmona Helio. "Estratificación social de la población trabajadora en Chile y su participación en el Ingreso Nacional, 1940–1954." In *Memoria en ciencias económicas.* Santiago: Universidad de Chile, Escuela de Economía, 1958.

Vásquez, Ana, and Ana María Araujo. *La maldición de Ulises: Repercusiones psicológicas del exilio.* Santiago: Editorial Sudamericana, 1990.

Verdugo, Patricia. *Interferencia secreta: 11 de septiembre de 1973.* Santiago: Editorial Sudamericano, 1998.

Vergara, Pilar. "Las transformaciones del estado chileno bajo el régimen militar." In FLACSO, eds., *Chile: 1973–198?,* pp. 65–104. Santiago: FLACSO, 1983.

Viera-Gallo, José Antonio. *Chile: Un nuevo camino.* Santiago: CESOC, 1989.

——. *La fuerza de las ideas.* Santiago: CESOC, 1993.

Vodanovic, Hernán. *Un socialismo renovado para Chile.* Santiago: Editorial Andante, 1988.

Walker, Ignacio. *Socialismo y democracia: Chile y Europa en perspectiva comparada.* Santiago: CIEPLAN-HACHETTE, 1990.

Walzer, Michael. *The Revolution of the Saints: A Study in the Origins of Radical Politics.* Cambridge: Cambridge University Press, 1965.

Warren, Kay. *The Symbolism of Subordination: Indian Identity in a Guatemalan Town.* Austin: University of Texas Press, 1978.

Weber, Max. *The Methodology of the Social Sciences.* New York: Free Press, 1949.

Wellman, Barry, and S. D. Berkowitz, eds. *Social Structures: A Network Approach.* New York: Cambridge University Press, 1988.

Wilde, Alexander. "Irruptions of Memory: Expressive Politics in Chile's Transition to Democracy." Paper presented to the Authoritarian Legacies Working Group of the Institute of Latin American and Iberian Studies, Columbia University, Buenos Aires, Argentina, August 27–29, 1998.

Williams, R. C. *Culture in Exile: Russian Emigres in Germany, 1881–1941.* Ithaca: Cornell University Press, 1972.

Winn, Peter. *Weavers of Revolution: The Yarur Workers and Chile's Road to Socialism.* New York: Oxford University Press, 1986.

Wintrobe, R. "It Pays to Do Good. But Not More Good Than It Pays." *Journal of Economic Behavior and Organization* 2, no. 3 (1981): 201–213.

Zerán, Faride. *O el asilo contra la opresión: 23 historias para recordar.* Santiago: Editores Paradox, 1991.

Selected Chilean Periodicals

Análisis (biweekly)
Apsi (weekly)
Caras (monthly)
Chile-América (exile journal)
Convergencia (monthly)
Epoca, La (daily)
Hoy Magazine (weekly)
Mercurio, El (daily)
Qué Pasa (weekly)
Segunda, La (daily)

Selected Interviews

Cecilia Aguirre
Angela Bachelet
Sergio Baeza
John Biehl
Sergio Bitar
José Joaquín Brunner
María Isabel Castillo
Alvaro Díaz
Andrés Domínguez
Hugo Fruhling
Ernesto Galáz
Manuel Antonio Garretón
Claudio González
Luis Guastavino
Jorge Heine
Carlos Huneeus
Jaime Insunza
Monica Jiménez
Marta Lagos
Elizabeth Lira

Norbert Lechner
Juan Pablo Letelier
Javier Martínez
Cecilia Medina
Juan Enrique Miquel
Oscar Montealegre
Isabel Margarita Morel
Roberto Moreno
Tomás Moulián
Máximo Pacheco
Antonio Palacios
Gabriel Palma
Osvaldo Puccio
María Eugenia Rojas
Juan Somavía
Teresa Valdés
Augusto Varas
Ignacio Walker
Eugenia Weinstein
José Zalaquett

INDEX

IRVINE SULLIVAN INGRAM LIBRARY
STATE UNIVERSITY OF WEST GEORGIA
CARROLLTON GEORGIA